The Creation of Settings and the Future Societies

Seymour B. Sarason

THE CREATION OF SETTINGS AND THE FUTURE SOCIETIES

BROOKLINE
BOOKS

THE CREATION OF SETTINGS AND THE FUTURE SOCIETIES
by Seymour B. Sarason

Copyright © 1972 by: Jossey-Bass, Inc., Publishers
433 California Street
San Francisco, California 94104
&
Jossey-Bass Limited
28 Banner Street
London EC1Y 8QE

Library of Congress
Cataloging-In-Publication Data

Sarason, Seymour
    The creation of settings and the future societies/Seymour·
    Sarason. --Rev.ed.
    p. cm.
    Bibliography: p.
    Includes index.
    1. Small groups. 2. Social institutions. 3. Social
    interaction. I. Title.
    HM133.S25 1988   302.3'4--dc19
    CIP 88-7255
    ISBN0-914797-49-2 (pbk)

Published by
Brookline Books, Inc.
PO Box 1046
Cambridge, MA   02238

This book is for my daughter, Julie Sarason,
in the hope that it deserves her.

Contents

Preface to Paperback Edition

With one exception, anything I have ever written was built on, or stimulated by, the research and ideas of others, past and present. That exception was *The Creation of Settings*, which explains why writing it was both pleasurable and anxiety-arousing. The pleasure (to the extent that writing can be a pleasure!) derived from the belief that I was formulating a problem that no one had conceptualized before. The anxiety stemmed from another belief: I was wrong, and I had simply not searched the literature sufficiently. So, until I wrote the last page of the manuscript, I continued to comb the literature to determine if anyone else had tried to describe and explain how new settings were created and with what consequences. Here and there I could find sentences and paragraphs relevant to the creation of settings but nothing that could be dignified as a conceptualization.

I was puzzled. I concluded that in a strange way my development as a person and as a psychologist had made the creation of settings a central focus in my thinking. That makes it sound more rational than it was. For one thing, I wrote the book somewhat less than a decade after I had created the Yale Psycho-Educational Clinic. I had experienced the creation of a new setting. Indeed, one of the stimulants to the creation of the clinic was to experience what the creation of a new setting entailed and why the process was so problematic in its outcomes.

But there was a "prehistory" to the clinic. My first professional position was in a new state training school for mentally retarded individuals. It was in all respects the most innovative insitution of its kind in this century. Why in a few short years did this new institution begin to go downhill and to become inconsistent with its original purposes? When I left the Southbury Training School in 1945 to go to Yale, the transformations that I had observed at Southbury required explanation.

I could not relegate Southbury to an unused past. There was something to fathom but I was unclear about where and how to begin. If I could not leave the problem alone, it was because of what was happening in the larger society in the years between coming to Yale and starting the clinic in 1961-62. Those were years in which new settings, especially in the public sector, were beginning to be created at an unprecedented rate, reaching an apex in the sixties. Why did so many of these new settings fail of their purposes? That in part explains why creating the clinic was intellectually important for me. But before the clinic and Southbury, the creation of settings had become salient for me because of my involvement in radical politics. Why did the Russian revolution fail, going from a vision of heaven on earth to an unrivalled tyranny in which scores of millions were consumed? What, if anything, did the Russian revolution and Southbury have in common? Why is it so frequent that the stated purpose of a new setting is transformed out of recognition?

The phrase and concept "the creation of settings" began to take shape when the creation of the clinic was becoming a reality. It was then that I realized that the creation of settings contained issues that go back to my earliest years. I recently completed *The Making of an American Psychologist: An Autobiography* (San Francisco: Jossey-Bass, 1988). One of the longest chapters is about the clinic. In it is this footnote:

> I defined the creation of settings as when two or more people *get together* in new and sustained relationships to attain agreed-upon goals. Where did that phrase come from? If this were only a personal autobiography I would devote a chapter to the purely psychological or private origins of the phrase. Chronologically, the answer begins with my curiosity about, and utter conscious ignorance of, how babies are created and born. Even now hardly a night passes without a dream containing visual themes of winding passages and the pursuit of exits. I did not connect the coining of the phrase until several months after the Psycho-Educational Clinic was created and I "heard" myself using the phrase somewhat repetitively. We live our lives. We are also lived by them. Freud was no fool.

The creation of a setting is, among other things (and there are other significant things), a process in which leadership is a strange, wondrous, mystifying amalgam of the truly private, the zeitgeist, place, and luck.

Nothing is more heartwarming to a writer than to receive letters from readers who say "you have described what I have experienced." Some of these were more than letters. I have received the most personal accounts of hope turned into disillusionment from individuals heterogeneous in the extreme: teachers and principals of new programs and schools, an administrator of a new nursing home, a professor in a new medical school, the president of a new community college, a lay person who started a respite-care service, a graduate student caught up in the creation of a new community mental health center, a nurse who helped create a new hospice for terminally ill people. If it is encouraging to learn that what you have written has helped others make sense of their experiences, it certainly has its downside.

As problem and process, the creation of settings has received some recognition and study. If the pace of the creation of new settings has slackened somewhat, it is still the case, I believe, that the pace is dizzingly high. I am, of course, gratified, that *The Creation of Settings* will now be made available to a wider audience than before.

Seymour B. Sarason
April 1988

Preface

When I have written a book before I could always assume that the reader was familiar with its contents, if not in its details or central theme, then at least with the domain of problems to which the effort purported to be relevant. When uncertain about this assumption, an author can choose a title which helps the reader to know where he is being taken. My experience with this book indicated that I could not make the usual assumption, and the title that made sense to me was not very illuminating to others. When in response to questions I said that I was interested in the creation of settings, I learned to expect puzzled expressions and even embarrassed silence. Sometimes a brave soul said: What does the creation of settings *mean?* Even my defining the phrase (by saying that it referred to *any* instance when two or more people come together in new and sustained relationships to achieve certain goals) did not seem to be enlightening. Sometimes I became so sensitive to the fact that my answer to friendly inquiries was mystifying that I tried to become concrete: for instance, marriage was the smallest instance of a setting, revolution the most ambitious, and in between was a fantastic array of types of new settings. I was interested, I would say, in the processes and problems common to the creation of settings which on the surface appeared to be radically different from one another. Far from being clarifying, this answer seemed to produce facial expressions suggesting that the listener now understood the problem: my grandiosity. And if to dispel such a notion I said that the creation of settings had hardly been formulated as a set of problems, that we lacked adequate description and analysis of the process, that too many people spent too much time trying to understand chronologically mature settings and were overlooking how they came into existence, that the creation of a setting could not be comprehended in terms of the psychology of individuals, that it reflected a fascinating amalgam of unexamined values and ideas—these were not very reassuring additions to some listeners.

It took me a long time to hit upon a helpful response. When I said that I was interested in why the bulk of new settings failed so early (literally or figuratively), why the intent to create something new generally confirmed that the more things change the more they remain the same, and why initial agreement on values (like love) was not enough to create and sustain a viable setting, the listener was likely to act as though he understood what I was after. If the conversation went on long enough, I frequently had to stop talking (willingly in these instances) and listen to a personal account of participation in a new setting which began in hope and ended rather quickly in what I call organizational craziness. I could always count on someone asking: Do you really mean that how a human setting gets created has hardly been studied or formulated? Interestingly this question was sometimes asked by professional colleagues who were experts in organizations and their problems. Their puzzlement was no less than mine had once been.

This book was written for two reasons. I had to order my experiences and observations about how people create a variety of settings. This may explain or justify why I wrote the book, but it does not explain why I considered it worthy of publication. That decision was based on the beliefs that although what I have had to say may not have been put in the most felicitous ways and that my formulations may be deficient in a number of respects, the problem I was grappling with was a crucially important one that deserved far more attention than it has ever received. This book is a plea for more study and understanding of a social activity that is peculiarly human. Although a part of me would like to believe that increased understanding of the problem will have widespread social effects, that it may help others fall less short of the mark than they ordinarily would, I have no illusions that understanding and knowledge inevitably result in the betterment of social man.

Inevitably this book has a large personal component. I have helped create several rather complicated settings, and these experiences provided me with more organizing ideas than I could find in the existing literature. Although part of me is undisguisedly in many of these pages, I would have exposed myself with much more reluctance than I actually felt if it were not that I made it my business to interview in some depth people who had also created new settings. In almost every respect what they told me in confidence confirmed what I had learned from my own experience. However, since my experience obviously was limited, I also learned from these individuals things which fitted in with but were not derivable from my experiences. I am indebted to these individuals for their time, candor, and permission to use their accounts with the appropriate disguises. For the most part they saw themselves as men of action—practical people who understood the real world and could move or change it. They prided themselves in being doers and, not infrequently, contrasted themselves with theoreticians whom they felt had precious little to offer them. In the matter of creating a new setting they were correct in their complaints that theoreticians (university people) had little to offer. But what they related to me amply demonstrated that they were far from being practical people if by that is meant having intimate knowledge of social realities and of how things "really" work. As one of these individuals said to me as we parted: "People regard me as a very practical guy, and I have agreed with them and have always considered it a compliment. And yet, what I have told you tonight doesn't fit, does it?" It didn't.

This started out to be a much bigger book. I intended to describe my experiences in depth, to use available descriptions and discussions by others (even though they were inadequate in many respects), and to pursue the question of why existing psychological, social, and political theory paid little attention to how settings were created (analogous to asking why it took so long for the phenomena of childhood to be recognized as important or why only in recent decades early infancy has begun to be seen in terms of cognitive processes). Once I began to write and to present my thoughts to various audiences, I concluded that the book I thought I should write might distract attention from the fascination and importance of the creation of settings. If I were to present and criticize existing organizational theory and try to demonstrate the inadequacy of personality theory as

a way of understanding the birth and early development of a social
setting and use descriptions by others together with long digressions
about why they may be misleading, I might end up with a book that
conceivably could bury the problem under the weight of controversy
and detail. This book, therefore, is written in a way that hopefully
allows the special and general reader to decide whether what I am
talking about is as important as I think it is.

     This is not a how-to-do-it book. Inevitably, however, as I
describe and analyze failures and successes, I take a stand on how
settings can be viewed and developed. I do not take stands to prove
that I am right, but rather to demonstrate that there is a universe of
alternatives to traditional ways of thinking. For example, when I assert
that the tendency to put up new buildings to house new settings is
frequently an invitation to disaster, it is not because I am in principle
opposed to new buildings but because I want to demonstrate that the
presumed need for new buildings can effectively obscure examination
of issues and assumptions that argue against construction. On the
very day that this Preface is being written, there appeared in the *New
York Times* (January 18, 1972) an account of three "new" public
schools in New York City: the first is housed in a former catering
establishment "specializing in wedding and bar mitzvah receptions,"
the second in a former factory "used for the manufacture and storage
of such products as mattresses, artificial flowers, and halvah," and the
third occupies the quarters of a former private school in the ground
floor of an apartment building. None of these has walls, and the
chancellor of the New York City schools is quoted as saying: "When
I see this, I am convinced we may be able to renew ourselves instead
of going the old route of cartoning off buildings into separate classrooms." Different assumptions about what a school can and should be
apparently were effective in inhibiting the tendency to want to house
new ideas in new buildings. The cost of these three "new" schools
was almost nothing compared to what new construction would have
required. These issues are discussed in Chapter Eight.

     A central theme of this book is that the social context from
which a new setting emerges, as well as the thinking of those who
create new settings, reflects what seems "natural" in the society. And
what seems natural is almost always a function of the culture to a
degree that usually renders us incapable of recognizing wherein we
are prisoners of the culture. Those who create new settings always
want to do something new, usually unaware that they are armed with,
and will subsequently be disarmed by, categories of thought which
help produce the conditions the new setting hopes to remedy. If we

accept the proposition that the more things change the more they remain the same, it is not because people will it or because of the perversity of the human personality but primarily because of what we think to be "natural," that is, so a part of us that it is inconceivable that things could be otherwise. Nowhere is this more clearly the case than in the creation of a new setting.

Conceptually the creation of settings belongs to no one discipline. Psychology, political science, government, history, sociology, architecture, city planning, the organizational-administrative fields— in each of these and other disciplines are individuals for whom this book will, I hope be relevant. Practically, however, individuals in most of these fields do not create new settings. They may consult with and study those who do, but only rarely do they personally experience the process, a fact which has advantages and disadvantages. One does not have to be a patient or a psychotherapist to say something significant about psychotherapy, and yet the most significant contributions have come from those who have been both. Creating a new setting gives a depth of meaning to the relationships of the human mind to the complexities of social organizations that cannot be gained by the most creative amalgam of thinking and imagination. In recent decades a number of academicians were drawn into the arena of social action only to return to their universities with varying degrees of bitterness and disappointment, aware as they never were of the gulf between theory and practice, between what is and what should be, between what they now know and what they should have known. I hope this book will help some people see these experiences in a different light and help others venture forth with a sensitive grasp of social realities. At the very least, I hope that it will enable them to approach these new ventures in the "outside" world with an understanding of the opportunities and traps that action provides. If like B. F. Skinner (see Chapter Twelve) they approach the design of new settings from the perspective of oversimplified theorizing that does not address itself to even the most obvious complications of action, they court failure. Many people like to quote Kurt Lewin's statement that there is nothing as practical as a good theory, as if that statement meant that theory was in some platonic sense superior to practice. Such a dichotomy and value judgment are nonsense, as Lewin well knew. Theory always reflects or says something about past actions, and it should always give rise to new tests in action. Valuing theory because it is theory is as mischievous as justifying action because it is action.

From the time the Yale Psycho-Educational Clinic was started and for the eight years of its formal existence the creation of settings was one of its central themes. I was part of as thoughtful, bold, and exciting a group of people as one will ever find. Directly or indirectly, they are all in this book. They helped shape my life and thinking. What I owe them cannot be repaid by or be reflected in words. They helped substantiate a theme of this book: you cannot create the conditions which enable others to change unless those conditions exist for you. Burton Blatt, Murray Levine, Dick Reppucci, Warren Bennis, and Brian Sarata read parts or all of this book and made suggestions which I am sure brought more clarity to it than it otherwise would have had. Their encouragement meant more to me than they know. Anita Miller was her usual invaluable self.

New Haven, Connecticut   SEYMOUR B. SARASON

CHAPTER 1

Creation of Settings

This book is about a set of related problems which, despite their frequency and importance, has remained relatively unrecognized and undiscussed to a surprising, if not amazing, degree. This is not because individuals have not experienced these problems in the most poignant ways or because society does not consider them to have fateful significances. I certainly do not want to give the impression that aspects of these problems have gone unrecognized or undiscussed, because there is a staggering literature which in one or another way approaches the core issues without stating them or, more frequently, stating them in ways which do not have productive consequences for the world of ideas and action.

I have labeled this set of problems the creation of settings that provisionally may be defined as any instance in which two or more people come together in new relationships over a sustained period of time in order to achieve certain goals. The most frequent instance, of course, is when two people enter into marriage. The most ambitious instance would be when people band together for the express purpose of creating a new society, and this could be a setting (such as a commune) encapsulated within a society or an effort to "destroy" the larger society and to create a new one. In between marriage and the creation of a new society there is, on the surface at least, a bewildering array of attempts to create new settings. For example, when legislation was passed to set up the Peace Corps, it literally meant that scores of new settings would have to be created: the central setting in Washington and scores of others in countries around the world. In each of these instances people would be brought together in what were for them new relationships over a sustained period of time to achieve certain objectives. The Head Start program is an example of a single piece of legislation authorizing the creation of hundreds (if not thousands) of discrete settings each one of which required that people be brought together in new relationships in order to achieve over time the objectives of the program.

The creation of a new university, hospital, clinic, school, or community agency is another example of the creation of a setting, and within each of them there is almost always found instances possessing the characteristics of the creation of a setting. For example, when a hospital decides to set up a new intensive-care unit, or when a university launches a new department, or when a community initiates a new program for the inner city we are again dealing with the creation of a setting. And then there is the business and industrial sector, where one can safely assume that new settings are developed with a very high frequency. It may be a new company, factory, restaurant, or store—the labels, overt forms, purposes, and size may vary in the extreme but almost always they possess the defining provisional characteristics of the creation of a setting.

In the past decade or so, more new settings (leaving marriage aside) have been created than in the entire previous history of the human race. It has never been very clear to me what people mean when they say that the world is changing at an ever accelerating rate. When pressed to elaborate, most people point to many technological advances, or discoveries, or events (such as the moon walk) which have had little or no effect on their lives but which they assume someday will result in a society markedly different from the one they know. Some people point to the plethora of social problems which seem to be overwhelming in their numbers and difficulty, although on reflection they realize that these problems are far from new in our society. Certainly there seems to be a sharpened awareness of what is happening in the world, but this is no warrant for the assumption that things are changing at an ever accelerating rate. It is likely that heightened awareness of problems feeds the hope that things are changing very quickly and that the problems will soon (that is, in the foreseeable future) disappear.

I would suggest that a major factor contributing to the belief that things are changing very swiftly is the perception that one cannot keep up with the new settings created daily to cope with one or another type of problem. The rate of setting creation is somewhat fantastic, and it is understandable, albeit incorrect, if we confuse this fact with real change. Such a confusion is analogous to one in which increases in Gross National Product are taken to signify the accomplishment of desired goals. It could be argued with some justice that the rate of setting creation reflects some kind of basic change in our society, but again this is quite different from arguing that swift change is the hallmark of our times.

The point I am making here was forced upon me most clearly through my experience in schools. What has characterized our urban school systems in the past decade is the dramatic increase in new "programs" the bulk of which possess all of the characteristics of new settings—a new type of school, or administrative department, or subject-matter department, or program for children atypical in some fashion, or a new resource center, and on and on. A reflection of this can be gleaned from the fact that during one week in one inner city school in New Haven ninety-three different people (excluding, of course, the full-time personnel of that school) entered the school to perform a service. The bulk of these people were each members of some kind of setting or program.[1] It is small wonder that those within and without the school system, particularly those within it, should feel that a lot of changes have occurred, using earlier years as a criterion for comparison. In fact, the older the teacher the more impressed he is with the way schools have changed, and here too when pressed one is directed to all the new instrumentalities which have been created to improve the schools.

Contributing both to the perception of accelerated change and the high rate of setting creation is the increased amount of time devoted to news on television and radio, particularly radio. In almost

[1] Words like *program, organization,* and *institution* are usually interchangeable with *setting.* Although each of these words evokes different images and somewhat different meanings, it seemed to me that *setting* was the least ambiguous and the most general. For some people the word *setting* has reference to a physical location (such as a stage setting), but I hope it is clear that although it is frequently the case that settings have a circumscribed physical space, it is not a necessary characteristic.

all of our large urban centers there is at least one radio station devoted to news around the clock, and it is my impression that over the past two decades all radio stations have increased the time given to news reporting. It is extremely difficult to listen to the radio without concluding that the problems of the world in general, and our society in particular, are multiplying fast and that this is also true for efforts to solve these problems. If there is a riot, there will, of course, be a commission to investigate and recommend new vehicles for solution. If a community discovers that it has a drug problem among its youth, again something new and different must be done. We are constantly being reminded that something bad is happening and that something new will take care of it, and it is the latter response which arouses hope in some who like to believe (who *have* to believe) that the desired change will take place soon. At the same time it arouses indifference or pessimism in others who have come to believe that the more things change the more they remain the same. The skeptical response to new programs or settings was best put by a colleague who characterized our urban school systems as "the fastest changing status quos."

But the very high rate of setting creation does not in itself mean that the creation of settings is a crucial general problem apart from the objectives each setting was set up to reach. That is to say, one could argue that the creation of a new university involves processes and problems that are so different from the creation of a new elementary school (or clinic, or stage production, or institution for the retarded) that it does not make sense to talk in general about the creation of settings, and therefore it cannot be regarded as a crucial *general* problem. There is the same kind of truth to this argument as to the one that says apples and oranges are different and not comparable. Apples and oranges are, of course, comparable, and it is precisely that way of thinking which goes beyond superficial appearances to seek communalities that is most productive of new ideas and a different view of the world.

What may lead us to regard the creation of settings as an important, if not a crucial, problem is consideration of the fact that at the same time that people today are aware of the increase of new settings they experience one or all of several feelings: skepticism about outcome, resignation to failure, anxiety about the future, and a subliminal fear that the general situation is deteriorating. Side by side are a kind of feverish initiation of new solutions and an anticipation of social disaster. In no way do I wish to suggest that this sense of unease and pessimism is attributed by people clearly or directly to the inadequacies of thinking behind the creation of settings, although this is usually

alluded to. Not a week goes by without the appearance of several
new books which attempt to explain why the increasing multiplication
of new efforts to deal with problems is likely to end in disillusionment.
Many of these publications are pitched at the level of the larger society
and involve critical analysis of specific values and value systems which
at one time may have been appropriate to and functional for the
society but are no longer so. The uses of technology, the traditional
criteria for judging economic growth, the changing social role of the
corporation, the significances of the rise of the so-called military-in-
dustrial complex, practices in the provision of health services, the usual
ways of thinking about and dealing with problems of race and poverty,
individual rights and actions on the one hand and centralized authority on the other hand—these are some of the issues, problems, and
polarities which are being examined and reexamined in terms of their
basic assumptions and values, with the aim of developing consciousness of new values without which it is believed the headlong dash to
disaster will not be averted. Currently, pollution and population
growth are the problems providing the most dramatic forum for raising the question of what is and what should be the relationships
among technology, social organizations, societal problems, and basic
values.

There are several reasons why I feel these critical analyses are
important. First, they reflect the more general feeling that things are
out of whack and in ways which make contemplation of the future
more like the experience of a nightmare than that of wish-fulfilling
fantasy. Second, they attempt to cut through to the basic assumptions,
unverbalized by most people, which seem to govern thinking. The
thinking of many people is usually unreflectively based on criteria of
"progress" that do not stand up under critical scrutiny. In fact, what
so many of these social analysts clearly agree on is the fateful role of
the unthinking acceptance of quantity and the passage of time as
criteria of "progress." The Enlightenment is drawing to a dark close,
and to some writers the close is not preparatory to a new era but to the
end of the human species. Even those (and they are a majority) who
do not share such a foreboding mood have difficulty generating or
justifying optimism, let alone enthusiasm.

The third reason why these social analyses are important can
be illustrated by imagining the following: through some magical
means it becomes possible quickly, if not immediately, to change the
values of all people in our society so that a reordering of priorities
becomes possible and the building of a new society becomes the order
of the day. Having "solved" the problem of values—*and that is the*

first basic problem—it is obvious that many settings will be drastically changed or eliminated and, equally obviously, that many new settings will have to be created. It would make life simple indeed if one could assume that agreement on values is the necessary *and* sufficient condition for the creation of new settings which are successful in terms of their stated objectives. The fact of the matter is that agreement on values may be a necessary condition but it is far from being a sufficient condition. Beyond values the creation of settings involves (among other things we shall later be discussing) substantive knowledge, a historical stance, a realistic time perspective, vehicles of criticism, and the necessity for and the evils of leadership. The creation of settings is not an engineering or technological task. It is also not one that can be accomplished by simply having appropriate or strong motivation. In short, to the extent that our imagined society is ready to restructure itself, it is faced with problems no less staggering or overwhelming or difficult than those with which it was faced before the magical transformation of values.

It may be that one of the many reasons some people have contributed to the utopian literature, and why millions today and in the distant past have been avid readers of these descriptions, is that it permits one to bypass the realities of the creation of new settings and societies.[2] What these literary utopias have in common is that they were brought into existence by an act of controlled fantasy, and they avoid the evils of creation by a process analogous to the belief in virginal birth.[3]

[2] Chapter Twelve is devoted to a critical analysis of B. F. Skinner's *Walden Two*, (1962) especially in light of his most recent, controversial book *Beyond Freedom and Dignity* (1971).

[3] Over the centuries the literary utopias have had a remarkable effect on the minds of people, if only because they have presented alternative ways of thinking and acting (as well as different value systems) which in the normal course of living would not occur to most people. Furthermore, these literary utopias have stimulated individuals and groups to attempt to bring these utopias into actual existence. There are aspects of society, technological and social, which were described in literary utopias long before they ever appeared in society, and although it would be erroneous to say that these literary utopias "caused" these changes, it would be equally erroneous to deny that they were not part of the historical context or intellectual tradition from which these changes emerged. For example, the goals of the current women's liberation movement were not only described in early utopian literature but were in fact implemented in some of the communes started in this country in the nineteenth century, a fact which does not establish cause and effect but does suggest that these writings and efforts at implementation are part of the historical context out of which the current liberation movement has emerged. As we shall see later in this book, the capacity of one's actions to be guided seriously and systematically by the knowledge that there *are* alternative ways of thinking and

Today we use the adjective *utopian* not only to suggest that something does not exist but also, and more important, that we do not know how to get to where we want to go, and it is the latter use which implicitly recognizes that knowing the goal is only the beginning of the journey. Wrapped up in the phrase *the creation of settings* are problems which precede chapter one in the published utopias.

But one does not have to make the point either by imagining a magical transformation of a society's values or by discussing literary utopias, because we are living at a time which is witnessing a marked increase in serious efforts to create settings (such as communes, mini-societies, collectives) encapsulated within the larger society but consciously and deliberately aiming to be different from that society. Like the literary utopias these modern efforts are powered by a rejection of conventional values regarding human work, behavior, and relationships, as well as by commitment to a different value system.[4] Unlike the literary utopias this new value system is tied to a commitment to action, to build somewhere "in the real world" a setting consistent with the basic values. About most of these efforts we know nothing; about others we have at best what one could call anecdotal evidence. We have no way of knowing with any degree of security the frequency of these efforts in the past two decades—how many never got beyond the initial organizational meetings, how many ceased functioning and at what point in their development, or how many of those no longer in existence were "successful" for at least part of the time. All we really know is that shortly after World War II, in part sparked by Skinner's *Walden Two* (1948), these efforts at creating truly new settings became increasingly frequent. Despite our ignorance a prediction can be made on the basis of earlier attempts to

---

acting—a principle so beautifully illustrated in the literary utopias—is a factor crucial to understanding the process of the creation of any setting.

[4] On the front page of the *New York Times* (December 17, 1970) under the headline "Communes Spread As The Young Reject Old Values" is a report which contains the following: "It now is becoming clear that the commune phenomenon, which began most recently in the late nineteen-sixties with the hippie movement, is growing to such proportions that it may become a major social factor in the nineteen-seventies. Nearly 2,000 communes in thirty-four states have been turned up by a New York Times inquiry seeking to determine how many permanent communal living arrangements of significant size could be found in the country, why they existed and who lived in them. That number is believed to be conservative because it no doubt missed some smaller communes and does not include hundreds of small, urban cooperatives and collectives." This article is only one of many similar ones contained in the *Times* over the past two years. In the Syracuse University *Daily Orange* for October 14, 1970, the banner headline on the front page is "Collectives Are Key To Revolution."

create new minisocieties. The early to the middle decades of the nineteenth century in this country were marked by the creation of scores
of "communes," the great bulk of which were religious in character
(see Holloway, 1966; Nordhoff, 1966). Like their current descendants
they were against prevailing values and for another set of values.
Although these earlier efforts are far from well described, the conclusion seems justified that the rate of success was low, and I see no
reason why one should expect any different outcome with the current
efforts.

A number of years ago my wife and I began to consider building our own home after concluding that whatever houses we had
looked at did not suit our purposes. The idea of building our own
home (as well as *owning* any home) was not anything for which my
background prepared me. In any event, we consulted an architect.
After one hour of discussion during which my anxiety and hesitation
must have been blatantly clear in the questions I was asking, he looked
at me and said in an admirably therapeutic manner: "You know, it
is extremely difficult to build a house that will fall down." In regard
to past efforts at creating new communes or collectives it is fair to say,
"It is very difficult to build a new minisociety that will stand up." The
discrepancy between the unfortunate fate of so many real-life attempts
to build a utopia and the success described in the literary utopias
signifies a number of things, not the least of which is that in the real
world agreement on basic values is far from adequate to the development of a viable, new social setting.

Most Ambitious Instance: Revolution

The crucial significance of the problem of the creation of settings can be illustrated further by turning to a class of instances which
in terms of scope and numbers of people who are or will be involved
is by far the most ambitious: the banding together of a group for the
express purpose of overthrowing a society and then of creating a new
one. When one looks over the history of these efforts (for example, the
Russian, American, French, Cuban revolutions) one can for our purposes describe, albeit in a grossly oversimplified way, several characteristics. Varying numbers of people are dissatisfied in varying ways with
the existing state of affairs and, again in different ways, clamor for
change. A number of groups is formed, in each one of which the
members, who previously may have had little, or no, or much knowledge of each other, agree to organize themselves in new and sustained
relationships in order to accomplish the task of overthrowing and
creating a society. The group (that is, the setting), initially quite

small, has a leader who usually brought the group together. The rules by which the group will be governed are relatively unverbalized and implicit, with the leader playing the most decisive role in planning and decision-making. The major tasks with which the group deals are many but one of the most important, because it involves the preservation of values, goals, and strength, is how to grow numerically—how to bring in more and more people and in ways which bring the group nearer to the goals of overthrowing and creating a new society. In point of fact the group is far more occupied with obtaining resources for overthrowing the existing structure than with what it does if and when it gains power. Throughout, those who comprise the setting share a sense of mission, of being different, of being superior, and of being in danger. From the very beginning, but particularly as the setting grows numerically and geographically, conflicts arise about goals, tactics, and communication, and the resolution of these conflicts may be accomplished, postponed, or be of such strength that members leave and form their own setting. At some point one or more of the groups, cooperatively or otherwise, achieve "power" and a new phase of setting creation begins.[5]

I have begun in this way in order to make the point that however adequate description might be, it misses the existence of certain basic assumptions which not only characterize the creation of settings but help explain why they fail or why settings vary so greatly in their accomplishment of stated goals. To illustrate what I mean we shall turn to a speech by Fidel Castro to the Cuban people on July 26, 1970. (This document was reprinted with an introduction by Lee Lockwood in the *New York Review of Books* of September 24, 1970.) As Lockwood notes, the speech appeared in Cuba's only newspaper with the banner headline "We Have Failed" and "in one of the frankest and most moving confessions of incompetency by a modern political

---

[5] It is anticipating later contents of this book to suggest here that the characteristics of the revolutionary group that I have presented are highly similar to those of any new setting. In describing other instances of the creation of settings the language and emphasis would be different from what I have described above, but the characteristics would be surprisingly similar. For example, the fear of being in danger from outside forces, the sense of being or wanting to be different and better or even unique, the desire to grow and amass people or things, to be primarily future oriented—these are some of the characteristics to be found in any instance of the creation of settings. Entering into marriage or starting a new university or new business is obviously different from organizing a setting for the purpose of overthrowing a society in order to create a new one, and yet they all share certain common characteristics or problems. Amoebas are obviously different from elephants, and both are different from man, but all do share certain common properties.

leader, Castro, before a crowd of half a million in Havana's Revolutionary Square, revealed to the Cuban people a devastating portrait of Cuba's economy in disarray. Then, characteristically, he placed the bulk of the blame squarely on his shoulders."

Essentially Castro makes the following points, illustrating each of them with facts and events. (1) There does not exist now, and there will not exist for a long time to come, enough *material* resources to meet the goals set by the leaders before and at the time of the revolution. (2) There does not exist now, and there will not exist for a long time, enough *human* resources to meet the goals set by the leaders before and at the time of the revolution. Concretely, neither in terms of education, technical knowledge, nor past experience are there enough people adequate to present and future tasks. "One of the many tragic things in our country . . . is our lack of cadres, of men with a high enough level of training and intelligence who are capable of carrying out the complex tasks of production." (3) The strongest motivation to succeed or overcome obstacles, even when it could be described as "iron will," has not only been insufficient as a solution but it has also resulted in the fact that "many comrades have worn themselves out, have 'burned themselves out,' as they say." (4) The revolutionary leaders had no idea of what they would be up against. "We could best be classified as ignorant. And we were ignorant—almost without exception (and I, of course, am not the exception)—all of us. . . . Most of the time we make the mistake of minimizing the difficulties, of minimizing the complexity of the problems."

In effect what Castro is telling us in this amazingly revealing document is that in the endeavor to create a new setting he wrongly assumed that agreement on basic values and goals, possessing the strongest motivation to succeed, and finally achieving power were the necessary and sufficient conditions for achieving stated objectives. Furthermore, Castro tells us, he and others could and should have known this from the beginning.

What Castro describes is in many ways similar to what is contained in Lenin's writings in the last months of his life when as a result of his cerebral stroke he could no longer be the active leader. These last months have been poignantly described in Lewin's book *Lenin's Last Struggle* (1968). Although most of what Lenin wrote during this period was not for public consumption, focusing largely on the power struggles going on in the party, and lacking Castro's subjective and ingenuous style, there emerges Lenin's recognition that the Russian Revolution was in danger of failing and for precisely the same reasons contained in Castro's speech. The document most similar to

Castro's speech is Lenin's (1968) paper "Better Fewer, but Better," in which he bemoans the lack of human resources appropriate to the tasks at hand and makes perfectly clear that agreement on values and objectives as well as the presence of the strongest degree of motivation to succeed are no guarantee for a successful new setting.

In discussing Castro and Lenin it was not my intention in any way to pass judgment on them or the new societies which they endeavored to help create, not because I am neutral in such matters, which I certainly am not, but because of two major considerations. First, to pass judgment would be to distract attention away from the major hypothesis that what these historical figures have said and written (that is, their diagnosis of the difficulty) is relevant to the creation of any new setting, large or small. The fact that they tell us what they learned, what they could or should have known, about the most ambitious instance of the creation of a setting should not blind us to the possibility that they have kinship to those who have far more modest aims. The second reason for not passing judgment is my awareness of one of the most important characteristics of those who create a setting: the tendency to oversimplify the question or the answer (or both). There is, I suppose, a third consideration, and that is that my own attempts to create settings have had the effect of reducing the strength of my tendency to pass judgment on others, particularly those caught up in efforts more ambitious than my own. Passing judgment is too frequently like "doing good" in that it enables us to feel virtuous and superior at the same time that it blinds us to the communalities we share.

Smallest Instance: Marriage

We know far more about how people have gone about creating a new society than about how two people go about creating the marital setting. We can always count on the historian, professional or amateur, to describe and interpret new settings which have or have had social significances. In fact, different historians may make their mark by focusing on differing aspects of the same event, and some by trying to bring the different aspects together to make a more comprehensible and comprehensive picture. We are not as fortunate in the case of marriage. One would expect that the processes by which two people create the marital setting would be extremely well described in the professional literature of the behavioral sciences, but this expectation is not borne out. There is, of course, a voluminous literature having to do with the ways in which certain aspects of marriage (stability, outcome, size, sexual behavior) are related to personality, intellectual, and social-class variables; and the number of books and articles written on marriage counseling is very large. Strangely, however, this literature contains very little illuminating the thinking, steps, and processes whereby two people enter into a sustained relationship, the problems they do and do not anticipate, the bases on which tasks are distributed and performed, their knowledge and use of resources (time, money, things), the "constitution" by which they will be governed, the vehicles for handling conflict, the factors which determine how they will handle "foreign relations," and how they view and manage numerical growth. Creating the marital setting contains all the issues and problems involved in creating any larger setting. The frequency of divorce, as well as the number of sustained but unhappy marriages, indicates that attaining stated objectives in marriage is probably no less difficult or frequent than it is in settings created for other purposes.

Why marriage, today at least, seems to be an increasingly frail institution is a simple question the answer to which is formidably complex, but for the restricted purposes of this book I would like to suggest that part of the answer is contained in Castro's explanation of the "mistakes" of the Cuban revolution—specifically, that the creation of the marital setting usually proceeds on the assumption that agreement on values as well as strength of motivation to succeed are the necessary and sufficient conditions to achieve stated objectives. Furthermore, and still following Castro's (and Lenin's) analysis, in creating the setting little or no systematic attention is given to the realities contained in such words as resources, knowledge, skills, foreign relations, and history. Indeed, love is not enough!

If the professionals have not viewed or studied marriage as the creation of a setting involving a series of definable issues and problems which exist regardless of the temperament, personality, and idiosyncrasies of two people, this is not true of our novelists and dramatists. Although they differ among themselves in what they emphasize and in how they relate marriage to larger social issues and forces, when one looks generally at what they have written they seem among other things to be saying that creating a viable marriage is quite complicated: its members oversimplify or ignore the realities they will face; these realities or problems are or were predictable; and their conceptual unpreparedness for what they will face not only contributes to stress but maximizes the tendency to explain everything in motivational or personality terms—and we are back again to Castro and Lenin. But these historical figures pinpointed something that is only implicit in most novels and plays, and it would go like this: the problems we are now facing stem in large measure from the way we thought and

the knowledge we did not use; it was not what was in our hearts but
what was missing in our heads; yes, what we felt and wanted, what
we were as personalities, were and are important, but what may kill us
is what we did not know but could or should have known.

I trust that no reader will interpret anything I have said as
maintaining either that marriage and revolution are the "same" or
that I have advanced anything resembling an explanation of either of
these phenomena. I also hope that the juxtaposition of marriage and
revolution—the largest and smallest instances of the creation of a setting—is not viewed as an idiosyncratic association on my part or the
straining for communalities by attending to superficial characteristics.
Such criticisms may turn out to have merit, but if they do it will not
be because of unreflective response to the fact that marriage and revolution are concretely and obviously different. Such unreflective response to that which is concretely or perceptually different is as unjustified, wrong, and intellectually confining as when some people
naively assume that artists and scientists think and work differently
because they use different materials, work in very different kinds of
places, and, of course, their end products are concretely and vastly
different. Furthermore, according to the stereotype, artists are primarily intuitive while scientists are logical, cerebral, and objective.
One does not have to deny differences in order to assert that examination of the processes and problems of artistic and scientific activity
reveals important similarities. For example, the idea that scientists are
not intuitive in their work and that, for instance, Michelangelo's Moses
did not involve a fantastic complexity of purely "cerebral" processes
and activity simply does not stand up under scrutiny. Clarity in these
matters is obscured by the tendency of some artists and scientists to
accept, because of ignorance or misguided pride, the stereotype.

To pursue the matter of marriage and revolution a bit further,
we can turn to another aspect which, in my experience, characterizes
the creation of settings—an aspect, incidentally, which has fateful
consequences for the life of the setting. Put most simply, this aspect
involves the belief (only later is the belief seen as a fantasy) that in
the lifetime of those who are creating the setting the point will be
reached when all major problems will have been solved, all major goals
achieved, and a conflict-free future assured. In short, whereas the
literary utopias occur by virtue of bypassing the realities of creation,
those who engage in the creation of settings will attain their utopia by
conquering the realities. As we shall see later in this book, the point at
which this belief is recognized as a fantasy—the point at which the
utopian myth founders on the rocks of reality—is crucial to all that

follows, if for no other reason than that adjustment to reality involves the necessity for change.[6]

American Constitutional Convention

The American Constitutional Convention of 1787 is one of the best-described instances of the beginning context of the creation of a setting. That the product of this assembly has been regarded as a landmark in the history of freedom and that it proved amazingly durable are important to our discussion only insofar as they suggest that the convention possessed clearly the major characteristics of the creation of a setting and in ways which vividly contrast with the creation of many other settings, large and small.

The participants in the convention were quite aware that their task was to provide the beginning and basic foundation to a new society or face the possibility that the aims of the revolution would never be realized. They knew that unless they succeeded in changing aspects of the relationships among individuals, groups, and states—and in ways which could be sustained in the face of thorny and deep-rooted differences—an unusual opportunity to change the course of history would be missed. If, as I shall discuss in a later chapter, those who create a setting almost always see themselves as different or special, as improving on what already exists or has gone before, as being the prisoners, so to speak, of a sense of mission, the participants in the convention felt this most poignantly.

Whether the United States in 1787 was in truth on the edge of dissolution is a question that will be argued among historians until the

[6] Leadership in a setting is always crucial but it becomes even more so at the point described above. The most serious situation is one in which the leader or the leadership is unaware that the point has been reached, while others recognize the point. Probably the more frequent situation is where the leadership recognizes the point has been reached but continues to act and talk as if this point has not been reached. What has and will continue to intrigue historians about the Russian revolution is what might have happened if Lenin had lived because, as Lewin (1968) has described, there are grounds for maintaining that in his final illness Lenin recognized, to a degree at least, that neither he nor the people could any longer act as if the aims of the revolution were being, or would likely be, achieved and that he had every intention of "going to the people." This, of course, is what Castro did in the speech I referred to earlier.

As numerous novelists have described, the point at which either or both members of a marriage recognize that their projected utopia will not be attained, and the manner in which the recognition is handled, is a turning point (for good or bad) in the quality of their setting. Giving up the myth of utopia is never easy, but when it occurs in the context of utter unpreparedness it can be shattering, and off one goes to the next marriage.

United States is no more. That a majority of the continental elite believed this to be the truth is the most solid, incontrovertible fact in the records of that year. A feeling in the bones that the United States was intended to be a full-fledged nation, a recognition that such a nation must have a national government, a loss of confidence in the capacity of Congress to heal itself and become such a government, a fear that the vast potential of the American people might never be realized, and above all a desire to bring the Revolution at last to completion—these were the principal political sentiments that carried Washington, Madison, Hamilton, and the rest down the dusty road to Philadelphia [Rossiter, 1966, p. 49].

Rossiter's book on "the Grand Convention" illustrates well some of the most important characteristics of the creation of settings, particularly in their beginning context, and I can only urge the reader to consult his book first to see how his descriptions justify the following generalizations and, second, to judge how in the reader's own experience with the creation of settings the generalizations are applicable and, therefore, in part account for success or failure, partial or complete. For example, Rossiter describes the four arrangements which "were especially important in fixing the style and procedures of the convention."

First, the voting was to be, as it had always been in Congress, strictly by states, with each state, no matter what its size and pretentions, having one vote. The Pennsylvanians, led by the two Morrises, had made it known informally in the first few days that they were tired of continental gatherings in which the smallest state had exactly the same voting power as the largest, but the Virginians, "conceiving" that an "attempt" to do away with equality "might beget fatal altercations," were able to "discountenance and stifle the project" at birth. They hoped that the small states, if not bullied right at the start, would come, "in the course of the deliberations, to give up their equality for the sake of an effective government." Although Madison and his associates were determined to do away forever with the confederate principle of one-state, one-vote, they recognized that they would have to accomplish this small miracle in a meeting organized precisely on that principle. Not wishing the meeting to end the day after it had begun, they gave in graciously and, as events were to prove, prudently to the small states.

Second, a decorum befitting a gathering of gentlemen was to be self-consciously maintained. Members were politely forbidden to whisper, read, or pass notes while one of their colleagues was speaking; they could be "called to order by any other member, as well as by the president": and the president himself was provided with special safeguards for his power and dignity. "When the house shall adjourn," one rule stated sententiously, "every member shall stand in his place, until the president pass him." One would like very much to have seen this sight.

If the proceedings were to be decorous, they were not, however, to be frozen. The members voted down a proposed rule authorizing "any member to call for the yeahs and nays and have them entered on the minutes," and provided, at the suggestion of Spaight of North Carolina, for orderly reconsideration of any decision already "determined by a majority." Thus they made it possible to feel their way toward solutions they could not immediately anticipate, by changing their minds as often and easily as men can in the presence of friends and rivals.

Finally, the Convention voted, on the prompting of Pierce Butler, to guard "against licentious publication of their proceedings." In search of privacy, which they knew they would need in abundance, the members voted "that no copy be taken of any entry on the journal during the sitting of the house without leave of the house. That members only be permitted to inspect the journal. That nothing spoken in the house be printed, or otherwise published or communicated without leave."

Although few delegates may have grasped the logic of their action clearly on May 28–29, the adoption of the so-called secrecy rule was the most critical decision of a procedural nature the Convention was ever to make. At the time George Mason found this a "necessary precaution to prevent misrepresentations or mistakes," and in later years Madison insisted that "no Constitution would ever have been adopted by the convention if the debates had been public." It is hard to disagree with these opinions. The secrecy rule stirred the imaginations and loosened the tongues of delegates on the floor, permitted them to take advanced positions and then to withdraw gracefully under fire, guarded them against both careless and willful misinterpretations of their groupings for constitutional solutions and political compromises, permitted one consensus after another to form out of a wealth of half-formed opinions and half-baked prejudices, encouraged them to express honest doubts about such sacred cows as the sovereignty of the states and the glories of the militia, and spared bravos like Randolph and Charles Pinckney the temptation of playing to any gallery save that of posterity, one that usually brings out the best in such men.

The remarkable thing about this rule is not that it was so readily adopted, but that it was so rigidly observed by the delegates and so uncomplainingly accepted by the press and public [i ρ. 141–143].

It is a glimpse of the obvious that in beginning to create a setting *some* implicit or explicit rules are necessary by which the individuals will be governed. What this excerpt about arrangements indicates is the importance given not only to explicit rules but to rules which would maximize candidness of opinion and protect the individual against the irrationalities of himself and others, and this in the context of acute recognition that there were major differences and problems which could not be expected to be discussed only on the level of cold reason and logic. It was not that they sought rules in order to be able to get on to solve problems, but that they had problems (and a prehistory) which required rules appropriate to their nature and possible solution.

What is even more remarkable is that the considerations which led to the rules by which they agreed to be governed—rules which not only reflected real problems but also conceptions about what man is and how he acts under certain conditions—are reflected in the document that finally emerges, that is, the conception of checks and balances and the vehicles of control against the abuses of too little and too much power. Earlier in this chapter I pointed out that one of the most frequent characteristics of the creation of settings is the belief that in the lifetime of those who are creating the setting the point will (or can) be reached when all major problems will have been solved, all major goals achieved, and a conflict-free future assured, and this belief ordinarily is adversely fateful for the setting. The success of the 1787 Convention may well be due in large part to weakness of such a belief among its participants and the strong presence instead of a conception of man, *and man in certain public roles,* that forced them to think about and devise ways which would both recognize and dilute the consequences of some of man's less pleasant tendencies.

It is both incomplete and too simple to explain what these men did by saying that they were as remarkable a group of people as has ever been assembled to do an important job and that such a group would distinguish themselves regardless of the tasks with which they were confronted. That they were remarkable in many ways goes without saying, but what I am suggesting is that as important as their personalities, maturity, and erudition were their ideas and conceptions about the good and the bad in man, particularly as he strives for, gets caught up in, and finally achieves political power. It really makes no difference, at this point, whether or not one agrees with these ideas and conceptions. What is important is that these men began to create a setting guided not by what they hoped man could be but by what they thought he was; not by assuming that shared values were necessary and sufficient for success but by contriving and inventing ways which might protect these values against man's tendencies to act rashly, selfishly, and corruptly; not by deluding themselves that the end product of their labors was adequate for all time but by specifically providing for change and orderly change which in principle could undo all they had done.

A related generalization which the 1787 convention illustrates well is the necessity for *anticipating problems and consequences,* an activity or process notably absent or found only in diminished degree in the creation of most settings. In fact, when one reads the proceedings one is struck by how similar they seem to be to the thinking of a scientist when he is planning a study, at least the thinking of a "successful" scientist: figuring out ahead of time the possible consequences of using or not using a particular variable or procedure, of the effect of one variable on another, and of the adequacy of controls against human and mechanical defects and failures. Anticipating problems and consequences is not a pleasurable activity, if only because it confronts one with how hard and long one may have to work, and this was certainly the case in the 1787 convention. Here again, the distinguishing feature was not only in "motivation"—because a number of participants wanted to get it over with and go home (the convention lasted from May to September and it was a steaming summer)—but in the *knowledge* that anticipating problems and consequences was acceding to necessity and not indulging a luxury.

A final generalization which characterized the convention, and again one found in small degree in the creation of most settings, was the realization that for any problem there was a wide variety of alternative solutions. Put in another way, there was no single correct solution (as in an arithmetic problem) but a variety of solutions and that it was important in arriving at the final solution to hear and consider as many as could be generated.

Because the concept of the universe of alternatives will loom large in later chapters, it may be helpful to the reader briefly to note several things about it. The first is its axiomatic nature: the kinds of problems which confront the creation of settings do not logically lead to one, and only one, solution. Second, the awareness and acceptance of the fact that there are alternative solutions make accommodation and compromise more likely, a consequence which is anathema only to those who have to believe that agreement on values leads in some inevitable fashion to only one way of implementing them in the solution of a problem. In the process of creating a setting, awareness and acceptance of the concept of the universe of alternatives, as well as sustaining such acceptance, are extraordinarily difficult. This has not been a problem in most instances of the creation of a setting either because the concept simply was not in anybody's head or because the awareness of alternatives was seen as complicating what was already a complicated situation—and it is usually only after failure and catastrophe have occurred that respect is given to the concept and then in the form of a postmortem on a dead setting. One of the differences between presight and hindsight is contained in the concept of the universe of alternatives.

Needing or striving for perfection, so characteristic of so many people creating a setting, is not compatible with the complications of the concept of the universe of alternatives. As Benjamin Franklin put it to the convention (Rossiter, p. 235):

Mr. President: I confess that there are several parts of this constitution which I do not approve, but I am not sure I shall never approve them: For having lived long, I have experienced many instances of being obliged by better information, or fuller consideration, to change opinions even on important subjects, which I once thought right, but found to be otherwise. It is therefore that the older I grow, the more apt I am to doubt my own judgment, and to pay more respect to the judgment of others. . . . Though many private persons think almost as highly of their own infallibility as of that of their sect, few express it so naturally as a certain French lady, who in a dispute with her sister said, "I don't know how it happens, Sister, but I meet with no body but myself, that's always in the right—*Il n'y a que moi qui a toujours raison.*"

In all these sentiments, Sir, I agree to this constitution with all its faults, if they are such; because I think a general government necessary for us, and there is no form of government but what may be a blessing to the people if well administered, and believe farther that this is likely to be well administered for a course of years. . . . I doubt too whether any other convention we can obtain may be able to make a better constitution. For when you assemble a number of men to have the advantage of their joint wisdom, you inevitably assemble with those men, all their prejudices, their passions, their errors of opinion, their local interests, and their selfish views. From such an assembly can a perfect production be expected? It therefore astonishes me, Sir, to find this system approaching so near to perfection as it does; and I think it will astonish our enemies. . . . Thus I consent, Sir, to this constitution because I expect no better, and because I am not sure, that it is not the best. The opinions I have had of its errors, I sacrifice to the public good. I have never whispered a syllable of them abroad. Within these walls they were born, and here they shall die. . . .

On the whole, Sir, I cannot help expressing a wish that every member of the Convention who may still have objections to it, would with me, on this occasion, doubt a little of his own infallibility, and to make manifest our unanimity, put his name to this instrument.

Thus far in this introductory chapter I have indicated that the creation of settings is a general problem the understanding of which may be extremely important, if not crucial, to what is and will be happening in our society. More specifically, I have maintained that the pessimism and cynicism with which so many people have come to view past and present efforts of our society to solve problems is, in part at least, implicit recognition that there is something wrong in how we have conceived of the countless settings which were created to deal with the problems. Although it would be stupid to deny that traditional values are being questioned, or that a new consensus about values is not emerging or is not needed, I have argued that describing the current malaise exclusively in terms of values obscures and even misses the point that consensus about values does not instruct one in how to create settings consistent with these values, and that is why the creation of settings is such an important problem.

Time and again I have observed the creation of settings (usually in the human service area) with whose basic values and aims it would be hard to disagree, only to see over time how optimism is replaced by pessimism, consensus by polarization, and passionate concern for values by a desire to exist. (When I report this I am not reporting what I felt but what those in the setting felt, and sometimes these feelings were paraded on the pages of the local newspapers.) Why so many new settings fail, and relatively quickly, is not easy to understand, and what I have tried to do in very brief fashion in this chapter is to suggest that part of the answer is in how people think: their knowledge, ideas, conceptions. Lest this be construed as another cliche, let it be noted that currently the two most frequent answers involve the role of feelings and values which, while inextricably related to thinking, are not synonymous with it. For example, an entire new industry has developed and flourished which centers on the problems of "relating" and "communicating," the assumption being that what is wrong in settings is that they do not permit, if they ever permitted, their members to express or communicate "true" feeling to each other. Consequently, in creating a setting or in "renewing" an existing one, the major problem is to ensure "open" communication and to make it possible for members to be in touch with their "true" feelings. Behind these statements is yet an equally vague set of other statements about "human" values, self-actualization, and the democratic ethos. But if all this leaves doubt about the nature of the intended cure, it is removed when one examines the variety of group dynamics utilized, and the variety is great indeed and growing proportionately with the size of the industry. What is intended and what becomes the focus of interest in these groups procedures are feelings, emotions, and affects —their quality, strength, direction, expression, and utility. In some of these group procedures attitudes and feelings toward authority and leadership become the magnetic center pulling and exposing the feelings of the group. The variety of procedures is great, as are the underlying conceptions, but what they all have in common is seeking the expression of "true" feeling in the group situation and a propagandistic flavor suggesting that an important answer is available to the ills of individuals and organizations.

There is, of course, some merit to these procedures and claims, but the implication that changing feelings and values is primarily the answer to the ills of individuals, malfunctioning settings, and the creation of more viable settings relegates ideas and thinking—the cognitive realm of human endeavor—to a secondary role. In stating the problem of the creation of settings I deliberately chose examples (national revolutions, marriage, utopias) which bring to the fore in obvious fashion the role of ideas and conceptions in shaping the future of the setting for good or bad.

One of the thorny obstacles to understanding and formulating the creation of settings is the lack of well-described instances. If one were to use the literary utopias as examples of description telling us how and why things were done, one would have to conclude that the number of adequate descriptions of actual attempts to create settings is almost nonexistent. There are descriptions, to be sure, but they are usually deficient on at least several counts: important areas of activity and thinking are omitted; what is described is usually fragmentary and (far more often than not) subject to all the limitations of retrospective thinking and description. The inadequacy of existing descriptions has several explanations, but surely one of the important ones, as will become clear later in this book, is that creating a setting is conceptually and action-wise as complex a task as can be undertaken, and if existing descriptions do not reflect these complexities—if they intimidate the would-be conscientious describer—it is all too understandable. Nevertheless, I would suggest that the complex task is made a near-impossible one by the lack of an organized set of conceptions which would help select and order data according to the basic problems confronting the creation of any setting. To arouse interest in this problem and to suggest what some of these basic conceptions may be are the aims of this book.

Plan of the Book

This book will not tell the reader how successful settings can be created, although in discussing instances of success and failure it is inevitable that certain conclusions will emerge that can serve as guides to others. The diagnosis of "mistakes" implies prescription for how they might have been avoided, and the analysis of "success" similarly conveys a prescription for action. In either case we must recognize that we are at a point where we must not pretend that our conclusions are a secure basis for action. The lack of such a secure basis should be no bar to those who wish to create new settings. Indeed it never has been, and the major purpose of this book is to try to begin to understand why this is so. What is it in our heads and our society that permits us to engage in as meaningful and important a task as the creation of a setting as if all that were involved was the proper compounding of motivation, technology, and hard work? This book is not in the how-to-do-it tradition. It is rather an attempt to bring order to my own efforts to understand my own experiences, and those of others, in creating new settings. The attempt is father to the hope that those disposed to action, and those disposed to think about and comment on such action, will become more conscious of the conceptual complexity of the problem.

As a result of my experiences and observations I have come to see what I consider to be basic processes and problems in the creation of settings, and I have found them to be productive not only in ordering my own experiences but in seeing the value of the existing literature. (In fact, one of the most personally exciting and instructive consequences of my experiences has been the sense of continuity and kinship with so much that has been done and written.) Consequently, each of the subsequent chapters concerns a problem or process as it is developmentally encountered in the creation of a setting, bringing in my own experience as well as those aspects of the literature deemed most relevant and illustrative.

Although, as the present chapter suggests, I see the creation of settings as a crucial general problem and one which contains most of the important issues of present and past social living, the remainder of this book is modest in scope because it will be largely about relatively small settings devoted to some form of human service. I shall, of course, be satisfied if what I have to say is regarded as a contribution in this restricted area, but it should already be obvious that I regard what I have to say as having much wider significance. I say this less because I am convinced that this is the case than because of the hope that others with wider experience and deeper historical knowledge will see fit to pursue the matter further. The direction our society and our individual selves takes is uppermost in most people's minds, but unless the compass that guides us has history built into it we will go in circles, feel lost, and conclude that the more things change the more they remain the same. The creation of settings is not peculiar to our society or times. One can only sigh and say "here we go again" when we see efforts to shape futures based on the rejection or ignorance of the past. For example, in the *New York Times* article on communes to which I referred earlier, it is noted, without comment, that many of these efforts are proceeding as if they have invented the wheel, robbing themselves of a sense of continuity and the possibility of truly helpful knowledge. Although the broad sweep of history will be missing from most of what follows, we shall see in the next chapter that the creation of a modest setting proceeds (in the local sense) ahistorically at its peril.

CHAPTER **2**

Before the Beginning

A history of a setting is usually not written merely because it is interesting but rather to explain the contexts of its creation and development, and such explanations have been of three kinds. The first is what may be called explanation in terms of a single, dominant personality; that is, the history of the setting is seen primarily as a function of some combination of a single individual's temperament, intellect, and motivations. For example, if you wish to understand the creation and development of the Ford Motor Company, you have to understand the kind of person Henry Ford was: his habits, ways of thinking, goals, values, and so on. Or if you want to understand how the Menninger and Mayo Clinics were created and developed, you have to know what the brothers Menninger and Mayo were like—their personal, intellectual, and professional histories. Or if one wants to understand "The Harmony Society," one of many religious-communist societies of the nineteenth century described by Nordhoff (1966), one has to understand its founder, George Rapp. The following typifies Nordhoff's emphasis: "Rapp was, with the help of his adopted son, the organizer of the community's labor, appointing foremen in each department; he planned their enterprises

—but he was also their preacher and teacher; and he taught them that their main duty was to live a sincerely and rigidly religious life; that they were not to labor for wealth, or look forward anxiously for prosperity; that the coming of the Lord was near, and for this they were waiting, as his chosen ones separated from the world."

The fascination as well as the limitation of this "human interest" approach are well put in Holoway's preface to the American edition (1966) of his delightful book *Heavens On Earth,* which contains discussions of many of the societies contained in Nordhoff's book:

Heavens on Earth was pleasingly received on both sides of the Atlantic, recommended by the Book Society in England and generally regarded as a stylish, entertaining and well-balanced account of the serious endeavours it describes. It is still, I believe, the only book on the subject which attempts to show the American phase of communitarian societies as part of a tradition stretching from Plato and the Essenes to the Kibbutzim, while trying to assign to each community its relative importance within the movement as a whole. From one point of view, I wish it performed these functions more fully. I would like to add a good deal of material relating these societies to the general social, political and economic history of the period and to similar communities contemporary with these in other countries. But I know that this would upset the balance of the book and diffuse the impact made by the communities themselves, thus leading to an entirely different kind of approach.

In this book I am concerned above all with the human interest which inevitably belongs to all those individuals who are brave enough to disregard conventional patterns of behavior and willingly face hardship and criticism for the sake of ideas and ideals which they believe to be right. When, as in the present instance, these beliefs are in conflict with most of the assumptions on which our civilization rests, the human interest is intensified. Although a more sociological approach might be of equal interest, I do not think it could be grafted onto this book in its present form. It seems best, therefore, not to meddle with this one in that way, and to leave the other project aside as a possibility for the future.

This quotation contains the essence of the second type of explanation which is that to understand the creation and development of a setting the most basic consideration is wrapped up in the word *Zeitgeist.* That is to say, and to say it loosely, the setting reflects what is in the air, and what is in the air derives from the existing social structure. Whereas the first explanation is primarily psychological, the second is sociological; whereas the first gives supremacy to intrapsychic factors, the second gives greatest weight to factors which are independent of any individual; whereas the psychological explanation tends to be put in a restricted or local geographical area, the sociological explanation may be put in the context of an entire nation or even transcend national boundaries.

The third explanation is a combination of the first two and its obvious reasonableness is matched by the obvious difficulty a single mind encounters doing justice to the first two explanations in an integrated fashion. However reasonable this type of explanation may be in principle, it requires making at least two assumptions whose validity is no simple matter to establish. The first is that one's working conceptions or theory of personality are sufficiently comprehensive so as to direct one to collect data relevant to those conceptions. The second assumption is identical to the first but what is at issue here is the adequacy of one's sociological conceptions.

In Chapter One, I already indicated that a major obstacle to our understanding of the creation and development of settings is the surprising lack of detailed descriptions of their "natural history." This lack may be attributed to the tendency to see the problem in terms of the personality of a single person or the characteristics of a small group, putting the problem in the realm of personality and the idiosyncratic and, therefore, making it not a general problem. It may also be attributed to the incompleteness or narrowness of sociological theory in that the creation of settings as a test of theory is not seen as a problem.[1] Some readers will be aware that there are thousands of professionals (sociologists, social psychologists, industrial psychologists, management consultants, "systems" engineers or repairers, operations researchers) who devote their days studying and trying to change myriad settings. Is it possible, someone could ask, that these people, involved as they are with the dynamics and intricacies of settings, have not come up with an understanding of how settings were created and developed? The answer, of course, is that it is impossible not to formulate ideas about how these settings came to be what they are. *What must be recognized, and in as crystal clear a way as possible, is that these ideas derive almost exclusively from observing and working with chronologically mature settings which are having problems.* To assume from the analysis of a chronologically mature setting that one can derive a valid and comprehensive picture of how the setting was created and

---

[1] *The Handbook of Organizations* (March, 1965) is an unusually large, comprehensive, and excellent summary of theory and research in regard to a variety of settings, including industrial, penal, educational. The creation of a setting or organization as a separate problem is not raised or discussed. Stinchcombe's (1965) chapter is the most relevant, but aside from stating in one paragraph why people create new settings, he says little about the developmental aspects.

developed is to make the mistake about which Freud long ago warned in relation to the psychoanalysis of adults: do not assume that the picture of early childhood one gains from treating troubled adults is identical, or even highly similar, to that one would gain from studying childhood. When Freud seized the opportunity (the case of Little Hans) to study a troubled youngster it was not only to test conceptions derived from working with adults but also to nurture the belief that something new would be learned and that the theory of development would take on new substance and scope. The consequences of this logic confirmed important aspects of his theory at the same time that they opened up new vistas in theory and practice.

The fact that thousands of people spend their working lives trying to help and repair troubled settings in itself establishes the creation of settings as an important problem, and in two ways. How do we account for so many troubled settings? To what extent are these troubles preventable?

New Settings Out of Old Ones

In this section I discuss new settings which are outgrowths of or additions to existing ones. The following are concrete and frequent instances. (1) A state Youth Services Commission which is to be responsible for the care of all delinquent and dependent youth sixteen years of age and below. Whereas before several different state agencies (such as, welfare, corrections, health) had different responsibilities for some of these youths, one new agency would be created in order to make for more coordinated care and programing. Aside from greater efficiency, and precisely because youth would be its sole focus, it is expected that the new agency would develop more creative, comprehensive, and effective programs. (2) A new school. Because of increased population in a part of the city, or the utter inadequacy of an existing school in a ghetto area, the Board of Education decides that a new school is necessary. Basically, the same situation may obtain in higher education: a university decides to have a new institute of social science, or a department or independent program in black studies, or a new department of computer science. (3) A new city, or state, or federal air pollution agency. Here, too, functions which were performed by different agencies, in none of which pollution was a major focus, are brought together in a new setting, and, of course, new functions are to be added. (4) A new Office of Child Development. I am referring specifically to the creation in 1970 of a new federal agency into which were placed existing agencies and programs concerned with children. Again the stated purposes included greater efficiency and more rational planning and programing. (5) A new state mental hospital, or new prison, or new city hospital. Here again these new settings may be to supplant inadequate existing settings or to meet increased need.

I have begun with these instances of setting creation not because I am interested (at this point) in them but because I wish to focus on some of the characteristics of the matrix of structures out of which the new setting has emerged and into which it is placed. The point I shall be making is not unlike the one which states that at birth the newborn has a history, not the least important part of which is the fact he contains something of each of his parents. Ordinarily, this glimpse of the obvious is of no particular significance unless at or shortly after birth there is something extraordinarily amiss, and then the obvious becomes a spur to thinking and action. Even if the rate of "amissness" among new settings is no greater than that among newborns and infants, and it probably is a good deal greater, we cannot avoid looking at what I have called before-the-beginning.

One of the clearest communalities among the types of instances listed above is that each arises from an existing organization of settings. Each of these settings, however different its purposes and functions may be, is by law or individual perception part of a larger setting. Each setting in the organization desires either to remain the same or to grow, depending on a variety of factors which need not detain us. The crucial fact is that each setting in part views itself in terms of other settings in the larger organization; that is, the settings are in competition with each other for resources which will enable them either to remain where they are or to grow. Part of each setting's time and energy is spent scrutinizing the other settings. In fact, each setting's "behavior" is in part based on the assumption that it is indeed part of a dynamic system which is ever changing and in which a change in one part is very likely to have effects on other parts of the system.

All of this is obvious, but what is not so obvious is that these characteristics obtain whenever there are limited resources to share, there are no agreed upon values strongly shared by all, and decisions and planning are the prerogatives of a very small number of people who perform these functions for reasons other than commonly shared values or goals. It is oversimple to view these characteristics as a *necessary* consequence of specialized functions which, for the sake of efficiency, require a bureaucratic mode of functioning. There have been instances of communes, relatively large in size and performing a wide variety of specialized functions, where these characteristics were not present, or only minimally so (Nordhoff, 1966). The point, however, is that the types of instances of setting creation listed earlier arise from an existing organization of settings in which competition for resources is guaranteed.

What can one expect, what indeed must happen, when to such an organization a new setting will be added? Not only did the existing settings have no voice in the creation of the new setting, not only is it obvious to them that limited resources will now be divided by a larger denominator, but some of these existing settings will give up functions and resources to the new setting because these and other functions will presumably be better performed in the new setting.[2] One need not resort to theory to conclude that what was already a dynamic system has become even more so and in ways which work against and not for the new setting. This conclusion is in no way based on considerations of personalities or power, factors that no doubt may alter the quantitative but not the qualitative aspects of the dynamics.

Certain aspects of what we are discussing are well illustrated by data from four cases of young adults with whom I once had a therapeutic relationship. In two cases the individuals had been married for a relatively short period of time, and in the other two they were shortly to be married and the therapeutic relationship continued for some time after marriage. In each case the couple lived with one of the parents because of economic necessity, and this arrangement was entered into explicitly on a temporary basis. Perhaps the most remarkable feature of these cases was that the parents with whom they lived were initially viewed and reported as being, if not enthusiastic, unquestionably willing to have the young couple live with them. Perhaps equally remarkable was that although each couple in some vague way expected that there would be problems, they had no doubt that they would be appropriately resolved. What emerged, of course, will be quite familiar to many readers. There were many problems and conflicts and everyone could not wait until other living arrangements could be made.

The details of the substance and strength of these conflicts are

[2] That existing settings usually have no voice in the creation of a new setting is par for the course. That I mention it here, and that it will enter into different aspects of our discussion, in no way reflects concern with courtesy or manner or some abstract notion of a democratic ethos, but rather the simple fact that ignoring the relationships of existing settings to a proposed new one is to change adversely the balance of positive and negative forces which any new setting faces. I disclaim the significance of courtesy, obviously not because I am against it, but because I have seen too many instances where the existing settings were treated courteously but with a ritualistic type of courtesy serving no other function than to avoid facing the existing realities out of which the new setting arose. As one individual said: "I touched all bases," an expression well describing the game he was playing.

less important than the fact that everyone agreed that "personality" was the etiological factor of greatest significance. I confess that I shared this view at that time (a good many years ago). It was only in retrospect that I came to see that an essential condition for what happened was that the parents had to deal with the problem of resources. That is to say, in terms of time, space, and things, they had to make some real accommodations; they had, so to speak, to give up part of what they had and they had little or no realization of what this would mean or what it would do to them. (There was some evidence that some of the parents may well have realized that they would have to share existing resources and basically did not want to do so.) Nobody at the time seemed to recognize that subdividing existing resources was a real problem not manufactured by personality. That personality can exacerbate or dilute the problem goes without saying, but it is all too easy to overlook that having to give up part of one's resources is a problem independent of personality, and to be unaware of this is asking for trouble.

A much more frequent instance of this point is when one has house guests for a weekend or more. Even when one looks forward to the visit, which is not always the case, there is at the end of a visit a feeling of relief that one's resources (my home) no longer have to be shared. It is not simply a matter that one's habits of living can be reinstated, which is true, but that the reinstatement has to do with the resources one owns.

But there is one other characteristic shared by the instances I listed in which the new setting arises from and is added to an existing organization of settings: it is expected that the new setting will perform better the functions previously performed by other parts of the organization—an expectation not ordinarily shared by the settings from which the functions have been taken.

We are led then to the conclusion, in relation to the types of instances we have been discussing, that the before-the-beginning period contains organizational dynamics which tend to work against rather than for the new setting in the sense that its heritage is marked by conflict, real or potential. If this seems obvious to the reader, as it should, let him ponder the point which we shall be discussing later, that those who are given responsibility for the new setting almost always proceed either as if the reverse were true or as if their heritage were truly virginal.

In light of what I have described one may ask how any new setting manages to arise from the organization of existing settings. The answer resides in large part in the consequences of the fact that the examples I gave all involved governmental organizations (administrative-executive) which are subject to three sources of pressure: public, legislative, and internal. Ordinarily, either because of particularly upsetting events which draw public attention or because of the organized efforts of certain individuals and groups, pressure is brought to bear both upon the legislative and administrative bodies to do something more than or different from what they are now doing. The response of the existing organization of settings is of two kinds: a willingness to do more and a denial that it is in any way responsible for inadequacies in the way the problem has been handled (the latter response usually based on the position that there had long been internal pressure to do more and that adequate resources were never made available to do what needed to be done). At the point when everyone agrees that something more needs to be done there begins the competition about who will get the new resources: will it go to an existing setting, will it be spread around, or will a new and independent setting be created? Many people and settings (internal, external, legislative) are strongly concerned with how the question will be resolved and the struggle can be quite intense. What we need to pay attention to is not only that struggle occurs and that conflict is present, but that among the many people who are interested and involved there are only a few who formally or informally have discernible degrees of power and influence. It would be misleading to view these individuals as engaged in a struggle for leadership because some of them have no desire "to win" in the sense of being asked to take over the new resources. A particular legislator or private citizen or representative of a certain community may wish to influence the final decision but not because he wishes to become the formal leader of the new setting. He may wish to influence where the new resources will go, the ways in which they will be used, and the kind of person who should be leader, but he does not seek to become the leader. At this point in before-the-beginning the conflicts center around substantive issues and administrative placement.

The decision to create a new and independent setting usually reflects two considerations: the opinion that the existing settings are inadequate for one or another reason and, independent of this, the awareness that the conflicts that emerged in the process of arriving at a decision were of such strength and quality as to make a new and independent setting the desirable possibility. And again we see that the new setting has a variegated type of heritage not the least important aspect of which is that the individuals and settings which comprise that heritage continue to be operative. As I indicated before, part of this heritage literally becomes part of the new setting. All of the rest continue to surround it.

Nonbureaucratic Origins

Some readers will have responded to the discussion of the first class of instances by saying, "That's bureaucracy for you, particularly public ones, and to expect successful outcomes for new settings which arise from and become part of that bureaucracy is to expect virtue to arise from sin; bureaucracy is sinful and contaminates all that it touches." There are, of course, philosophers and religions who assert that virtue only arises from sin, provided that one is capable of learning lessons and that the criteria of sin are clear. The point is not whether the assertion is true but rather that one has to be very clear about what is virtuous and sinful. To say that bureaucratic organizations are "bad" may be true but it is certainly not the whole story. For example, the fact that the types of settings discussed in the previous section may fail (let us assume they have) cannot be understood solely in terms of bureaucratic organizations because that does not explain why the before-the-beginning phase in the creation of a setting is so frequently ignored by those who create the setting. One might rather expect an exquisite sensitivity to this phase because those who are asked to create the settings usually have been reared, so to speak, in bureaucratic organizations and should be expected to know the importance of confronting history. But such confrontation of history is, in my experience, rare, and if such human error and ignorance are not simple consequences of bureaucratic organization, it suggests the real possibility that the creation of a setting even in the context of nonbureaucratic organization is by no means assured. Without denying at all that the type of existing organization from which a new setting arises is extremely important, I am maintaining that its fate is in part independent of type of organization.

To illustrate this point let us look at another class of instances of the creation of a setting: (1) a new commune or collective; (2) a new private college or, more frequent, a "free school" or "free university"; (3) a new city under private auspices (see Eichler and Kaplan, 1967); (4) a new clinical service or program initiated by parents of afflicted children (see Graziano, 1969).

These instances have several characteristics in common. First, they are not a consequence of public clamor or a public problem which directly produces pressure to create *this* type of setting. Each of these settings reflects in some way a public problem, and in the minds of those who create the setting there may be a sense of urgency that they do something about the problem, but there is no external pressure on *them* to create the setting. Second, the felt need for the setting as well as the decision to try to create it is that of a single individual who is and remains, for some time, the leader, the organizer, the mover. Third, there is a guiding idea which lends distinctiveness to the proposed setting and which, in one way or another, is considered to be better than or superior to the ideas behind existing settings. Fourth, the competition between the new and existing settings is viewed minimally, or not at all, in terms of limited resources but rather in the realm of ideas and values. Fifth, the chances of success for the new setting are considered high precisely because it is outside the influence of existing bureaucratic organizations which would dilute, or subvert, or abort the superior ideas or values.

What the class of instances has in common with the previous one is the characteristic of superiority of mission, that is, competition in the realm of ideas or values with the clear implication that the new setting will be better than existing ones. In all other respects the two classes of instances appear to differ so that one is forced to ask if it makes any sense, in regard to the second class, to talk of a before-the-beginning phase. After all, if one of the characteristics is that one individual possessed the idea and started the process of creating the setting, it would seem that the before-the-beginning phase would involve us purely in personal history rather than in the dynamics of existing settings. Furthermore, if it is only a matter of idiosyncratic personal history it would suggest that arriving at generalizations about this class of instances would be extremely difficult, each history being so different from all others.

In discussing the before-the-beginning phase in the previous section, it was pointed out that the problem which ultimately gave rise to the new setting was external to the existing organization of settings (for example, city, state, federal). That is to say, things happened "out there" which set things in motion. But this is equally true for the present class of instances, except that the external happenings are neither by law nor tradition the responsibility of the individual who will start the setting. The important point here is not that the individual sees a problem "out there" but that he sees the problem as in part due to existing modes of organization. For example, if I were to decide to create my own school for children, it would in some way reflect a diagnosis of what is wrong with existing schools (Sarason, 1971). That is to say, before the idea of a new school ever occurred to me I would have had knowledge of and experience with the existing schools. That I worked in these schools on a professional basis is one kind of experience and source of knowledge, but it may be equally important that I *lived* in these schools as a pupil for a number of years. As in the first class of instances, the new school I create will inevitably reflect characteristics of the fact that I was part of existing schools. Would I think the same about the new school if I had gone to private instead of public schools? Would not the fact that these two types of school are usually organized or structured differently make some difference in how I think about the new school?

From time to time I have asked a class of my students to imagine that they want to start a new school for children; they should think about it for a while and then give forth with their plans. Since the task always is presented after previous meetings centered around educational issues, the task I give seems relevant to them. The class usually consists of men and women some of whom went to private and others to public schools; needless to say, they vary in personality, experience, and so on. They come up with all kinds of ideas and plans but they invariably have one thing in common: in the new school all the children are in one place. When I point this out to them with the statement that one could imagine a school in which different groups of children were in very different locations (just as many children go to a geographically separate place we call a nursery school which is apart from all other "school" children), the response is usually one of puzzlement or surprise. The point is not that I could or do seriously justify such a plan but that the characteristic common to their plans is a reflection of their previous experience with the existing organization we call school.[8]

What we are beginning to see is that in this class of instances there is a before-the-beginning phase, that it does involve the nature and structure of existing settings, but that its relations to and effects upon the creation of the new setting are not obvious. It is not obvious in the same way that categories of thought are not obvious; they are the unquestioned, even unverbalized, aspects of thinking that ensure that the new will have some of the features of the old.

Earlier when I was discussing a new setting which arises from

---

[8] Sarason, Zitnay, and Kaplan (1971) have made the same point in regard to building. That is to say, almost always when a public agency decides to provide additional services for a large number of people (such as the mentally retarded or mentally ill) it includes money for a building program. That there are alternatives to new buildings or that the very processes involved in building work against developing adequate services are usually never considered —more correctly, they cannot exist as possibilities in the minds of people. A new institution automatically means a new physical structure. We shall be discussing this further in Chapter Eight.

and becomes part of an existing organization of settings, I concluded that confronting its history for the purposes of understanding and dealing with it was crucial for its future. In that context, however, confronting history has relatively clear meanings. But what would confronting its history mean in cases where the new setting does not arise from an existing organization but rather from the mind of one individual (or even from those of a small group)? What would confronting its history mean if I decided to create a new school? What did it mean to George Pullman in 1880 when he decided to create a model town (Buder, 1967)? What did it mean to James W. Rouse when he decided to build Columbia in Maryland, or Robert E. Simon, Jr., in Reston, Virginia (Eichler and Kaplan, 1967)? What does it mean to those who have created new communes or minisocieties? Unfortunately, on the basis of existing literature it is difficult, and often impossible, to answer these questions. I shall attempt to give the outlines of an answer, therefore, not on the basis of specific instances but on the basis of conclusions I have come to by personal experience and observation. If what I have to say is largely in the nature of "shoulds and oughts"—what one should confront—it reflects primarily what others did not do, errors of omission which later seemed to contribute to problems and failure. Put in another way: I am more concerned that the reader see that confronting history is an important phase in the creation of a setting than I am in whether he agrees with my way of analyzing it.

If I decided to create a new school for children (or if I decided to start a commune), I should be aware that I was not the first person in human history to start such a venture. I may think that my guiding idea is historically unique, a hope nourished by an ahistorical stance, but what would permit me to ignore the obvious fact that there have been countless others, past and present, who created educational ventures, some of whom succeeded while others failed? My observation is that, in fact, there is always a more or less dim awareness that there is a relevant history of past endeavors but this is largely ignored or, more correctly, it has no conceptual significance. Sometimes there is a keen identification with past endeavors but largely in terms of ideas and values and not in terms of their development, organization, and problems.[4] The point I would emphasize is that almost always,

---

[4] Long before I started the Yale Psycho-Educational Clinic I was aware that the first clinic in this country was started in 1896 by Professor Lightner Witmer in the department of psychology of the University of Pennsylvania. I always considered him one of the really great pioneers in the mental health field, albeit largely unrecognized today as such by others. Hopefully, some of

if not always, there is some degree of awareness that there is a relevant history but that far more often than not the perceived relevance has to do with values and goals which in no way instruct one as to the problems of creation. Here again one can use the Constitutional Convention of 1787 for illustrative purposes because so many of its participants, particularly the leading ones, had a most highly developed sense of history in relation to the task which brought them to Philadelphia. They not only saw themselves in relation to past historical events and periods in which the forces of freedom and tyranny were in conflict; they not only identified with the ideas, values, and traditions of past individuals who fought for freedom; but they also confronted this history from the standpoint of what lessons could be learned about success and failure, about the relation of theory and practice. No one had to tell them that there was a relevant past; they saw as an important part of their task determining in what ways this past was usable.

Someone might say: "Really, all you are saying is what any researcher or scholar does and teaches his students to do: before proceeding to deal with a particular problem one should scrutinize what others have said and done about that problem. It is not enough to know that the problem has a history. One has to know this history in a way so that its dilemmas, mistakes, and solutions can be used productively now." That *is* all I am saying, but it must be recognized that it can be said only because there is a long tradition which makes this way of thinking and acting second nature to the researcher or scholar. Such a tradition hardly exists in relation to the creation of settings, and it will not exist until this problem area becomes formulated and the object of research and scholarly studies. It is my impression that when highly qualified researchers and scholars, even eminent ones, have engaged in the creation of a setting there often seemed to be no transfer of the historical stance from their special area of expertise to that of the creation of the particular setting. I mention this only in

---

my own writing (Sarason and Doris, 1969) and that of the Levines (1970) will rectify somewhat Witmer's unrecognized achievements. The point of all this is that when I started the Yale clinic I very consciously identified myself as in the Witmer tradition, professionally and personally. He was one of my heroes and I wanted to be like him. The very name of our clinic as well as its emphasis reflected this identification. However, it never dawned on me to try to find out how and why his clinic was organized the way it was, the problems he encountered by virtue of being in an academic department, how he and those around him "lived together" and maintained themselves intellectually and financially, and what contributed (and when) to its decline and Witmer's role in this.

regard to the argument that those who create settings are usually "action people" in whom the historical stance is weak or nonexistent. This is a variant of explanation in terms of personality, and while there may be some truth to it, it is clearly not the whole story.

Let us now turn to another aspect of confronting history by attending to the implications of the characteristic that the new setting has a "superior" mission; that is, it competes with existing settings in the realm of ideas and values. To discuss such implications I shall present an excerpt of a "case history" contained in an article "Clinical Innovation and the Mental Health Power Structure" by Dr. Anthony Graziano (1969). Although this is not a clear example of the class of instances we are now discussing, it illustrates well certain principles characteristic of such instances.

About eleven years ago a small group of parents sought treatment for autistic children and found available only expensive psychiatrists or the depressing custodialism of back-ward children's units at the state hospital. Local clinics were of little help since they operated on the familiar assumption that their services were best limited to those who could "profit most" from therapy, and, given a choice between a rampaging psychotic child and one with less severe behavior, the clinics tended to treat the latter and send the others off to the state hospitals. Unwilling to accept either deadly placement (private therapists or state hospitals), parents cast around and were eventually referred to the "experts," that is, the same clinics and private-practice psychiatrists who had previously failed to help those children. They were nevertheless still considered to be the proper agents to carry out a new program, now that a few determined lay people had thought of it. This is an important and recurrent point, suggesting that any new mental health service or idea, regardless of its origin, is automatically referred back into the control of the same people who had achieved so little in the past, perhaps insuring that little will be done in the future. The territorial claims of professionals, it seems, are seldom challenged, despite what might be a history of failure, irrelevance, or ignorance.

Following some two years of work, the lay group arranged with a local child clinic to create special services for autistic children. The result, a psychoanalytically oriented group program, operated uneasily for four years, amidst laymen-professional controversy over roles, responsibility, finances, and, finally, the program's therapeutic effectiveness. The lay people, rightly seeing themselves as the "originators" of the program, felt that they were being "displaced" by the professionals. The professionals, on the other hand, saw the laymen as naive, not recognizing their own limitations and trying to preempt clearly professional territory. Threatened and angered, both sides retreated to positions which were more acrimonious than communicative. "Don't trust the professional!" and "Beware the layman!" were often heard in varied ways.

Hostilities grew, the groups split, and, after four years of their cooperative program, these two groups, the "insider" professional clinic with its continuing program and the "outsider" lay group now determined to have its own program, were directly competing for the same pool of local and state funds.

The clinic, embedded within the professional community, had operated for some twenty-five years and espoused no new, radical, or untried approaches. It argued that it was an experienced, traditional, co-operating part of the local mental health community; that it was properly medically directed; that its approaches were based on "the tried and true methods of psychoanalysis." The clinic based its arguments on experience, professionalism, and stability as a successful community agency, and offered to continue the accepted psychoanalytic methodology.

The "outsiders," having acquired the services of a young and still idealistic psychologist who was just two years out of graduate school, contended that because psychoanalytic approaches had not resulted in significant improvement for autistic children the community should support any reasonable alternative approaches rather than insisting upon the pseudo-efficiency of a single program to avoid "duplication of services." One alternative was proposed, the modification of behavior through the application of psychological learning theory, that is, teaching adaptive behavior rather than treating internal sickness. Further, because this approach was psychological, it therefore would properly be psychologically and not medically directed.

Thus they criticized the establishment and proposed change, attempting new approaches based on a psychological rather than medical model, and insisting on including poverty children in the program. Naively stepping on many toes, they said all the wrong things; one does not successfully seek support from a professionally conservative community by criticizing it and promising to provide new and different services which are grossly at odds with accepted certainties, essentially untried and, in many respects, ambiguous. Early in 1963, to offer psychological learning concepts as alternatives to psychoanalytic treatment of children and to insist that traditional clinics had failed to help low-income children was not well received. From the beginning, then, this group, henceforth referred to as ASMIC (Association for Mentally Ill Children), were cast as "radicals" and "trouble-makers."

Hoping to avoid competing within the clinical structure, ASMIC proposed to the local university in 1963 a small-scale research and training project to develop child-therapy approaches from learning theory, and to select and train nondegree undergraduate and master's level students as child group workers and behavior therapists. It was hoped that, after a year or two of preliminary investigation, federal support would be available through the university. Approved by the chairman and the dean, the proposal was rejected at the higher administrative levels because (a) the project was too radical and would only create continuing controversy; (b) the local mental health professionals had already clearly indicated their opposition to it; and (c) the university, always cognizant of town-gown problems, could not risk becoming involved.

The message was clear: the project was opposed by the local

mental health professionals, it had already caused controversy, would create more, and the university was no place for controversy! (sic)

Thus denied the more cloistered university environment, ASMIC moved to compete within the closed-rank mental health agency structure, where they soon encountered what we shall refer to as the United Agency. That agency's annual fund-raising campaign is carried out with intense publicity, and donating through one's place of employment seems to have become somewhat less than voluntary. Operated primarily by business and industrial men the United Agency had some million and a half dollars to distribute to agencies of their choice, thus giving a small group of traditionally conservative businessmen considerable power over the city's social action programs.

Having been advised that ASMIC's proposed program could not long survive, the United Agency's apparent tactic was to delay for a few months, until ASMIC demised quietly. That delaying tactic was implemented as follows: (1) The United Agency listened to ASMIC's preliminary ideas but could not act until they had a written proposal. (2) A month later the United Agency rejected the written proposal because it was only a "paper program"! (3) ASMIC's program was started and expanded but after 6 months of operation was again denied support because it had been too brief a time on which to base a decision. The group was advised to apply again after a longer period of operation. (4) After a year of operation ASMIC's next request was denied on the basis that the program had to be "professionally evaluated" before the United Agency could act. And who would carry out the evaluation? The local mental health professionals, of course. ASMIC objected to being evaluated by their competitors but agreed to an evaluation by the State Department of Mental Health, although they, too, had previously refused to support the program. This was to be the "final" hurdle and, if the evaluation was positive, the United Agency would grant funds for the program. (5) Completing its professional evaluation the state department returned a highly positive report and strongly recommended that ASMIC be supported. Apparently caught off guard, the United Agency was strangely unresponsive, and several months elapsed before the next request for funds was again deferred, on the basis that the question of "duplication of services" had never been resolved. (6) After additional state endorsement and high praise for the program as a nonduplicated service, the United Agency rejected ASMIC's next request, replying that if the state thought so highly of the program, then why did not they support it? "Come back," they said, "when you get state support." (7) Six months later and nearly three years after starting the program, ASMIC had a state grant. The United Agency then allocated $3,000.00 which, they said, would be forwarded as soon as ASMIC provided the United Agency with (a) an official tax-exemption statement, (b) the names and addresses of all children who had received ASMIC services, and (c) the names of the fathers and their employers.

For three years ASMIC had met all of the United Agency's conditions; they had provided a detailed proposal, launched the program, had successfully operated for three years, had expanded, had received high professional evaluations, had resolved duplication-of-service issue, had provided the exemption voucher but could not, they explained, provide confidential information such as names, addresses, and fathers' places of employment.

The United Agency, however, blandly refused support because ASMIC was, after all, "uncooperative" in refusing to supply the requested information.

ASMIC's final attempts to gain local mental health support were with an agency we will call "Urban Action" whose function, at least partly, was to help ameliorate poverty conditions through federally supported programs.

Arguing that the city had no mental health services of any scope for poverty-level children, ASMIC proposed to apply and evaluate techniques of behavior modification, environmental manipulation, and selection and training of "indigenous" subprofessionals, mothers, and siblings, to help emotionally disturbed poverty-level children.

The written proposal was met with enthusiasm but, the agency explained, in keeping with the concept of "total community" focus, more than one agency had to be involved. They therefore suggested inviting the local mental health association to join the project, even if only on a consultant basis. The mental health association, of course, was comprised of the same professionals who had opposed ASMIC's program from the beginning. Skeptical but nevertheless in good faith, ASMIC distributed copies of their proposal to the mental health association, again referring something new back to the old power structure. Five months later a prediction was borne out; the mental health association returned the proposal as "unworkable" and, in its place, submitted their own highly traditional psychiatric version, which was ultimately rejected in Washington. Those poverty-level children who received no mental health services in 1963 still receive no services, and there are no indications that the situation will be any different in the next few years.

The "outside" group, its new ideas clashing with the professional establishment, repeatedly encountered barriers composed of the same people and never did receive support from the local mental health agencies, the United Agency, the university, or the Urban Action Agency. For the first two years it subsisted on small tuition fees and a spate of cake sales organized by a few determined ladies, and eventually did receive significant state support from the departments of education and mental health. Thus it carried out its programs, in spite of the opposition and lack of support of the local mental health professionals.*

If anything is clear in this description it is that the proposed new setting viewed itself, and was viewed by others, as stating a superior mission—it would do a better job with these children than existing agencies had done. The young and idealistic psychologist would show the establishment how *really* to render help. Although there was competition for resources, the major source of competition was in the realm of ideas. But what significance does this have for confronting history? Graziano implies an answer to the question in his phrase "naively stepping on many toes." What he seems to be saying in a refreshingly candid manner is that he could (or should have) have known before he started what he bitterly learned later. What he could have known was that there was an existing structure or pattern of relationships among existing settings, that they had some ideological communalities, and that tradition and history were reflected in these interrelationships. But these are things Graziano could have known about particular agencies in a particular community. There is a more general thing that was knowable and that is that human history is replete with instances in which new ideas and settings have been aborted precisely in the ways Graziano so delightfully presents.

What if Graziano knew all this before he began the negotiations with the existing structure? Obviously, and I mean obviously, if he *knew* these things it could only be because his *ways of thinking* (assumptions, conceptions, theories) were different from what in fact they were, and his ways of proceeding would have been different.

In his thoughtful discussion of the case history, Graziano makes quite clear how the bureaucratic dynamics of the existing mental health power structure work against new settings based on new and competing ideas. However, there are two aspects of the problem which he does not illuminate. The first is that the dynamics he describes are independent of ideology. That is to say, if the theoretical positions had been reversed and Graziano had been committed to a psychoanalytic orientation and the existing organization of settings had been committed to a behavior modification position, the same script for the drama could have been written. In fact, if one were sensitive to history, one could write innumerable ` histories in which psychoanalysts, beginning with Freud, experienced in relation to the then existing mental health power structure precisely what Graziano experienced and described. The second aspect he does not address, except by implication, is the question: Was the end result of failure due *only* to the interorganizational dynamics he so well describes? It is easy to come away with the impression that he accepts such an explanation, except for his admission of naivete. It is not clear whether he means that the end result was knowable and that he never should have proceeded, or does he mean that he should have known with what he was dealing and that his strategy should have been different? If it is the former it is tantamount to saying that different ways of thinking and acting are differences which make no difference; if it is the latter, it is saying that the end result is a function of interorganizational dynamics *and* how one thinks about and deals with them. The fact of the matter is, of course, that the new setting did receive support, not from the local power structure but from the state one, suggesting that the interrelationships between the two power structures were not the same, or as close, or as ideologically cohesive as those among agencies comprising the local power structure. My own knowledge and observations of the Connecticut scene support the conclusion that the way state and local power structures relate to a new setting is similar, if not identical, to the response of either to a proposed new setting arising from within its own midst. In short, any proposed new setting confronts a preexisting complicated structure of relationships, parts of which work against and parts work for the creation of the new setting. Although earlier in this chapter I emphasized the negative or interfering effects of the existing organization of settings on the new one—stating that the new setting has a heritage of conflict—this emphasis has to be tempered somewhat by the possibility that this heritage is not all negative. The very fact that the new setting reflects some preexisting conflict within and between existing settings suggests some potential support for the new setting.

There are three aspects to the term confronting history. The first is a way of thinking that points one to the past on the assumption that where one is (in relation to the proposed setting) does not solely reflect chance factors. I mean more than the fact that at any one point in our lives our past is playing a role, an obvious point we all recognize although we struggle in different ways and degrees to avoid its recognition. What I am placing greater emphasis on is that an individual's relation to a proposed setting involves or implies actual or potential relationships with many other settings and this totality has an understandable past and a significant future. It is my observation that the more an individual (or small group) is aware of *his* relation to the proposed setting, in terms of *his* personal history, the less he is able to perceive that personal history as an incomplete explanation of the present. There is much more that has been set off or is now occurring in the earliest phases than is contained in the needs, motivation, and goals of an individual.

The *principle* involved here is similar to one with which psychotherapists are familiar and that is that the meanings which can be attributed to what a patient says far exceed what a literal interpretation of his words signifies and, furthermore, that these verbalizations have to be viewed in relation to the therapist as well as others. When Freud advised the analysts "to listen and not listen" he was saying that

a lot more is going on than the patient's words denote and that one
has to learn how to become aware of these other significances. In fact,
one of Freud's enduring contributions is the rationale he developed for
how and why the analyst adopts a stance maximizing the "information" he gets. The same principle obtains in the earliest phases of the
creation of a setting. The individual's *personal* way of thinking of the
setting can obscure what only later becomes obvious—that a lot more
was going on "out there" than is given in the personal or subjective
way of thinking.

A second aspect of the term *confronting history* is implied in
the first and that is that one is always dealing with a history of structured relationships. It can be counted on that the new setting reflects
the history of relationships among diverse but related settings. A distinction can be made here between those settings which have, and will
continue to have, relationships with the proposed setting and those
which will not have such relationships. In the latter case the relationships are seen as developing in the future and, therefore, requiring no
action in the present, a view not always shared by the settings whose
role has been put into the future. In fact, it is rare that one reads a
newspaper without learning about some group protesting its exclusion
from the planning of a new setting. The future can be history.

The third aspect of confronting history is that the individual or
small group assuming or given responsibility for the new setting utilizes
this historical knowledge for actions which maximize the chances that
the new setting will be viable and in ways consistent with its values
and goals. The problem is not how to have a live and functioning setting but how to have one which is true to its purposes.

The significance of the before-the-beginning and the confronting of history is illustrated in *Jean Monnet and the United States of
Europe* (Bromberger, 1969). Specifically, the book deals with Monnet's role in the creation of three new settings: the European Defense
Community, Euratom, and the Common Market. It is, of course, impossible to summarize the many details, actions, and ideas involved
in these settings, and I do not doubt that other books on these settings
would have different emphases and give a different picture. For our
purposes here it really makes no difference whether or not one regards
this book as complete or incomplete, or whether one agrees or dis-
agrees with the purposes of these settings, or even their subsequent
history. What this book does do is to describe exceedingly well how in
the earliest phases of the proposed settings every idea and action on
the part of Monnet and his colleagues seemed to reflect an exquisite
sensitivity to history. It is as if at every step of the way they viewed

history as containing forces both for and against them and saw that their major task was to deal with both. Their attention to detail, their use of history to anticipate consequences, and their learning from failure (European Defense Community) are in startling contrast to what characterizes the earliest phases of most new settings. The fact that the settings described in this book were international in scope and of far greater significance for men than the creation of a new school or a new city should not obscure their basic similarities. Just as the theory of the organization of the atom is basically similar to the theory of the organization of the universe, the theory of the creation of a small setting will be highly similar, if not identical, to that of a much larger one.

Another extremely well-described example of the before-the-beginning phase and the confronting of history is contained in *The Big Machine* by Robert Jungk (1968). The title of the book refers to an international laboratory centering around a mammoth proton synchroton which "breaks up" particles under heavy bombardment, producing new and different particles. This extremely large and expensive instrument was established by a dozen European states through the European Organization for Nuclear Research, known as CERN. To develop and maintain this international laboratory required building a small city outside of Geneva, Switzerland. I wish here only to note that Jungk explicitly focuses on the prehistory of the setting, primarily because the more he came to know the setting the more he was intrigued with how it ever came to be in the first place.[5] Although

---

[5] Jungk's handling of the prehistory phase is superior to that of the Brombergers in terms of detail, scope, and balance. This may be due to different purposes: one is essentially the biography of a man while the other is that of a setting. It may also reflect the fact that Jungk is a formally trained historian while the Brombergers presumably are not. For example, Jungk became aware at one point that there had been certain objections to the first plans. "Nowhere had I read anything about these objections to the first plans for CERN; they had come to me in the form of hints from Auger. Was there any written documentation? Presumably not any longer, thought Jean Mussard, for the records in which the objections of the Copenhagen group could have been found had been discarded by UNESCO, together with other dispensable documents dated earlier than 1956, in a general clearance of its files. I found the information quite depressing. It was not the first time I had been met with the disappearance of sources of the history of science, because of lack of interest. Scientists ordinarily exhibit little feeling for history and make no effort to preserve their personal records. My imagination conjured up visions of fierce 'paper wolves' lurking in the basements of UNESCO and all the other large organizations, waiting to tear to shreds all the letters, memoranda, and plans of the early days of the world's first supranational laboratory. A few days later, I paid a visit to a lady of the editorial staff of *Impact*. She led me, with a smile, into a neighboring office. There on a desk lay huge, half-untied bundles of memoranda,

he never states it explicitly, one gets the distinct impression that Jungk could not understand how this productive, exciting international community ever emerged from the history and traditions of the participating European states. It never should have come into existence! But Jungk makes clear in his discussion of prehistory why and how it came into existence, and a large part of the answer is the exquisite sensitivity of a small group of individuals to the history and traditions of the past and present settings.

We have discussed the earliest aspects of the creation of a setting on the implicit assumption that they are significant for later phases, based on the expectation that there will be later phases. This, of course, is not the case because many proposed new settings never get beyond the earliest phases. They abort, and it is my impression that their frequency may be at least as high as those that are "full term." There are many different reasons for this but in a number of these instances the reason is contained in the dynamics of the earliest phases. It is understandable but unfortunate that these aborted attempts are rarely if ever described or reported, and we are, as a consequence, robbed of the opportunity of understanding better the sources of failure. Just as a lot has been learned about biological development from the study of spontaneous or induced abortions, we could learn much from the study of aborted attempts to create a new setting. For example, I have known a number of instances of aborted efforts the failure of which has usually been attributed to external difficulties—to individuals or groups too hostile or too powerful or even too indifferent to the proposed new setting. There has always seemed to be truth to the way these external forces have been characterized, although it is quite a leap to conclude that they "caused" the failure. This, too, is reminiscent of biological development where for scores of decades (and centuries) the trauma of birth was viewed as "the cause" of the atypical development and early death of many infants. After all, since birth is no easy matter, and in some cases an inordinately difficult one, it was easy to attribute injury and malformations to the birth process. It was not until systematic studies of spontaneous abortions were done (among other types of studies of embryos) that it became apparent that in many, if not most, cases, birth was difficult because of already present malformations.

---

minutes, letters, and newspaper clippings: the documents of the 'Technical Bureau, the nucleus of CERN. For once, praised be the slowness of the bureaucracy! Thanks to it, this treasure had not been transformed into refuse long ago" (p. 47). It is my impression that such digging was not characteristic of the Brombergers, perhaps because of their somewhat idolatrous view of Monnet.

I have tried to make clear that the creation of a setting is no easy matter and that already in its earliest phases there are built-in obstacles and conflicts. I do not wish to leave the impression that all that is required for clear sailing is that one understand and confront these difficulties, as if their nature and strength can by appropriate thoughts and actions be neutralized or eliminated. Life indeed would be more agreeable if external social realities were so responsive to whatever one considered the correct way of thinking and acting. Having said this, however, it is important that we recognize that aborted efforts to create a setting may not always, or even frequently, be due only to the fact that our external worlds present us with difficulties. Our own ways of thinking about what we wish to create may be as much of an obstacle as external hostility or indifference.

My purpose in this chapter has been to emphasize that a proposed new setting always arises in some relation to existing settings; that there are characteristics of the new setting (such as superiority of mission) and concerns of the existing ones (such as ideology, concern for resources) which ensure some conflict and competition; that regardless of whether the proposed setting arises from an existing structure or arises outside of one, it reflects in its purposes or functions or ideology some aspect of traditional conceptions; that its heritage of conflict contains positive and negative forces; and that confronting its history is not a matter of esthetics—all of this comprising the before-the-beginning phase. In the next chapter we shall discuss another phase of development in the creation of a setting, a phase no less thorny or complicated than the one we have just discussed. As we shall see, there is much support for the saying of grandmothers about the children: "When they are small you have small problems and when they are big you have big problems."

CHAPTER 3

The Leader and
the Beginning Context

Although I shall be talking of leaders in this chapter, it will not be for the purpose of understanding them in a psychological or phenomenological sense. I take that up in detail in later chapters after the more general sociological and developmental aspects of the creation of a setting have been presented. Choosing a leader is obviously a crucial process and one in which personality and contextual factors fatefully begin to interact, but at this point our interest must focus less on the leader as a personality and more on the organizational matrix in which he becomes embedded. Put in another way, we shall try to understand the guiding conceptions which seem to underlie the creation of a setting in terms of several questions. How is the leader of the new setting chosen? What is his time perspective? What are the consequences of how he defines the beginning point? I examine these questions in regard to both those instances where the new setting emerges from an existing organization of settings and those in which the idea for and the development of the new setting is that of one person in the sense that it is unambiguous that in terms of possessing material resources, or in intellectual contribution, or moral stance one individual assumes and is given leadership. What is most obvious in both types of instances is that there is and must be a leader, and although the scope and means of exercising leadership may be vague and ill-defined, there is no question in anyone's mind that a leader is necessary. This, however, is in marked contrast to the creation of the marital setting or some communes or collectives, where the issue of leadership is avoided, or not formulated as a problem, or explicitly denied as a necessity. One does not have to be an acute observer of the current scene to know that our younger citizens, particularly the college population, do not look favorably on the leaders they encounter or with whom they must work. Ambivalence is the term appropriate for the attitude of some, while for others the basic attitude is one of denying the necessity of leadership. It is the latter attitude which has sparked the creation of new minisocieties. It is not fortuitous that we are also witnessing the resurgence of the women's liberation movement which at its core involves issues concerning the ways in which leadership is assumed, given, and exercised. Whenever the issue of equality among people is at issue, that of the basis of leadership is in the background. The tendency for those entering marriage to avoid the issues of leadership or to deal with it indirectly not only has significance for that setting but also for the creation of those settings which ordinarily are viewed as basically different.

Choosing the Leader

In those instances where the leader has been part of the earliest phases, particularly when he has played an influential role, one would expect that the problems of transition from one phase to another would be different from those in which the leader has not been part of the earliest phases. In fact, the often-stated preference to "choose from the ranks" or to "promote from within" reflects two assumptions. First, the more knowledge the leader has of the earliest phases and of the existing organization of settings, the more smooth will be the implementation process and the more successful will be the new setting in achieving its purposes. Second, choosing from within avoids the morale problems that can occur when an outsider is brought in. Both assumptions have a surface plausibility which does not stand up in practice as frequently as one might expect.[1] It would be helpful if we knew how

---

[1] Phrases like "promote from within," "get the right people," or "get

frequently both assumptions are invalidated by subsequent events, but here again we have no data by which to judge. Using my own observations as a guide I would have to say that this "common-sense" way of thinking is invalidated enough times so that we are required to examine the two assumptions critically.

Let us start with the first assumption by asking this question: in seeking a leader what does one mean that he should have knowledge of the earliest phases of the new setting as well as of the existing organization of settings? In light of our discussion in the previous chapter the answer to the question involves far more than sheer knowledge, if by knowledge is meant facts, procedures, the uses of power, and even expertise in relation to the particular substantive problems the new setting is intended to meet. The thrust of our discussion was that several things were necessary: a way of thinking which mirrored the complexity of interests and conflicts out of which the new setting has emerged, the internal and external groups which are or will be affected, and the necessity to confront these problems in ways which will not interfere with achieving the purposes of the new setting—and by confronting I did not mean resort to power as a way of resolving issues, or compromise which subverts the goals of the new setting, or ritualistic diplomacy. What I have been saying is that the choice of the leader involves far more than considerations of personality or even professional competence or intellectual ability. But here we run into the following problem: the individual or small group who have to choose a leader frequently do not themselves possess the kind of understanding or ways of thinking which I have indicated the new leader should have. Leaders usually choose leaders, and if those who choose do so without real understanding of the dynamics and ramifications of the context out of which the new setting has emerged, it is no wonder that wrong choices are made.

A number of years ago the board of education of a small city built a new school in a ghetto area. There was much fanfare about the new school, particularly the ways in which community agencies and neighborhood groups would be involved. It was explicit that this was not to be a school encapsulated and isolated from its surroundings;

someone who can ensure and lead" reflect well the kind of understanding available to someone interested in the creation of settings. These phrases, like most of folk wisdom, have a kernel of truth. The truth, however, is not always helpful, a point exemplified well by these kinds of phrases. Folk wisdom is also readily at hand to explain why settings fail: "poor leadership," "poor organization," "poor morale," and "rigidity." Just as facts are not necessarily the same as the truth, the truth is not necessarily the same as understanding.

parents would be involved in a variety of ways, and a number of professional individuals and groups (both within and without the system) would give their services. The choice of the principal was obviously crucial, as was the opinion of the superintendent that no one of the individuals currently a principal was appropriate or adequate. He wished to promote from within and he chose a young, white male who had been teaching in a ghetto school where he had the reputation of being community oriented and on good terms with the parents of the neighborhood. After interviewing the young man the superintendent was convinced that he would really create an "open" school responsive to the needs of its pupils and their parents, and the young man was appointed. Within two years after its opening the principal was removed and transferred to another school, largely as a result of parent pressure and demonstrations.

How do we understand what happened? As soon as the principal's appointment was announced, two of the heads of programs within the school system began to meet with the new principal with the purpose of making their services available to the new school. The heads were quite frustrated with their relationships to existing school programs and eagerly looked forward to the opening of the new school as an opportunity to render what they considered to be more meaningful and productive service to ghetto children. At the same time a member of the Yale Psycho-Educational Clinic began to meet with the principal and for the same reasons. Within a matter of several weeks all discussion ceased when it became apparent that the new principal viewed these discussions as an intrusion on his rights and plans which were never clear. If anything was clear it was that the principal had already made the transition from owning *his* classroom to owning *his* school. This interpretation did not seem to be supported by the fact that in the summer before the school opened the principal visited many homes in this ghetto area, introduced himself, and expressed the hope that parents would truly involve themselves in the school's activities. Not long after the school opened, parents encountered what we and others had experienced the previous spring.

To understand what happened requires that we look at the superintendent who was an extremely bright, forthright, courageous individual who knew his own mind and generally got what he wanted. There was no doubt that he believed in "open" schools which reflected community needs and opinions, but there was also no doubt that he truly did not comprehend what this meant in action. For example, he never made any effort to know this particular neighborhood in terms of its formal or informal organizations, its changing character in terms of militancy, or the differing views held about what the new school should be. Certainly this part of the community was not "involved" by him. It is also true that although he knew of the dissatisfaction of his closest aides with existing principals and "their" schools (they would not long have remained aides if they felt otherwise), he tended to view this in personality terms; that is, most principals were rigid, authoritarian, and resistant to change and innovation. Although he may have understood in some abstract sense that part of the problem inhered in history and traditions as well as in the consequences of a hierarchically and centrally organized structure, in practice he viewed the problem as solely a manifestation of clashes in temperament and thinking between individuals. I am sure that when this superintendent interviewed the person whom he later appointed as principal, they both concluded that there was a meeting of minds about what the new school should be. That neither of them—by virtue each of experience, style, or ways of thinking about theory and practice—truly knew what this agreement meant in the world of action contributed to the subsequent disaster. By his own lack of intimate knowledge of the community on which the school was placed, by his own inability to focus on what the problems were between a school and various special services within and without the system and how these should be dealt with, by his tendency to view intrasystem problems as resolvable by "proper" motivation and agreement on values—in short, by his way of viewing things—the leader chose a leader unprepared for the task ahead.[2]

Let us now examine the second assumption—that promotion from within is better for morale than importing a leader. This assumption suggests that those who are choosing a leader are sensitive to or knowledgeable about the feelings and opinions of those in the existing settings. But what is frequently the case is that the sensitivity is much more in relation to importing a leader than it is to the consequences of promoting from within.

[2] The problems and dilemmas of the classroom teacher who becomes a principal are more complex than I can go into here. This is taken up in greater detail in my book *The Culture of the School and the Problem of Change* (1971). One of the major points emphasized and illustrated in that book is that a surprising number of school personnel have as superficial an understanding of the school setting as most outsiders, a fact which goes a long way in explaining why schools are, as one colleague said, such fast-changing status quos. It is as if the higher up in the administrative hierarchy an individual climbs, the more he forgets what life was like. It is not that people get promoted to their level of incompetence but that promotion so frequently renders the individual increasingly unable to use past knowledge and experience.

Although it does not involve the creation of a setting, the point here is well illustrated in the university, where promotions from within are very frequent. Take, for example, the situation where a department has a number of assistant professors and has an opening at the associate level. Those who must choose an individual for promotion are almost always aware that if they were to bring in an outsider, or even if it became known that this possibility was being considered, they would have a morale problem on their hands. Although they are also aware that choosing one from the ranks will not produce indifference among those not chosen, this awareness is usually transient and does not give rise to actions which *directly* deal with the opinions and feelings of those not chosen. That the awareness is transient is probably due to the fact that those who must choose were once "chosen," and they feel that there is little one could say or do that one would make those not chosen feel better. This is a way of thinking which does not distinguish between the need to make a person feel better and the obligation to help him confront reality. But how does one understand the fact that there is usually no sensitivity to the fact that those who are already at the associate professor level are not indifferent to a newcomer who is now in competition with them for the highest level of appointment? The situation is usually complicated by the fact that not only is there competition for a limited number of positions but there is also competition among the different areas of the discipline.

The point of all this is that when leaders choose leaders, they create a morale problem regardless of whether they choose from within or without, and to choose as if this were not true is an example of the gulf that can exist between knowledge and action. It is almost always the case that the leaders who choose "know" the hierarchical structure of the existing settings and the reality of limited resources *and* the psychological consequences of both. At the point when they must act (choose), however, this knowledge is frequently not utilizable or even available. Consequently, the leader who is chosen for the new setting receives no help in directing him to problems which stem from the origins of the new setting. As we shall see later in this chapter, this lack of direction facilitates the tendency for the new leader to be almost exclusively future oriented, that is, to view his assumption of responsibility as the true beginning point rather than as a point in a continuum of events and processes.

How and why the leader was chosen, and what the guiding conceptions were of those who choose and the one who was chosen, are not questions relevant only to the need to describe and understand what went on in the earliest phases. They are questions which are also relevant to the understanding of later events and phases in the new setting. It would be more correct to say that when I have examined published accounts of new settings I have been forced to ask these questions in order to understand some later events. This is not to say that I believe that early events "cause" later ones in some simple or direct way, but rather that early events suggest the presence of ways of thinking that initiate or continue processes contributing to some extent (or facilitating) the occurrence of later events that are obviously significant or fateful.

But, one must ask, why is it that published accounts are so deficient in illuminating these questions? There are three major reasons. First, the guiding conceptions did not *require* close attention to these questions. Second, they would require description and discussion of touchy, conflictful, or downright messy events and relationships which writers would prefer to avoid—a motivation which is as mischievous as it is understandable. Third, particularly when what is being described and discussed is intended as a scientific effort, the writer tends to accede to a tradition in which he presents events and history as being a function of a rational mover—the writer. If he does not present himself in this way, at least he can explain everything that happened as having rational causes. There is a fourth reason which in many ways is the most important for understanding the creation of a setting and will be taken up in detail in a later chapter. Very briefly, it is that in the writing of the history of a setting, particularly one devoted to some form of human service, evaluation of the setting is almost always in terms of what was done for "others," and the question of what happened to those who created and manned the setting —how they were affected and changed by the history and conditions of the setting—is barely discussed because it is not seen as relevant to the major purpose which is to help others.[8] When one's focus is, so to speak, on an end product which is given or delivered to others, one writes with an external rather than internal orientation. The fact that

---

[8] From the earliest days of the industrial revolution criticisms were voiced about the dangers of evaluating a factor in terms of the quantity and quality of its end product independent of what the consequences were for those who worked there. Today, of course, the consequences of that separation are apparent and are the basis for what many consider to be the crisis in western society (regardless of the political ideology and social structure of the countries which comprise it). It is ironic that we have been and still are far more aware of the issue in regard to the industrial setting than to those involved in human services. From time to time we are confronted with the issue in regard to educational institutions and those devoted to dependent or deviant individuals (Blatt, 1970), but the confrontation is a usually very transient one, and little changes.

both orientations are ever present and interrelated is recognized, but if the justification for one's work is what one did for others, it is expected that the picture of the setting qua setting gets slighted.

Yale Psycho-Educational Clinic

To illustrate some of these points I shall draw upon my experiences in founding and directing the Yale Psycho-Educational Clinic until 1970. A number of colleagues and I (Sarason, Levine, Goldenberg, Cherlin, and Bennett, 1966) published a book describing the thinking behind the activities, failures, and accomplishments of the clinic. It was a very big book full of detail about where and how we worked with others. I think it is fair to say that in part we viewed that book as an attempt to convey to readers the social, professional, and intellectual origins of the clinic. It is also true that we wrote the book because we thought we had something to say, because we felt we had demonstrated something, and, of course, in good missionary style we thought others ought to be doing what we were doing. Both before and after the publication of the book many people around the country asked to visit and to get a firsthand picture of what the clinic was and to see how we worked. Their interest was in what we were doing with and for others, and *that* was their conception of what the clinic was as a setting. There can be no doubt that our book contributed to this conception, and that book described the clinic as well as the detailed job history of an individual describes that individual.

But, someone could argue, was not the book helpful to some in the same way that a detailed job history is to a prospective employer? Did we not tell people what they wanted to know or what they felt they needed to know? In addition, the argument could go, why should the reader be interested in the history of the clinic as a setting —its origins in a certain university and university department, the conflicts surrounding its origins, the agreements made, the positive and negative attitudes toward it, and the relation between the origins and the ending of the clinic? Why should people be interested in this kind of a history? One of the more obvious answers, of course, is that such a history could be helpful to those who wished to start a similar setting in their university. To be sure, not all universities and departments of psychology are the same in terms of values, traditions, and resources, but it is not an impetuous act to assume a fair degree of similarity so that the history of the Psycho-Educational Clinic would be relevant to similar efforts elsewhere.

For example, our clinic represented a marked departure from the traditions and practices of our department of psychology, which had never had any kind of clinic of its own, let alone one working in neighborhood employment centers, classrooms, ghetto "work crews," and helping to create residential youth centers and new regional centers for the mentally retarded. Obviously, and I mean obviously, such a departure could not be viewed without hesitation, ambivalence, and some reluctance on the part of the department faculty who had to approve the new venture. There were three reasons for approval. First, in varying degrees the faculty had some positive attitudes toward what was proposed. Second, the bulk of the resources necessary to start the clinic would not come from departmental or university funds. Third, and in some ways most important, I was a professor in a department and university which, fortunately, took seriously the idea that professors should be encouraged to do what they want to do, especially if it did not mean cutting the resource pie thinner—a blend of freedom and constraint which, to say the least, is not without its problems. In short, *I* could have *my* clinic as long as I was willing and able to finance and lead it. Consequently, when after seven years I no longer wished to remain as director, the department was faced with the question, did it want *its* clinic?[4]

This fragment of history will strike a familiar chord in the minds of readers knowledgeable about universities. It is likely that every department in every university in this country has had a setting the origins of which were similar to those of the clinic, and with similar problems of existence. I have heard many individuals talk about such experiences with rancor, disappointment, and feelings of rejection as though what happened was primarily explainable in personality or motivational terms. However understandable such reactions may be, they completely miss or obscure the point that the origins of the setting involved differences or clashes between traditions. To proceed as if this is not the case, as if reason and good intentions will triumph, is as

---

[4] At the time this book was being written it was not at all clear what the fate of the clinic would be. If it does continue, it will be not only because of what we were and demonstrated or because attitudes in the department changed, but because of the consequences of events in the rest of the university and New Haven (May, 1970), events which mirrored more general trends in our society and made our clinic look both relevent and respectable. I mention this because it is too easy to view conflict and its resolution, particularly when one has been part of it, as only or even primarily a clash of people and personalities when, in fact, there is always a larger, more impersonal matrix of forces at work. I am not denying the role of personality, but only saying that it is never a complete explanation of the origins, development, and fate of a setting. I suppose that the tendency to emphasize personality is that it has a visual salience not possessed by a concept like matrix of social forces.

realistic as expecting the Pope to succumb to the persuasiveness of an atheist's logic, or vice versa.

Another item not contained in our book was that I was aware, not to the extent I am now, that what I was embarking on involved or would involve a clash of values and traditions. In fact, this awareness made me willingly accept the responsibility of seeking and getting funds because it would help us maintain flexibility and independence. Indeed, I wanted *my* and not *their* type of clinic. I did not want to attract the traditionally oriented psychologist who tended to view research in what I considered a narrow fashion and who viewed the world of social action as at best an avocation and at worst a violation of the scientific tradition.

Embedded in the origins of the clinic was a difference and even conflict in values and traditions that determined the kinds of people who would be there. Knowledge of this was not only relevant for those who wanted to start a similar clinic but also for those who "only" wanted to understand how we worked as we did; but none of this was in our book. Countless times we told people where and how we worked with others. If asked *why* we worked as we did, our answer was usually in terms of either theory or the needs of people "out there," and, of course, these were relevant but not complete answers. That an important part of the answer to the why question was contained in the origins of the clinic was rarely made clear, certainly not in the book. For example, the clinic never had more than five faculty members, each of whom taught a normal class load in addition to a much greater amount of time spent in supervising graduate and undergraduate students. But teaching time, however defined, was miniscule compared to the time given to performing services in various field settings (day and night). The clinic was not a part-time affair, and the phrase *total involvement* could be used advisedly. One of the explicit arguments or reservations that departmental members had about approving the creation of the clinic was that it would become just that: a clinic performing services with research and scholarly functions playing very secondary roles or, worse yet, playing no roles at all or resulting in publications which were sloppy, unscientific, and could tarnish the high reputation of the department. The fact that I never considered these reservations groundless is less important than the fact that they deeply influenced why we worked as we did in terms of time and motivation. We felt under fairly constant trial and scrutiny, and not only from our own department, because the creation of the clinic quickly (really almost immediately) surfaced antagonisms from other clinical settings within and without the university. In fact we encountered much that Graziano did (see Chapter Two) except for the momentous fact that we were not financially dependent on these other sources. As is true for so many new settings, we felt embattled and superior, possessing only ourselves as the resource on which we could depend. The point of all of this is to indicate that our published answer to why we worked as we did (and why we enjoyed it) was very incomplete and particularly in regard to the issues surrounding the origins of the clinic and ever present in its existence.

But there is another telling aspect to the incompleteness which should give pause to those who "only" want to know how effective we were with those we sought to help, and who regard the bits of history I have given as more in the nature of biography or gossip than of "data." The issues which surrounded the origins of the clinic, the differences in values and traditions which maintained a gulf between the clinic and the department, the differences in orientation and practice between the clinic and other, older clinical settings—these factors, alone and together, facilitated our entry into many of the settings in which we had hoped to work precisely because these settings perceived us as being different from most of Yale and other community agencies. Assuming that we were significantly helpful to these settings, the explanation is not contained only in terms of our personalities, orientation, and technical skills. These *may* be the most significant factors but whatever weights one assigns to them cannot obscure an important fact: we were well received in some of these settings and that reception, and all it implies, was not irrelevant to any explanation of what we did and why. But that is hardly discussed in the book; and that is also true of the relation of Yale to the New Haven community. Leaving out description and discussion of the clinic as a setting, and emphasizing a great deal what we did with those we sought to help, we eliminated "historical and ever-present clutter" and, needless to say, significant information which from any theoretical point of view is not optional but mandatory.

It would have been easy for me, and perhaps more interesting for the reader, if in discussing the creation of the clinic I described clashes and conflicts in terms of individuals and their personality characteristics. That I did not do so was not only because it may hurt people or because I am aware that my personality diagnoses may be wrong or that it could become one grand *argumentum ad hominem*, but because I felt that what needed emphasis was that the creation of settings (in its earliest phases) almost always (if not always) takes place in a context containing conflicting ideas and values, limited resources, a sense of mission and superiority on the part of some and a need to preserve tradition on the part of others, the need to protect the setting from outside influences, and that this context almost always includes, or quickly is seen as impinging upon, a large number of existing settings. This matrix of factors is rarely described and discussed with the clarity required if one is to understand what a setting is and does, as well as its development and fate. There was one other reason for my emphasis on what may be called the sociological matrix of origins of settings and that has to do with the relationship between conception and practice. It is a difference which makes a big difference if those who create or become part of a new setting conceive of the process only or primarily in individual or personality terms (an individual psychology) or in terms of the matrix of factors I have presented. (The same, of course, is true for those in the existing organization of settings from which the new one emerged or for those in other types of settings upon which the new one impinges.) I shall have more to say about this in a later chapter. Suffice it to say at this point that both conceptions tend to have drastically different effects on tactics and strategy, time perspective, patience, personal stability, and the way one makes sense of one's experience and describes it to others. To be sure, it is not a question of choosing one or the other conception but rather the degree to which the dominance of one distorts the picture and shapes the future.

Ward H

Ward H is the title of a book by Colarelli and Siegel (1966), and it is one of the most comprehensive and thoughtful presentations of the creation and development of a setting in the area of helping services. For our purposes here the reader needs only to know that Ward H was a setting created in a state hospital in order systematically to implement a way of living for mental patients and staff that reflected a particular set of conceptions about the nature of chronic schizophrenia. This way of living was to be quite different from what would be the case in the rest of the hospital. A pilot study had produced heartening results and approval was given for one of the existing wards to be restructured and developed according to the guiding conceptions of the project directors.

The authors early state: "In July 1960 the Ward H project became a reality." From that point on in the book the description and discussion of the new setting are unusually comprehensive and stimulating. But up to that point three things are briefly discussed: the pilot study in 1959, guiding principles, and the innovative climate which characterized this state hospital. And now let us listen to what the authors say at the end of the first year of what turned out to be four years of life in "an adventure in innovation."

At this time there also developed a new series of crises. Earlier in the year the anxiety the aides had about their newfound authority had been evident in a continuing series of crises. By the end of the year, however, this anxiety had been dealt with. Now, however, anxiety became evident in the supporting professional staff and manifested itself in several crises and withdrawals from the ward. It became evident that the social service, adjunctive therapy, and nursing departments were withdrawing in part their investment in the program. A supervising nurse who had contact with the program told the project directors that she could intellectually appreciate what was being done and thought that it was worthwhile, but personally could not participate in it because of its discrepancy with her background and training. The ward nurse who had been with the project since the very beginning quit quite suddenly. The problem of the supervising nurse's withdrawal and the ward nurse's resignation were the first concrete difficulties the project had encountered over the role of the registered nurse in this kind of program, a problem that was to become most difficult for the project to resolve. It was difficult to pinpoint the source of these anxieties in the professional staff; evidently there was an ill-defined frustration present throughout this group which precipitated these withdrawals and needed to be attended to without delay. Another major area of problems at this time centered around the relationships between the project and the rest of the hospital. When the project had first been presented to the hospital staff it had been received very warmly and enthusiastically. Now, after a year, the enthusiasm had waned considerably and there was a discrepancy between the current attitude of the hospital toward the project and the initial one. The project seemed to be serving as an irritant in the daily operation of the hospital and cooperation was increasingly difficult between the various departments in the institution and the project itself. One of the activities the aides and patients had wanted to perform was the painting of the ward; this project caused conflict with the painters in the maintenance section of the hospital. The business office had difficulty in dealing with the unusual work orders from the ward and there was a series of problems over payment which patients and relatives owed for hospitalization. Probably the most obvious difficulty in the relations with the the hospital came over the project's contact with the clinical services. Thus, for example, it took nine months to replace the nurse who had quit on the ward. Concern was expressed by the medical personnel of the institution; they wondered how medical responsibility could be kept intact when in reality the physician assigned to the ward had no personal contact with the patients who were his legal charge. How could the doctor be held responsible for what happened to his patients when he was not able to see them? [p. 67]

Similar statements could be quoted from subsequent years. Toward the end of the book we are told that "the project terminated

September, 1964. It was not possible for the hospital to absorb it as an isolated social system; however, those aspects of the Ward H project that were compatible with the ongoing system were absorbed."

In light of our earlier discussions in this and the previous chapter, the reader will not be surprised by the questions I found myself asking after I finished reading *Ward H*. Although the project became a reality in July 1960, what were the issues, problems, and conflicts which marked its prehistory?[5] To what extent were the project directors aware of and able to confront the fact that the new setting would emerge from and become part of an existing organization of settings that had long-standing traditions and practices at variance with the new setting which, if successful, would establish the superiority of its mission? (From all available evidence the project was very successful.) Was the inability of the hospital "to absorb it as an isolated social system" related to issues, problems, and conflicts contained in the earliest phases of the new setting? Did the creation of the setting result, as seems likely, in a redistribution of existing limited resources?

These questions are not answerable for the same reasons they were not answerable by our book on the clinic: you cannot answer questions you do not raise, and for the reader it makes no difference whether that is due to the incompleteness of one's conceptions, or misplaced emphasis, or politeness. And yet the answers to these questions bear on the life and death of settings devoted to human service. Just as in psychotherapy you cannot treat a patient who does not show up,

---

[5] How writers pinpoint the beginning of a setting is quite revealing of implicit ways of thinking. To say that Ward H became a reality in July 1960 suggests two things: that a setting exists or begins only when it performs a service for others, and whatever precedes that point is "just" history or, as it now is more fashionable to say, "tooling up," a technological way of thinking that separates means and ends and bears more relationship to words than to external reality. In this connection it is important to note that the guiding principles for Ward H that Colarelli and Siegel discuss are guides to how one can understand and therapeutically respond to the chronic schizophrenic, and nothing in these principles guides one as to how one creates the appropriate setting. To say that Ward H began on a certain day is as meaningful as to say that John Jones became a schizophrenic on a certain day or that a revolution took place on a particular day, week, or month (Edwards, 1927). I became sensitive to these points because a couple of years after the "beginning" of the Psycho-Educational Clinic I found that I had difficulty answering the apparently simple question: when did the clinic begin? For quite some time the simple answer to the simple question was July 1963. What was producing difficulty for me was the dawning awareness that it all began in the fall of 1961 when my proposal was under discussion, setting off a train of events and processes which ensured that the present always contained history. As any Broadway buff knows, opening night is special but it is not the beginning.

similarly a helping setting which dies, or fails to be born, cannot be helpful.

Domination by the Future: The Timetable

One of the points I have been emphasizing is that a setting is usually seen as having a function in relation to others external to the setting and that one of the consequences of this is that it even determines the definition of the starting point. Embedded in this way of thinking, and a consequence of it, is an orientation to, even a preoccupation with, the future. It is true that this orientation isolates or de-emphasizes the past but that is a point that no longer should require emphasis.

Once a setting "starts," all kinds of things begin to happen or have to be done. A building may have to be planned and built, or some space may have to be found, or rented, or renovated. Personnel may have to be located, interviewed, hired. Various kinds of materials have to be procured. Rules, regulations, and policies have to be formulated, if only because they have to be communicated to prospective employees and clients. Financial resources have to be garnered, budgeted, and spent. Who will do what, who will be responsible to whom, and what kind of timetable will be set for accomplishing this and that are questions that are asked and receive some kind of answer. All of this takes place and is perceived in relation to primary and secondary goals which are in the immediate and distant future.

Those who are creating the setting always have a timetable. It may have narrow or broad limits, but a timetable is always there and influences how activity in the present is perceived. In many instances the timetable is rather fixed and inflexible because the sources of funds require a definite timetable, but it may also exist less because of the requirements set by others than because of certain characteristics of the leader. I have seen many leaders of new settings whose implicit or explicit conception or theory about the creation of a setting apparently permitted them to set a definite timetable. Almost invariably these have been people who were for the first time in their lives in a position to create a setting, and it probably would be more correct to explain their timetable on the basis of ignorance than on the basis of conceptions and theories. Wish-fulfillment and ignorance explain far more here than do words like *conceptions* and *theory*. Their cognitive approach seemed based on the same principles as those involved in making a car move: you open the door, you get in, you shut the door, you put the key in the ignition, you turn the key, press the gas pedal, and the car moves. Another example, more related to the creation of settings, is the way many people approach building their own home. Decide how much money one wants to spend, the kind of home one wants, hire an architect, draw up plans, get a contractor, agree on a beginning and finishing date, and then one is ready to move in. That it rarely, if ever, proceeds in this way, that many people have had to move in before the house was ready, or live in a hotel until the house was really finished, or spend a year or so after moving in bludgeoning the contractor to really finish the job—these possibilities were not contained in their "theory" of house building. The point, of course, is that as events begin to invalidate the time perspective, the handling or response to the present can become invaded by all kinds of factors which disrupt relationships and sometimes even result in aborting the whole affair.

A second characteristic of leaders that can result in a definite timetable emphasizes personality more than cognition, although these are never separate from each other. That is to say, there are people who must structure the future timewise and adhere to it. To the outsider this may appear to be authoritarianism (and it may be) or forcefulness (and it may be) or stubbornness (and it may be), but it also may be viewed as a compulsiveness manifesting itself in a structured future from which one cannot or should not deviate.

Although the reasons for it may vary, the existence of a fairly definite timetable can and usually does have an enormous influence on the beginning context. For one thing, the feeling of pressure begins to build as it becomes apparent that the setting being created does not and cannot develop in a vacuum and is dependent upon and must establish and negotiate relationships with a variety of other settings. For example, I have observed a number of instances of the creation of a new nursery school where the leaders became more and more frustrated as they were required to spend time in regard to fire department regulations, health department criteria, and city or state educational requirements. When in addition to these legal and administrative "obstacles" (which is the way they are experienced) the leaders were required to gain some kind of support or help from existing settings, and this not only took time but involved all kinds of policy and substantive issues, I observed reactions compounded of anger, anxiety, and even despair, as it became apparent that the timetable could not be adhered to. The pressure "to get started" and to view anything before "the beginning point" as *merely* secondary steps to a primary goal frequently has several consequences. First, it can result in the decision to bypass issues, individuals, and existing settings. Second, it can facilitate compromises, willingly or otherwise, which will shape the future. Third, it can create or exacerbate conflict or dissension in the small group formed by the leader to create the new setting. The existence of a fairly definite timetable usually creates a present dominated and tyrannized by a future which when it arrives is not the one imagined.

Examples (humorous or otherwise) can be found in the creation of the marital setting, specifically that period between the decision to get married and the marriage ceremony itself. There have been many young couples who have wanted to get married quickly only to discover that society is not always organized so as to be accommodating to individual desires. There is, of course, in most states some kind of health criterion which must be met, a certificate to be obtained, some kind of waiting period to be observed, and, of course, making sure that whoever performs the ceremony is empowered to do so. If either of the partners is below legal age, matters become psychologically and legally more complicated. But all this is as nothing compared to the parental and familial complications which are obstacles to a quick and simple marriage. What the young couple usually conceive as a simple process amenable to *their* timetable can become an obstacle course which postpones the starting point at the same time that conflict and controversy appear with their divisive effects either on the couple or their families or both. It does not have to happen this way; it just does a lot of times. I have known young couples who sensed what was in store for them and bypassed it all by quietly going off and getting married, with the not infrequent result that what was bypassed appeared later in different ways.

Creating the marital setting, like creating other types of settings, quickly becomes enmeshed with other settings, and its development is in part a function not only of how these relationships are conceived and managed but also the nature of the time perspective that is implicit or explicit in the conceptions.

In the previous chapters as well as in the first part of this one I emphasized in different ways a historical perspective and the necessity of confronting the history of the setting. What I have just been stressing is the crucial significance of the ever-present future time perspective, particularly one which either for internal or external reasons is fairly fixed. There is always a future-oriented time perspective and, in fact, the enthusiasm and sense of mission characterizing a new setting are largely a reflection of an orientation to a future point which when reached defines success. The fact that a particular type of timetable can have adverse consequences should not obscure the more general point that there is always a relationship between orientations to the future and the development of the setting in the beginning context. What is rarely made clear in descriptions of new settings is the nature of that perspective, its basis, or its consequences. Having an orientation toward a future is not a matter of choice either in the life of an individual or a new setting, and, let us not forget, there is nothing good or bad about an orientation toward the future except as it determines the ways in which it influences how our experience of the present interferes with or facilitates the achievement of our purposes.

Being caught up and dominated by the future seems almost to require no explanation. After all, a new setting is created to accomplish a future objective and one should expect those in it to strive toward it and vigorously so. If obstacles are encountered which postpone the accomplishment of goals, one should not expect an attitude of kindly tolerance. Some might say that what would require explanation is when those in the new setting are not acting as if they have been stimulated, galvanized, or motivated by the purposes which have brought them together.

This type of explanation is incomplete because it does not take into account some factors discussed in earlier chapters. That is to say, this explanation does not consider the fact that the attractiveness of the future resides not only in the nature of its goals but in its presumed superiority to what existed in the past. The creation of the Yale Psycho-Educational Clinic, for example, reflected the opinion that it was needed to demonstrate ways of thinking about and performing services that would be different from and superior to those services rendered by existing settings. Whether or not, or to what extent, this was true is less important than the fact that it was assumed to be true and that the staff attracted to it also believed that they had an opportunity to engage in something superior to what they had been doing previously. Our high hopes could only be understood by looking both at where we were going and where we had been. Related to this, of course, is another point I previously stressed: the prehistory of a new setting almost always contains conflict and controversy about how problems are being handled, and the creation of the new setting is implicit recognition of some kind of failure or inadequacy on the part of the existing organization of settings, hence the importance of confronting history. One of the most important consequences of the situation in which the new setting is dominated by the future is that awareness and remembrance of prehistory, as well as the significance of confronting history, are diminished or nonexistent. Whereas at one time the future was seen as intimately related to, and an outgrowth of, a particular set of past conditions and experiences, this perceived and experienced relationship tends to fade out of the picture as the new setting is born or starts up, begins to organize itself, acquires material and human resources, encounters problems and pressures internal or external, and perceives that the accomplishment of future goals may be postponed or only partial. When the present is dominated by concern about future goals, remembering and confronting history become a luxury. To the extent that present concerns reflect history—and in the beginning context present concerns always reflect history to some extent—denying or avoiding the relationship may satisfy individual needs but this should not be confused with changing the social realities.

Earlier in this chapter I sketchily described and discussed the origins of the Yale Psycho-Educational Clinic in terms of its relationship to an existing organization of settings, emphasizing how these origins contained various kinds of conflict and differences of opinion. The substance of these differences rather clearly indicated what some future problems would be. First, that unless our activities were frequently and meaningfully communicated to the department of psychology there would be no basis for changing people's attitudes. This would be particularly important because the clinic would be housed away from the departmental offices. Second, because we would be physically separated from our department, the ideological gulf could be widened to the extent that we at the clinic viewed ourselves as different and superior and utilized the separation in ways ruling out sustained discussion; that is, we could erect barriers which could facilitate the self-fulfilling prophecy that we were superior and misunderstood. Third, the kind of staff necessary to accomplish our goals would be those with interests and orientation which would make their stay and promotion at Yale problematic. From the very beginning I felt a deep sense of responsibility to these young faculty we would attract because they would be putting in an inordinate amount of time, energy, and thought over and above the normal duties of a faculty member, and to feel that their chances of remaining at Yale were small was quite bothersome to me, which was less important than what that would mean to them. There was a selfish component to this in that I had no intention of remaining forever as director of the clinic. If those who joined the clinic could not stay on, I would be faced at some future point with a personal dilemma.

All of this was quite clear during and after the prehistory phase. It was also quite clear that these problems had to be faced and there were different ways to do this. That I did not handle these issues at all well is a fact explainable by two factors. The first can best be put in terms of personal pride; I resented having to justify our existence to those whom I perceived to view themselves as "our betters." This is a particularly good example of how an individual's needs can obscure the distinction between the needs of an individual and those of a setting.[6] The second factor is one I have been emphasizing in this section and that is the ease with which one becomes almost exclusively concerned with a present laden by a conception of a future which leaves little room for pondering and dealing with the past. With what community settings should the clinic establish relationships? What should be the financial arrangements? What should be the role of students? Will we be able to cover research expenses? What if our services are not wanted or renewed by a setting? How shall we determine whether or not, or to what extent, we succeed or fail? Will what we write be viewed as only anecdotes or superficial description? Will we really be able to conceptualize what a community is and the dimensions along which it is organized? Can we really avoid in our own setting what we think characterizes so many settings, that is, ways of relating, thinking, and talking which defeat the purposes of personal and intellectual growth? Will we really be able to judge ourselves not only by the "good" we do for others but by how much we learn? Will we be able to capitalize on failure? These are only a fraction of the questions which almost daily concerned us, and they only reflect those kinds of questions which came from within us. It would tax a gifted taxonomist to describe and classify the questions and problems bombarding us from without, most of which in one way or another involved our goals and our future. In dedicating my book (*The School Culture and the Problem of Change*) to three people who played crucial roles in the creation of the clinic I said "especially for the first two years of the Yale Psycho-Educational Clinic when it was not at all clear we would make it." The phrase *making it* well suggests how caught up that small group was with an anxious future.

The reader who has not created a setting or participated in its earliest phases may have difficulty appreciating how in the beginning context the future overwhelms the past. This does not mean that this is part of an inevitable process but rather that it is very frequent. I am

---

[6] There are those who have characterized what I am saying as unduly charitable to the department of psychology. Such a characterization only makes sense if one thinks in either-or, black-white, right-wrong terms. That the department was playing its traditional role rather well goes without saying but this should not cause one to overlook that I did not handle matters in the best possible way. Candor requires that I admit that from the very beginning I did not view our chances of winning "as being even modestly high," a view not conducive to building bridges. If I knew then what I think I know now about the creation of settings, I would have acted quite differently, if for no other reason than that I would have a more adequate conceptual basis for controlling personal needs and motivation—and that is the significance of understanding and conceptualizing the creation of settings.

also not suggesting that the consequences of not confronting history are always serious or that they forever adversely affect the development of the setting. Neither I nor anybody else has any firm basis for determining how and to what extent settings have been adversely affected or died as a result of treating the past as just the past. Similarly, we have no way of knowing how many settings are aborted in their earliest phases because of the failure to deal with their historical origins.

It would be unfortunate if the reader concluded that my primary purpose in this and the previous chapters was to suggest that the creation of a setting was an obstacle course in which the role of the outside world was to see in how many different ways the purposes of the setting could be frustrated or scuttled. It would be equally unfortunate if the reader concluded that my major purpose has been to demonstrate that creating a setting is a personally demanding task for those who are responsible for it. That it is a demanding task which forever changes those who cope with it goes without saying, and this in large measure explains why most of those who do it once are wary about doing it again. My major purpose rather has been to suggest that the difficulty of the task is to an undetermined extent a consequence of the fact that we have not known how to think about or conceptualize the problem and so we do not have available in our heads a set of conceptions telling us what we may expect and what we might do. Those who create settings have, of course, conceptions about what will be involved but in the main they reduce to four factors: strength of motivation, values, personality, and power. These are as important as they are incomplete. What is missing and needed are conceptions which put these factors into a historical, sociological, and developmental or longitudinal context reflecting the supraindividual realities. At the present time creating a setting is akin to the rearing of a child and having little or no conception about the nature of development in its motoric, linguistic, cognitive, and physical-health aspects. It can be done and those doing the rearing will learn a great deal—far more, it is likely, than the child. Love is not enough in rearing a child or creating a setting. As a colleague remarked, "The heart can make up for a lot of inadequacies but an empty head is not one of them." Creating a setting is as much an affair of the head as it is the heart, the lesson which Castro so eloquently discussed in relating the failures of the Cuban revolution.

A Caution about Phases and Stages

There is far more to the beginning context than has been raised in this chapter. As in the previous one, this chapter had as its theme the problem of how continuity and history are perceived and the adverse consequences of denying or evading or simply not recognizing the problem. Before going on to other phases and problems the reader must be cautioned about an unreflective reaction against which he must guard, if only because authors frequently do not. It involves the belief that there are stages or phases which are distinct, bounded, and real. The fact that I have labeled and discussed a prehistory phase and a beginning context sounds "natural" enough and may lead the reader to view them as occupying different points on a time continuum; that is, one phase precedes and shapes the next one, old problems are transformed or resolved and attention is now attracted to problems akin to the next phase. This is akin to the reaction we frequently have when we drive past a road sign telling us we are now in a different state. Somehow the sign makes us feel that we have experienced a real change at the same time that we are aware that our feeling is not justified. There is, of course, some external basis to the concept of phases or stages—just as the highway sign signifies a real political-legal change—but one must be very careful not to overemphasize discontinuities and to underemphasize continuities.

A more serious error, particularly in regard to the creation of settings, is when an external observer utilizes the concept of stages in a way so as to blind him to the possibility that issues and problems of a later stage were present in the minds of some in an earlier stage. They may have been present in varying degrees of clarity but the important fact is that they existed in some form long before they became discernible in ways which permitted us to characterize these ways as a stage. For example, in the next chapter we shall be discussing the problems and characteristics of early growth in terms of the formation of the small core group which will bear major responsibilities for the development of the setting. Obviously this is not a problem characterizing or encountered in the prehistory stage or the beginning context (at least in its earliest phases). But this does not mean that long before the task of forming the core group arises there was no one (such as the leader or the leaders who chose the leader) who had thought about how this task should be handled. In fact, in the instance in which the new setting arises from an existing organization of settings, some of the most important decisions about the formation of the core group have been made by virtue of long-standing traditions and regulations. Some leaders who are chosen willingly accept being governed by these traditions and regulations, while others (sometimes before they accept the leadership) are thinking about getting around these traditions and regulations long before the task is at hand. A presumed advantage of creating a setting not embedded in an existing organization of settings —an advantage which may exist in the mind of the leader long before the core group has to be formed—is that one has much more freedom to form the core group in desired ways.

The point I am making is that the concept of stages of growth is so a part of our way of thinking that we fail to see that at the same time that it says something about the external world it also distorts it. There is nothing wrong in this as long as we remain aware that we are, so to speak, employing a conceptual sword which cuts both ways. Still another consequence of thinking in terms of stages of growth is that it frequently lulls us into accepting the idea of inevitability of process or outcome, an unfolding in which the shape of the future is already determined. The fact that things develop in a certain way is not synonymous with the statement that things *must* develop in a certain way, as if nothing can stop or alter the process. To believe this is akin to saying that because an individual has an inborn genetic defect which indisputably has adverse developmental consequences there is nothing one can do in the face of the inevitable, a statement which confuses what is with what could be. Modern genetics, of course, has altered this way of thinking and this would not have been possible if what *is* had been viewed as what *had* to be.

Initially it had been my plan to write this book in two parts: first a description of the modal ways in which settings seem to be created, and then a discussion of alternative ways of viewing the task. This plan turned out to be extraordinarily difficult to follow not only because of the relative lack of descriptive data but also, and more important, because description of the process constantly posed and exposed the contrast between what is and what could be. To have persisted with the plan to begin with description may well have created in the reader the impression that a developmental order meant an inevitability of process and outcome: two follows one, three follows two, four follows three, and it is all preordained by the nature of the system. Just as most people believe that the way in which we use numbers is the way nature ordained them to be used, so do we tend to view any regularity as the natural order of things. Elsewhere (Sarason, 1971) I have pointed out that practically everyone accepts it as natural that children should not go to school on Saturday and Sunday. If we are challenged to defend this regularity we are nonplussed because it does not seem to require explanation. In fact, when I have challenged people on this score some respond by saying it is a ridiculous question. It is precisely when we feel that something does not require explanation that we are very likely confusing what is with what has to be. The significance of this is that it should direct our attention not only to what people think but the degree to which what people think is based on deliberate consideration of what could be. It is one thing to proceed as if there is only one way of thinking about the problem, and it is quite another thing to be aware that one is choosing a course of action from a universe of possibilities. These different ways of thinking and their consequences are central to our discussion in the next chapter on the formation of the core group.

CHAPTER 4

Formation of the Core Group

At the beginning of this book I provisionally defined the creation of a setting as involving two or more people brought together in new relationships for a sustained period of time to achieve stated objectives. I used the word *provisional* for a number of reasons not the least of which was that utilizing a time criterion (*when* two or more people) was a convenience which could distort the historical continuity of events and processes. Another reason was that the definition simply did not and could not mirror the diverse human or group contexts from which a setting can emerge. Earlier I emphasized the instance in which the new setting emerges from an existing organization of settings, a leader is chosen by other leaders, and so on. To a lesser extent I also discussed the instance in which the new setting is the idea and creation of a single person. These instances far from exhaust the different social contexts out of which a new setting emerges. For example, many communes have grown out of an earlier network of informal relationships which may or may not have had the characteristics of a group.[1] That is to say, before the point at which the decision to create a new setting is made, those who will be part of it will have had various types of relationships, and in some instances the person who becomes the leader may or may not have been in that role in the informal group. This is also frequently true in the creation of new businesses and private educational enterprises. This is also true of new political groups which emerge out of informal relationships and then take on the characteristics of an organized setting for the purpose of attaining political power. This purpose may be achieved through conventional or revolutionary means, but in both instances previous relationships affect to a certain degree the course of development, although the effects are not always the same. In his illuminating book *Charismatic Leadership in the Third World,* Lacouture (1970) states: "While strife produces heroes, it also opens up severe internal conflicts. Even though the leader knows that his claim to authority is justified and based on past performance, he harbors an extremely suspicious attitude fostered by years of outlawry and imprisonment. One would think that the grim experience of revolutionary violence would have a cleansing effect in the domain of power. But the relations between former battle-comrades are often more strained than those between individuals who attain power by conventional paths. The contrasting situations in Algeria and Morocco illustrate this." Leaving aside the issue of means, the fact that a setting emerges from previous informal interpersonal relationships introduces factors that are not present when members of the core group in the new setting have had no such previous relationships.

Although it is of obvious importance and deserves extended study and discussion, I shall not attempt to list and discuss the variety of social or group origins from which a setting emerges and develops. I mention the problem here because I believe that differences in types of origins are most clear in their effects on the formation and nature of the core group which will have the most responsibility for creating and developing the new setting. In this chapter I shall as before focus primarily on the two types of instances which I know best: where the new setting emerges from an existing organization of settings, and where the new setting represents the ideas and efforts of a single individual. In the former a leader is chosen, while in the latter he

[1] See, for example, Yaswen's article "Sunrise Hill: Post Mortem" (1970).

chooses himself; in both instances he is faced with the task of forming a core group.

Predictable Problems Between the Leader and the Core Group

If it were possible to observe and record what a leader says or does as he goes about forming a core group, several things would become quite obvious. The first is that he thinks in terms of a core group: usually a handful of people who will be closest to him interpersonally and statuswise. They will be "his family" to whom he delegates responsibilities and powers second only to his own; he is quite aware that if he chooses badly he jeopardizes the future of the setting. But what does a leader mean when he says he has "chosen" a member of this group? If one asks leaders what they mean by this statement, by far the most frequent answer is that the individual has been chosen to do a particular job—to utilize his knowledge, experience, and skills so that the purposes of the setting will be realized. What this answer reflects—and what independent observation and records would demonstrate—is the emphasis placed on the formal task and the purposes of the setting. That is to say, there is a match between what needs to be done and what the individual can do. This would be a reasonable enough answer except that it ignores the fact that the individual and the leader will be in what is for them a *new* relationship, one that involves far more than is covered in the term *doing the job*.[2] Whether or not they can live together, whether or not their styles are congruent, whether or not their personal needs and goals clash—these are not questions contained in the answers which leaders give about why a person was hired. The assumption, of course, on the part of both the leader and the core individual is that these questions have been answered. The usual history of the relationship between leaders and core individuals does not suggest that the questions were asked or validly answered. In fact, for more often than not the questions were not even posed because they are experienced as personal, conflictful, unpolitic, and unanswerable except by the passage of time. What underlies all of this, however, and permits easy answers to difficult questions is a

---

[2] This is also the case where the leader and the core group previously have had informal relationships, such as in a new political group. What is so frequent and strange in these instances is the mutually shared fantasy that the transformation from the informal to the formal group will not involve them in new relationships, thereby bypassing the difficult, troublesome, but necessary task of anticipating problems and establishing ground rules for dealing with them.

belief we discussed in an earlier chapter—that agreement on values and motivation is seen as surmounting or preventing future difficulties.

The safest and most obvious prediction one can make about the relationship between the leader and a core individual is that there will be problems. The sources of these problems are many, among which personality is but one. When these problems will arise and what their specific character will be are not too predictable, but that is less a problem than the failure to anticipate that there will be problems and that ground rules can be developed to deal with them—not to eliminate but to deal with them.

Imagine the situation in which you have requested and received a large grant to support a long-term research project. It will be necessary for you to hire a number of people to assist in carrying out the purposes of the project, and some will be highly trained and sophisticated individuals capable of independent thought and action. How would you conduct the process of attracting and hiring these individuals? The word *attract* well reflects the basic set likely to govern the thinking of both you and the individual who is a candidate. That is to say, *you* are likely to describe the situation in the most favorable light and *he* is set to hear what is attractive to him. It is a set conducive to your putting your best forward and his perceiving the attractive aspects of the possibilities. The purposes of the project, the different ideas to be studied, the scope of the individual's responsibilities, salary, office space, and secretarial help—these are some of the things which in varying degrees of detail will ordinarily be discussed. What are likely to be bypassed or only alluded to are predictable problems which can cause conflict and disruption precisely because there was no prior discussion of and agreement about how the problems will be handled. For example, grants are given with the expectation that research findings will be made public, and research papers or books are essential for establishing a reputation and a basis for promotion, yet you and the candidate may never even discuss the problems of publication. The fact that there will be publications permits one to ask certain questions not as an exercise of fantasy but as a recognition of reality. Whose names will be on the publications? If there is more than one name, in what order shall they be? Who will have primary responsibility for writing? What if there are disagreements about what is included, style, and interpretation of the data? If a book will be published, how will royalties be apportioned? Anyone familiar with research settings can point to instances in which these questions become problems with serious consequences for the leader and his core group. That these questions are rarely if ever discussed at the point when one is choosing a member of the core group is not a matter of ignorance but rather of denial powered by the belief that where there is good will predictable questions will not become serious problems. As lawyers can tell us, substituting good will for mutually agreed-upon ground rules is as secure as skating on ice the thickness of which is unknown.

The point of this example is not only that certain issues are predictable, or that certain decisions will have to be made, but that they will be based on rules of governance. More often than not, such rules are rarely discussed and formulated ahead of time, or if they are it is so general or indirect that the ground is laid for the most frequent complaint one hears in any setting: "There is a communications problem." The failure to communicate has diverse interacting sources, but in my experience the most important is the failure of two people to anticipate and discuss how predictable issues affecting them both will be handled. As a result, these issues are usually faced and "resolved" in the worst of all situations: when feelings are high and smoldering conflict and controversy are present. It is facile and fashionable to attribute interpersonal conflict to differences in personality, undoubtedly because personality is always a factor and because no two people are alike. But that is precisely a basis that should compel people to recognize that there will be problems stemming from differences in personality and that these types of differences will inevitably be affected and manifested differently in relation to different nonpersonality issues that will arise.

The creation of the marital setting again provides illuminating examples because the types of questions and problems which the couple will face are fairly predictable. When will the marriage take place? Where will it take place, what kind of a ceremony, and who will be invited? What will be their financial resources and how will that affect where they will live and what furniture they will buy? Who will do what kinds of housekeeping chores? How will money be apportioned for food, clothes, savings, recreation, and socialization? How frequently and for how long shall parental visits be? Will there be children, and if so, what will determine when the first child will be conceived? How will decisions be made and will there by any decisions which will not be made jointly? When one considers the myriad aspects of human behavior which have been studied, is it not strange that there has been practically no systematic study of these and other questions which will confront the couple? In an unpublished study of relatively newly married college students, Robert Karlin (1971) found that it was around these questions that couples were having difficulty but that they tended neither to have anticipated them nor to have discussed how they might handle them. In light of what we know about the frequency and causes of divorce, as well as sustained but unhappy marriages, Karlin's findings are hardly surprising. In typical style we tend to "explain" such findings in terms of youth, immaturity, and personality clashes. Youth are not supposed to be foresightful and realistic; they plunge ahead on the assumption that love is a sufficient and necessary resource to cope and overcome what difficulties reality will put in their paths. But this is precisely what I am claiming characterizes the thinking of many of those who create a new setting, even though they may be chronologically mature people, presumably wise in the ways of the real world. Time and again I have observed the leader and his core group enter into what is to be an enduring relationship grounded in (if not suffused with) enthusiasm, good will and a problem-free view of their future relationships. There are several reasons why this is so. First, the tendency to view the new setting as different from and superior to other settings generates an enthusiasm and sense of mission which color the future in a quite rosy way; that is, superiority of ends is confused with superiority of means. Second, and related to the first, it is usually true both for the leader and core group that the attractiveness of the new setting inheres not only in what the new setting promises but in their disappointment in their previous settings. They are not only "going toward" something but "running away" from something (not unlike many marriage partners). Third, it is simply not part of their thinking to view the creation of the setting as a set of developmental problems which are fairly predictable and about which one can formulate ground rules so that when these problems occur the element of surprise is diluted, and past discussion can serve as a basis for discussion in the present. Fourth, even when there is more rather than less awareness of these developmental problems, discussion of them at the point when the core group is formed is made difficult precisely because they are problematic, will arouse differences of opinion, and may require decisions and compromises with which some may not want to live. Anticipating problems and forging a "constitution" by which the leader and the core group will be governed are intellectually and interpersonally difficult and demanding processes. One result of the processes may be that some individuals will choose not to join the setting, a consequence as revealing of ideological as of personality differences.

The strength and consequences of the initial enthusiasm have been well described by Yaswen (1970) in the course of his discussion of the failure of a particular commune:

These meetings concerned themselves primarily with two subjects: policies and personalities. In the area of personalities, we attempted to learn more about one another and to draw out the first reactions that people had to each other at that early stage of familiarity. Although we did come up with some significant communication—in which some mild interpersonal conflicts were uncovered—no one thought much of them. We felt assured that, on the basis of the great amounts of love which we already felt for each other and the importance of the endeavor we were commonly undertaking, all such petty conflicts could somehow ultimately be resolved. Also there was precious little, at that point, to dislike about each other, for in truth we really did not know one another.

The issues of community policies, however, proved somewhat more difficult. We began by asking each prospective member for his reasons for joining the community and what he expected of it. What followed was a sequence of some of the most beautiful descriptions one could hear of the plight of our kind in the mass-society and of the potentialities of utopia. It was a sharing of visions, an occurrence painfully lacking afterwards. But the trouble was that visions are vague. It is very easy to feel commonality with a person when he says that what he wants are peace, truth, health, and beauty. But the problem of how best to strive for them remains (as it has for millennia). When we tried to tackle that problem, the paths disturbingly started to divide. First of all, we had to define what we meant by such terms as peace, truth, health, and beauty. As might be expected, the various views represented were far more multifarious than we originally thought. The discussion of the least particle of them promised to be without end and, moreover, without even the possibility of an end. It was indeed frustrating for people with such fire and enthusiasm to have to sit upon their hands and quibble infinitely over the picayunes of how their great vision should crystalize. This was combined with the sense in all of us that, in spite of our particular differences, we shared something so deeply unutterable as to make such discussions pedantic and unnecessary. So we abandoned these discussions before the fact. We felt that there was no alternative to the actual working out of our differences through activity rather than debate.

So when the Conference ended, Sunrise Hill stood as an extremely nebulous though intensely exciting idea. Those further interested were to meet at the site on July 4, 1966. If later events proved the sagacity of the Sunrise Hill project questionable and the groundwork spindly, we who were involved must be pardoned for having partaken too headily and unreservedly of that intoxicating "Yes" spirit that pervaded the Heathcote Conference. The founding of Sunrise Hill was mainly an act of faith; there was little of prudence in it.

Predictable Problems Within the Core Group

I have talked of predictable problems between the leader and a member of the core group. The same points are as applicable to the relationships *among* the members of the core group, except that the task is more difficult for them because ordinarily they have no basis or vehicle (independent of the leader) for anticipating problems and forging ground rules. When these problems arise it is the leader to whom the core members come for a decision, a practice which sounds reasonable (as it sometimes is) but in practice has the effect of rendering the core members increasingly unable among themselves to anticipate and manage problems peculiar to their role relationships. Furthermore, since the decision of the leader usually means that some core members "win" while others "lose," divisions among the core members are increased and their capacity to anticipate and manage other mutual problems is decreased. There are leaders, of course, who desire this state of affairs but in my experience they are less common than those who either do not perceive what is happening or simply do not know how to help core members handle their mutual problems differently. When a leader makes a decision about something which has divided the core members, he has done just that: made a decision. He has not addressed himself either to why the core members were divided or the consequences of his decision in future mutual problem-solving.

The core group is usually not chosen at one time but rather serially. The order in which they are chosen is not a trifling matter either to the leader or the core group because the order usually reflects, or may be perceived as reflecting, a scale of importance. The importance which a core member places on his position is not only determined by his scale of importance or title but also by his perception of how the leader views them, and in many instances *when* the core member was chosen is given a good deal of weight. If the core member has not been among the first to be chosen, his sense of importance may also be determined by how the already present core members view (or he perceives them as viewing) his position.

The order in which core members are chosen may have another consequence fateful for the development of the setting and that is the development within the core group of the insider-outsider, friend-stranger dichotomies. When a new member is added to the core group, he perceives, and correctly so, that the existing core group is a group; they have come to know each other, they have established working and personal relationships, and they have some sense of group identity. The group already has cohesiveness and a history. At this point the new member is both a stranger and an outsider. He perceives a core group in which he does not and cannot feel "core." In my experience the fact that the new member feels as a stranger-outsider and the fact that he is so regarded by the others are practically never explicitly discussed or faced. And yet from the moment he joins the group everyone

is in varying degrees thinking about how and to what extent he will
"fit." What actually takes place will be a function of the dynamics of
the existing core group and the new member's conception of group
structure and behavior. It obviously makes a difference if the new
member views the existing group as a happy, tight-knit family (as he
likely was told) or, the other extreme, as a group of individuals already
heterogeneous in terms of power and resources. The important point
is that the new setting usually has no explicit way of facing and dealing with this process of growth. The guiding myth is that the fact that
the new member was chosen is evidence enough that he will "fit." But
in most cases this is a myth of the leader not always shared by others,
particularly when the new member was primarily chosen by the leader.

A core member is attracted to a new setting because he has
concluded that it will provide him the opportunity to work and develop
in ways superior to those in his old setting. Just as it is extremely rare
for those creating a new setting to say that they are merely replicating
what has heretofore existed elsewhere—something new, different, and
superior has been added—the core member does not come to the new
setting just to do what he has done before. Both the leader and core
member think of the future in terms of discrete tasks and responsibilities; that is, each core member has his special role. What is so unrealistic about this view can be seen by stating the two assumptions
(or myths) underlying it. First, doing one's job is *not* (or only minimally) determined by how other core members do their job. Second,
the resources available to the setting are sufficient to allow each core
member to do his job in the way he wishes. The first assumption is
never true, and the second only very rarely true. And so we have the
situation where core members are brought together because each can
do "his thing" whereas reality quickly confronts them with the fact
that this modern-day equivalent of rugged individualism is not possible without conflict, controversy, and disruption—precisely those
characteristics of living which disposed some to leave their previous
setting. Everyone, of course, recognizes and verbally supports cooperation and better communication, but they also recognize that the appropriate motivation somehow has not give rise to a desired state of
affairs. This recognition is usually short lived and is replaced by the
belief that indeed not all core members have the appropriate motivation. And we are back to the type of solution (appropriate motivation)
which initially proved inadequate as a basis for expecting that the core
group would be able to cope with and surmount the problems which
could divide them and defeat the purposes of the setting! What practically never gets recognized is that most of these problems were pre-

dictable; they could have been discussed at the outset, tentative ways of dealing with them could have been developed, and a realistic set of constitutional arrangements could have been forged. As I indicated in the earlier discussion of the American Constitutional Convention, dealing at the outset with problems and issues that exist or may exist is not a panacea but it is far more productive than denial, silence, and cliches about virtue and an untroubled future. The statement that a society based on law is preferable to one based on men is quite applicable to the creation of a new setting. For the most part a law comes into being as commentary on the past and as a preventive in the future. Laws may be unwise, but they are always rooted in or are a response to some aspect of social practice and reality. Settings are created and developed far more on a vague concept of man than they are on a concept of law rooted in the realities of what usually happens or what possibly can happen.

I have focused on the developmental problems of the core groups as a kind of corrective to what are perhaps its most obvious characteristics: high enthusiasm, sense of mission, the stimulation of novelty, the challenge of personal and professional growth, and the anticipations of the consequences of success. These are no less important than the problems and processes I have described but their obviousness can too easily obscure the subtle unpleasantries and divisions which, depending on a variety of factors, can later become the most obvious characteristics of the setting. How often has the reader heard core people talk about their setting in terms of "the good old days"? It frequently turns out, of course, that the good old days were not *so* good.

Many years ago I came to work at a new institution for the mentally retarded. This new institution was dramatically different, ideologically and architecturally, from all other institutions serving this population. Even before it opened its doors it had a distinctive reputation, and from shortly after it opened there was a constant stream of visitors from around the world. Certainly I chose this job from among several because of its innovative programs, ideology, and striking appearance. I was getting in on the ground floor; I was to be one of the core group.

I was the youngest member of the group and the last to be chosen, facts which then had absolutely no conscious import for me. I had met the superintendent and the core members and I perceived them as a highly integrated group quite conscious of the opportunity and challenge ahead of them. The superintendent was a most remarkable and inspiring man who, if he had not been the visionary, ethical, and humane individual he was, could have sold and resold the Brooklyn Bridge at least several times a day. When I was offered and accepted the position I felt quite lucky. I was joining a dedicated, close-working group of people who were going to demonstrate to a certain segment of the world what an institution for the mentally retarded should really be. In none of the discussions or negotiations leading up to my first day of work was there ever a discordant note or any reference to any existing or future problems. They were all obviously good people and so was I.

I could in all honesty describe the early years of my stay as among the most stimulating and rewarding periods of my life. Intellectually and professionally each day seemed somewhat like an adventure, and the next day was something to look forward to. Whatever one means by a sense of personal and professional growth I experienced. In fact, it never dawned on me that I would ever want to move on. When I look back on those early years it is with a sense of gratitude and pleasant memories.

That is one way of writing personal history, but like most personal history it is true, selective, and misleading. What it does not contain is that I was a core member in name only, rarely, if ever, consulted about anything. I was always on the outside looking in and "in" was quite fascinating and complicated because the core group was markedly heterogeneous in terms of influence, understanding of policy and goals, strength of striving for power and resources, attitudes toward the superintendent, and their approach to children. What initially seemed to be a cohesive group was, in fact, conflict-ridden on all kinds of issues. Each member was caught up in the problem of boundaries so that, operationally speaking, cooperation consisted of staying well within one's departmental walls. In all informal conversations one could pretty much count on the appearance of the theme that things were not going as they should; there was a marked discrepancy between reality and original intentions and between public rhetoric and private knowledge. Whereas in the early months of its existence it could be said that each core member was almost exclusively concerned with the needs of children—he existed, so to speak, for the children—not so slowly but surely this concern became less and less exclusive. I have often thought that if each member of the core group had been asked confidentially to state what his corrective measures would be, the solutions would have had at least one thing in common: a new core group would be chosen. According to them the problems did not inhere in structure, in how the group was formed, in the ambiguities of its constitutional arrangements, or in the absence of problem-anticipating attitudes and vehicles but in the personalities of people. *Argumentum ad hominem* was the sole diagnostic instrument. Depending on how one remembers and writes history, the good old days were neither so good nor so bad. For me and the institution they were both, but as time went on the bad became ascendant.

Let us take another example but this time from the theater. A stage play for the commercial theater is an instance of the creation of a setting, bringing people together as it does in new relationships for a sustained period of time to attain certain objectives, such as fame and money. There is always a leader (director) and almost always a core group: two or more principals. Most productions fail of their purposes. The usual explanations are very similar to those advanced for what happens to other types of settings. The basic idea may be blamed, or the director, or the actors, or a too sophisticated or too backward audience, or heartless critics. The specific example I have chosen concerns the first English production of Shaw's *Pygmalion,* about which Huggett (1969) has recently written an uproariously humorous account. Interestingly enough, the title of the book is *The Truth about Pygmalion,* because it is a book detailing how this setting came about and specifically the history of the relationship between the writer-director (Shaw), on the one hand, and his core group (Mrs. Patrick Campbell and Sir Herbert Beerbohm Tree), on the other hand. In almost all respects Huggett's story illuminates the problems and processes which I have thus far described in the creation of settings, with the important exception that opening night was a magnificent success despite the fact that what happened bears resemblance to a bloody military campaign.

Several aspects of the account are relevant to the present discussion. The first is that Shaw not only knew what he wanted but anticipated most of the mammoth problems he would encounter with two of "the most outrageous egos the theatre has ever produced"— Shaw, of course, being the third.[3] There was never any doubt in anyone's mind where Shaw stood and how decisions would be made. There could be (as he knew there would be) pouting, yelling, scream-

---

[3] Huggett states: "It is unlikely that Shaw would have rushed to take charge of the production if he had known in advance just how much trouble he was going to have with his two stars." This conjecture is not supported by the account. No doubt that Shaw's patience and assertiveness were taxed, but the overwhelming impression one gains is that Shaw was *never* surprised at the ingenuity of Mrs. Campbell and Sir Tree to try to have things their way. For example, anyone who reads pages 85 and 86 of Huggett's book will, if and when his laughter subsides, conclude that Shaw knew exactly what he was up against and his cards were always on the table.

ing, and even occasionally quiet discussion, but there was no ambiguity about how irreconcilable stances would get resolved. Little or nothing was hidden on or under the table; every conflict was out in the open and all of London was following the affair. The constitution was informal, crystal clear, and observed.

The following quotation is not, as Huggett suggests, peculiar to the theatre but characteristic of new settings.

Shaw bluntly refused to entrust his brainchild to the splendid but capricious talents of the great actor-manager, let alone those of his leading lady. He insisted on directing *Pygmalion* himself. The seeds of discontent were thus planted, preparing the way for a really magnificently explosive situation. The duet of personalities was now a trio, and the music which thundered and screamed round the Dome of the famous theatre was as dramatic and as colourful as the play which inspired it. . . .

At the beginning, as it usually is in the theatre, it was all sweetness and light, declarations of mutual esteem and promises of good behaviour. "Oh goodness, we're in for it and let's be *very* clever," wrote Mrs. Pat to Shaw after the first rehearsal. "Tree's fixed and you can manage the lot of us and then indeed you'll be a *great man*. Tree wants to be friendly and his admiration for you and the play is ENORMOUS. I'll be as tame as a mouse, and oh, *so* obedient. I wonder if you can get what you want out of me—I feel a little afraid" [p. 52].

The third aspect is more subtle, and that is that the two actors had no way (Shaw provided no way) for cooperating or resolving their differences except through Shaw. This was no problem as long as Shaw was around, but after the play opened to magnificent notices and long lines of people clamoring for tickets, Shaw took off on a vacation. It took letters from Mrs. Campbell (they could as well have come from Sir Tree) to bring Shaw back, because both actors had refashioned their roles in his absence. Most commercial productions in the theatre fail, and each season several of them are so utterly without merit that one wonders how, as is sometimes the case, well-known, sophisticated producers, directors, and actors could have been persuaded that it was all worthwhile and destined for success. These instances are never described or studied in the detail they really deserve from a theoretical point of view. However, from gossip, rumor, and anecdote several sources of disaster can be identified: conflict in leadership (producer vs. director, director vs. core group), conflict within the core group, and the capacity of people to depend on hope and luck as correctives against reality.

Little and Cantor's *The Playmakers* (1970) contains additional examples illuminating the problems involved in the creation of a setting, particularly the clash between individual and overall purposes or goals and the initial euphoria:

> Actors work with each other and their collaborators in the theater according to very specific, largely unwritten, and universally recognized commandments. If one were to codify the major actors' commandments they might read something like this: Thou shalt not "upstage" a fellow actor; nor interrupt his speeches; nor move conspicuously on his lines; nor ruin another actor's laugh by any means, motivated or otherwise; honor the playwright and read the lines as they are written.
>
> Such rules are elementary, recognized by all actors. And they are broken all the time. Since an actor is instinctively tempted to think a play is about him and that his role is the key part, he frequently "improves" on his lines. As an actress acknowledges, "This abuses the material, abuses the other actors, abuses the directorial concept." The older playwrights find improvisation intolerable and "Method" actors the worst offenders; Paddy Chayefsky doesn't appreciate spontaneous line-readings by actors. He says, "I really wouldn't mind, if only most actors didn't improvise such lousy lines."
>
> It is the director's job to hold the actors not only to the words but to the theme of the play, and not allow them to go wandering off into quixotic self-expression. A good director must resolve the conflict between his higher allegiance to the overall concept and the actor's fierce drive to interpret the play in terms of his own part [pp. 106–107].

Shumlin finds that a special atmosphere obtains when rehearsals commence. All is euphoric, the cast and collaborators are alight with optimism. There is a great coming together with single purpose, says Shumlin: "Everyone involved throws himself into the pot: flesh, bones, color of hair disappear. . . . It is a remarkable thing that takes place. It happens right away, and in my experience it always happens. People are not conscious of it at all. I recognize it, because as the director I have already shaped the play in my own mind. Maybe something will be a little wrong—something about the play, an actor in his part. But spiritually the thing will still happen. Each will have cast himself into the forge in which the metal, the amalgam, will be made, as they are modified by the play and as they themselves modify the play."

As rehearsals continue, euphoria dissolves and a change comes over the members of the cast. Shumlin notices that the actors begin to rely on their own judgments. They begin to question, to criticize, to analyze, as they grow more confident of their own abilities. At this stage, by thinking of himself at the expense of the group, an actor can be destructive. "Now," Shumlin says, "the director must hold a firm hand over the cast. He can be rewarded by the creativity that comes out of the actor exploring his own way, but he must find a tolerable level of permissiveness. You very quickly recognize when an actor has more to offer than you originally expected of him."

In the last days of rehearsal, the great coming together of the early days must repeat itself. The end meets the purpose of the beginning as the deadline approaches. "This factor creates its own dynamic," says

Shumlin. "Time is rapidly diminishing. And this works to re-create the spirit that existed on the first day." The cycle is complete, and a show is born [pp. 156–157].

Except when it dies an early death.

For Whom Does a Setting Exist?

The problems I have described in the formation and development of the core group are largely a consequence of the emphasis of one factor and the ignoring or deemphasis of another. The factor that is emphasized, indeed is viewed as central, is the job that needs to be done: to provide some kind of service or product for others not part of the setting. Whenever I have asked people what the purpose of their setting is, the answer I invariably get is in terms of delivering something to somebody—something people want.[4] In fact, since the people know that I already know why their setting exists, their response is usually accompanied by a good deal of puzzlement. After all, if you work in a child guidance clinic, what other purpose can you have except to provide services to children and families. If you are a teacher in a school, obviously you are there to help children learn. What other purpose can a state hospital or reformatory or prison have than to rehabilitate its inmates? If you are starting a shirt factory, your job is to make and sell shirts.

It all sounds both obvious and natural: the major purpose of a setting inheres in what it does for or provides to others. There are two types of settings, however, in which the question is not always answered in this invariant way: the church and the university. There are many in both of these settings who would claim that as important as any service they may provide to others are the creation and maintenance of those conditions which enable those in these settings to further *their* development regardless of the demands of the surrounding world. The current crisis in both of these settings can be viewed as stemming from pressures (from within and without) to make "internal salvation" secondary to rendering practical services to others.[5]

---

[4] This is not wholly true, of course, because a good deal of the efforts of the advertising industry is to *make* people want things and services.

[5] See, for example, the dialogue between Daniel Berrigan, S. J., and a psychiatrist (*New York Review of Books*, April 8, 1971). Berrigan poses the internal-external conflict in this way: "But it seems to me that Roman Catholic identity as such is unimportant, given the times and the real issues. . . . I have no continuing interest whatsoever in what you might call the internal questions of the Catholic community, whether that be the question of parochial schools or the question of birth control or the question of celibacy; we look upon such

The factor which is ignored or deemphasized in the creation of a setting, specifically in the formation of the core group, consists of two ingredients: the professional and personal growth and change of its members, and the ways in which their mutuality can enhance this growth and change. The issue is not in stating or valuing these factors but in viewing them as secondary to what one does for others. In almost every instance of the creation of a setting I have observed, these factors have been quite secondary to the concern with what is provided for others outside the setting. And yet the greatest source of disillusionment and disruption within the setting is a consequence of having ignored or deemphasized these factors. To the extent that a setting becomes more and more focused on its relationships to the outside world, it increasingly loses sight of what it can or must do for its own members. This development is inevitable in those instances where the setting was conceived and justified only in terms of what it does for others.

The fantastic rise today of the commune movement can be understood as a recognition of and reaction against the deemphasis of this internal factor, that is, how people can live and work together so as to enhance their personal and intellectual development. "We cannot do for others, we cannot change others, until we learn how to do for and change ourselves"—this is the underlying theme which historically has preoccupied those who have started communes. (It is also the theme which accounts for our literary utopias except, of course, that they bypass the problem of creation in the real world.) What is so fascinating and instructive about the history of communes is the seriousness with which they have faced the problem, and the high rate of failure. There are many reasons for the high rate of failure but at this point I wish only to note that recognizing the problem is no guarantee of success. Creating a commune and creating an establishment-type setting conceptually and developmentally have far more in common than has been recognized. The fact that their values have been worlds apart has successfully obscured the questions they have in common, among which are how to anticipate problems, how to choose

---

matters as in essence retarded questions of a community that still has to catch up with Christ's invitation that all men come join Him, and be with Him—in all their variety. And how sad it is that in the face of the terrible, terrible issues which face this planet's two billion human beings, some in the Church, priests and bishops as well as laymen, continue to be so utterly self-centered, so narrow, so uninterested in others, so aggrandizing—in the name of Jesus Christ!" With a slight change in wording Berrigan's position would reflect well the way in which many people feel the university must change in relation to society's problems.

and form a core group, and how to attain and maintain clarity about the rules of governance. With the caveat that there is no simple explanation either for the success or failure of a commune, the ways in which these questions were posed and answered seem related to the fate of many of them.

The reader will recall that when we were discussing the earliest phases in the creation of a setting, a major theme was the importance of dealing with the past. In the present chapter, in contrast, the theme has been the importance of anticipating and preparing for future problems of a predictable sort. Those who create settings have the problem of dealing in the present with problems of both the past and the future. In practice, however, this tends not to be experienced as a problem because the "pull" of events is toward getting started, forming the core group. The emphasis on getting started and getting to the point where the major purpose of the setting is being realized (such as delivering a service) works against thinking about and dealing with the crucial aspects of the past. This takes place not only because getting started is rooted in the pressures of reality but also because the crucial past always contains some conflict and controversy. Conflict and controversy will also be in the future but, as I have tried to show in the formation of the core group, they are no less avoided or skirted in thinking and planning than those of the past. I have no doubt that if studies were done of the discussions between the leader and each of the core members in the process of recruitment, past and future sources of conflict and controversy would rarely be found to have been subject for discussion. I also have no doubt that if one followed up this study with one on the developmental histories of these core groups, it would be found that most of their serious problems (and failures) had their origins in what could have been but was not discussed or faced.

The Narrow Present

Only those who have never created or participated in the creation of a setting can underestimate the myriad details which must be handled and the flow of problems which never ceases. Just as the rate of growth of the human organism is greatest in the first two or three years, the earliest months or the first year or so of a setting (depending, of course, on the type of setting) are characterized by very speedy growth. This rate of growth is not conducive either to remembrance of the past or to concern with other than the near-term future. When the realities of today require solution in order for tomorrow to go smoothly, it is not easy to keep in mind and to deal with the crucial past and what appears to be a distant future. The present is not only more "real" but it also has a literally compelling quality which makes it seem as if it is more important than the past or future. Dealing with the present is seen as practical and dealing with the past and future (except in fantasy) is seen as impractical and a luxury. It is sometimes the case that dealing with the past and future is considered important, but it is rare for this to go beyond verbal acknowledgment. As Charles Darwin says in *On the Origin of Species:* "Nothing is easier to admit in words than the truths of the universal struggle for life, or more difficult—at least I have found it so—than constantly *to bear this conclusion in mind*" (Hexter, p. 381). Hexter (1968) uses this quote from Darwin in the course of an enlightening discussion of "accessibility" as a persistent problem for the writer of narrative history. What Hexter says about the obligations of the writer of history to his audience is in principle identical to what I have indicated is an obligation of the leader to the core member. "The writer of history needs to be always watchful to see that pertinent previous generalizations, pertinent patterns of action previously identified, and pertinent parts of the story . . . come to bear for the reader at places where they are enlightening and revelatory." When the writer of narrative history fails to do this we get, as Hexter points out, dull history; when the leader fails to do this the development of a setting is jeopardized.

Although this preoccupation with the narrow present is understandable, it is hardly justified by its consequences. Let me illustrate this by describing the creation of a type of setting I have witnessed many times.

Practically everyone, within and without the schools, automatically assumes that becoming principal of a new school is much to be preferred over assuming leadership of an older school. The reasons seem obvious enough: a new school is expected to have better physical facilities; school personnel, children, and parents will take greater pride in the new school; the principal will have greater freedom to organize things his way, that is, it will be easier for him to innovate and to depart from past practices; the principal has more of an opportunity to choose teachers who fit in with his plans; he will not have to deal with an entrenched faculty who, because of their loyalty to a previous principal (or other reasons), are not likely to change their accustomed way of doing things. The fantasy that one is starting "fresh" is shared both by principal and teachers, a fantasy that engenders a great deal of motivation, enthusiasm, and much hope that life in this school will be different from life in their previous schools. But why call this a fantasy? It is a fantasy because it denies certain aspects of reality and because its wish-fulfillment aspects overwhelm and obscure what would be required to achieve change. I shall illustrate this by using a number of opportunities I and others at the Yale Psycho-Educational

Clinic have had to observe or participate in the development of new schools.

(1) From the time of appointment until the formal opening of the school the new principal spends almost all of his time in what can only be called housekeeping matters: ordering books, supplies, and furniture, assigning rooms, arranging schedules, negotiating the transfer of students from other schools, interviewing and selecting prospective personnel, making up bus schedules, etc., etc., etc. Particularly in the case of the principal new to his role the complexity of housekeeping is more than he imagined and was prepared for. In very quick order the principal sees as his major goal—a goal determined by others but which he fully accepts and in relationship to which he has increasing anxiety—opening the school on time and in good order.

(2) Up until the opening of school the bulk of the meetings in which the principal participates are with administrative personnel not only for the purpose of setting up house but in order for the principal to learn the rules and regulations relevant to whatever decisions he must make and plans that he has. The principal views these meetings—which are frequently with those responsible for his appointment or with those who can be helpful with the plethora of housekeeping matters—in terms of accommodating to the roles and power of others ("the system") and not in terms of seeking how to use the system to achieve his purposes.

Let us pause for a moment to emphasize a major consequence of what I have just described: up until the opening of the school the principal is not concerned with such issues as what life in a classroom should be, how teachers will be related to decisions and planning about educational values and goals, the role of parents and neighborhood-community resources, the handling of problem children, the purposes of evaluation, and other issues that bear directly on the educational experience of all those who have or should have a vested interest in a school. In fact, up until the opening of school there is precious little discussion of children or education. From the standpoint of the principal, however, the issues I have listed tend not to be issues about which he is set to do anything, or very much. It might be more fair, in some instances at least, to say that the principal is concerned with these issues but he is acutely aware that he does not know what to do about them, a problem we shall have more to say about later. If in the situation we are describing the principal was not so totally absorbed with matters of housekeeping and organization, he would be faced that much earlier with questions that will later plague him: in what relationship should he be to what children experience in classrooms? How does he get certain teachers to change their practices and attitudes: what does one do when one feels that a problem child is a reflection of a problem teacher? How should he handle the situation in which a complaint by a parent about a teacher may be legitimate? On whose side is the principal: child? teacher? system? neighborhood? It is extremely important to note how the principal asks these questions (and other questions) of himself because the form of the question assumes that he and he alone must answer the question. It is not in his head—and nothing in his previous experience would put it there—that these are the kinds of basic issues that he and his faculty must face, discuss, and resolve because these are the kinds of issues that affect all and, if they remain private, will contribute to the personal and intellectual loneliness of all, including the principal who escaped from one kind of role loneliness to another. To think and act in these ways would be an example of changing certain aspects of life in a school. But we are here also touching on the issue of the power of the principal, and as we shall see later, his view of it operates in ways antithetical to changing life in a school. But let us now return to the opening of the new school by the new principal.

(3) There is nothing the new principal in the new school desires more than an "orderly" opening, a desire particularly strong in the neophyte who feels, and who regards others as feeling, that his worth will be judged by how smoothly things go—identical to what the neophyte teacher experiences when he begins to teach his first class. Smoothness of operation tends to become an end in itself, and anything and anyone interfering with smoothness are not favorably looked upon.

(4) A variety of problems inevitably arises concerning parents, children, teachers, and various assortments of visitors, formal and informal. But of greatest concern to the principal are those with teachers who have changes to suggest, difficult or problem children they wish to discuss and about whom they want the principal to take action, or emerging conflicts with other teachers about procedures and practices. In addition, it is at this time that the new principal begins to be aware that his teachers, whom he may have had an important hand in choosing, are far from a homogeneous group in terms of the way they relate to the principal, the way they handle problems, and the way they relate to each other. It is not one big happy family, but the principal has no basis in thinking and training for realizing that this is inevitable in any organized group. More important, however, the principal has no way to handle these problems except by avoiding them, or handling them, usually indirectly, on a one-to-one basis as they come up.

I can summarize our observations and experiences by saying that by the end of the first year, life in the new school is remarkably similar to that in old ones: what children experience in classrooms, the quality of relationships among teachers and between them and the principal, the relationships among parents, community, and the school, the criteria by which everyone judges themselves and others—in one of these can one discuss a difference that makes a difference [Sarason, 1971, pp. 115–18].[6]

I chose this example because it illustrates that creating a setting involves myriad details and requires attention to practical matters and, in addition, because it points up the degree to which the preoccupation with a narrow present is determined by the existing organization of

[6] The best description and analysis of the creation of a new school are by Smith and Keith (1971). The tragedy they illuminate confirms in all essential respects what I have to say in this book about the creation of settings. Their book was published after mine was written and it was not possible for me to summarize their account. I had some knowledge about their study and refer to it briefly on page 203.

settings out of which the new one is emerging. There is a much less obvious point to the example and that is that the preoccupation with the narrow present is facilitated by the absence of any organized set of conceptions which recognize the significance of the crucial past and the more distant future. In other words, it is *not* a case of making a virtue out of necessity because that would suggest that some kind of conscious choice among competing needs was made. It is like building a home and *then* deciding how to live in it.

I have seen a few instances of new schools (and other types of new settings) where there was some recognition of these issues as well as a determination to avoid the fate that the more things change, the more they remain the same. But here, too, the pull of perceived reality was seen as the decisive factor subverting good intentions. In fact, as important as perceived reality was the absence of vehicles for translating intentions into practice, vehicles which not only would reflect intentions but could cope with and control the conflicts such vehicles produce. As soon as the process is begun whereby the crucial past and the significant future is formalized or "constitutionalized" the present becomes even more difficult and therein lies both its hope and danger—danger because the issues involved are difficult and troublesome; hope because they are at least on the agenda.

Growth and Differentiation

Thus far I have identified several sources of difficulty between the leader and the core group as well as among the core group members. The basis and order of recruitment, the absence of problem-anticipating and problem-resolving vehicles, the myth of unlimited resources and an untroubled future, specialization of function, competition among core members for resources and influence on the leader, the pull of the present realities and the ignoring or postponement of dealing with the crucial past and future—all of these have the potential of fragmenting and disrupting the setting in its infancy, however camouflaged these factors may be by enthusiasm and the sense of mission and growth. It is my contention that this potential is, unfortunately, very frequently realized and gives rise to that all too familiar discrepancy between public rhetoric and private feeling, the gnawing knowledge that the new setting is not as different from the old setting as one had hoped, the sense of aloneness in the context of "togetherness," and a felt separation between what one is and what one does.

But now we come to another question: what takes place when each member of the core group, each of whom has a specialized function, faces the task of recruiting *his* group? I emphasize the word *his* advisedly because just as the leader viewed the core group as having a special relationship to him, so does the core member view "his people." There are two mutually reinforcing sources of specialness here: specialization of function or interest and specialization of relationship between the core member and his group.

The answer to the question of how the core member faces the task of recruiting his group is essentially the same as in the case of the leader when he formed his core group. That is to say, he goes about the task in those ways which maximize the sources of difficulty I enumerated above. In creating his subsetting he recreates precisely those conditions which he so often experienced in the core group. What would be surprising would be if the core member went about the task differently, because that would reflect a way of thinking and an adherence to a set of values quite different from what is true of most leaders and other core members.

The modal way of facing the task is only minimally explainable in terms of personality or style, or by pointing to administrative charts or structure, or by invoking "bureaucracy" as the etiological factor. The explanation resides much more in traditional ways of thinking which simply do not permit consideration of alternative conceptions. It is not that alternative conceptions do not exist, or that if they exist they are considered impractical, but rather that the possibility of alternatives is not even entertained. This will not seem strange to those who explain things by simplistically assuming a one-to-one relationship between "the system" and how those within it think. What gets confused is how people within a particular setting think and act and how they *must* think and act. That is, there really are no alternatives; it is all a function of the characteristics of the setting, and the individual in theory and practice has no choice among alternatives. So, the argument runs, if individuals cannot even think of alternatives one has only to look for the answer in the characteristics of the setting. I have discussed this issue in some detail in my book *The Culture of the School and the Problem of Change* (1971) in relation to school principals. What I illustrate in that discussion is that although the great bulk of principals in a particular system may think and act alike and resist an alternative conception about their role by saying that the system will not permit it, one can usually find at least one principal who has long been operating on the alternative conception.

I am not erecting rugged individualism as an explanatory concept. I am denying the validity of a position which states that the settings with which we are all familiar *inherently* give rise to one, and only one, way of thinking. When one sees time and again core members form their group in the same way as leaders do, it is understandable (but not correct) if one concludes that only external necessity or structure are at work.

Another observation is relevant here. I have known a number of individuals who previously were core members in different types of settings and whose unhappiness with themselves, their work, and colleagues was at a high level. To talk with them about their setting was like being on a grievance committee. They had one other thing in common: they either made or were given the opportunity to create their setting (such as a business, a school, a university department). They could now do things *their* way; they could now implement alternative conceptions of how things should be. It would be nice if I could say that I studied these individuals and their new efforts in a systematic way. I did not. But I have talked with them, and in several instances I had the opportunity to talk with their core group and other workers. It would be nice if I could say that when these individuals left their old settings to start a new one they created something discernibly different. The answer is overwhelmingly in the negative. They did not produce mirror images but the resemblance was unmistakable. When I happened on one occasion to present these observations to a professional group, a member of the audience, a marriage counselor, said: "My God! It is just like repeated marriages. You think they have learned. They think they have learned. And again disaster."

In forming his group the core member ordinarily does not have the leader's degree of freedom. In fact, fairly frequently it is in the process of forming his group that the ambiguities in the constitutional arrangements between the leader and the core member surface in the form of unambiguous disagreements as to policy, values, goals, and privileges. But something else of greater import takes place at this time and it is contained in the question: Whose group is it? From a legal or administrative-chart standpoint the leader, the core member, and his group would have no difficulty answering the question by saying that the group "belongs" to the leader. It is the leader who is responsible for all that goes on, and therefore, the answer continues, it is his group. But this answer confuses authority with belongingness. In practice the core member views it as his group; that is, they belong to him and owe him allegiance, and the group usually feels the same way. The significance of this is subtle and momentous: *the purposes of this group become far more primary than the purposes of the larger setting.* This is not an intended consequence, of course; witness the sloganeering by the leader and the core group about everybody working in a common cause. The fact that core members and their groups have specialized functions obviously contributes to this unintended consequence, but it does not explain the extent of the gulfs among the different groups. It sets the stage and even the outlines of the script but not the drama. That is determined by several factors which I have already discussed but not in relation to each other. First, the problem is rarely discussed or anticipated, and even more rarely are ways of dealing with it devised. This is as true between the leader and each core member as it is among core members. Despite the fact that they encountered the problem in their previous settings, it remains vague and unformulated as a task to be dealt with. Second, to the extent that the relationships among the core group members are determined by conflicts around limited resources, influence with the leader, and disagreements about values and goals, the core member (wittingly or unwittingly) tends to view and use his group in terms of these conflicts. (It is my impression that there is usually a noticeable tendency for the core member and his group to have similar attitudes toward other core members.) Third, to the extent that in creating his subsetting he recreates precisely those conditions which he experienced (or experiences) in the core group, the core member has facilitated the process whereby he and his group become internally oriented; the group's functions and relationship gain primacy over the purposes of the setting.

When the question to whom a group belongs surfaces, it reflects a conflictful past, and for shorter or longer periods of time it can have disintegrative and demoralizing effects which defeat the purposes of the setting and everyone in it. This will be comprehensible to the reader if the question is put in terms of a familiar setting: a public school. To whom does the school belong? Up until a decade or so ago this was not a public issue. Within the school system it has *always* been a conflictful issue. Did it belong to the superintendent? Supervisors? Teachers? Principal? (I am not raising the legal or administrative-chart type of question which, in the case of the public schools, has a far from simple or a clear answer.) In practice the answer was clear: it and everyone in it belonged to the principal. It was *his* or *her* school, as any candid superintendent or supervisor would admit (Sarason, 1971). The children knew it, the parents knew it, and so did the teachers. Granted that it was *a* school in *a* system, that it was related to other schools in the system in diverse ways, that its goals were presumably the goals of the system, and that its allegiance and responsibilities went beyond its physical boundaries. As is not unusual, what one grants or intends should not be confused with what is. The school belonged to the principal. But the world was changing and what had always been an internally conflictful (but restricted) issue became truly public, in addition to which parents, students, and teachers were providing new ways of answering the question. (At the time this chapter was being written New York City announced that students would participate in the choice of high school principals.) This history and its consequences are not explainable by the structure of the school system, and as I point out in my book on the school culture, changing the structure of a school or a system without changing the quality of life in a classroom is another unfortunate instance of ignoring the basic questions of the values and purposes of schooling. However, far more important for our present purposes is the little recognized fact that practically every suggestion and demand for change which the different interest groups have made could have been instituted a long time ago. The obstacle was not structure but rather values and a way of thinking which ruled out alternative conceptions of what a school might be, even as time went on and it became apparent that the storm clouds were not going to go away. Not so incidentally: most of the current suggestions for change in our schools were built into the school John Dewey created in 1896 at the University of Chicago (Sarason, 1971).

My description and discussion of the formation of the core group, and its growth and differentiation, do not make a pretty picture, and it is one that has been drawn by countless others past and present. There are those who have viewed the picture and concluded that man's imperfections are both inherent and irremediable and that trying to make silk purses out of sows' ears is a task for fools and not for those who want to get things done—a view unable to account for the instances in which the sow's ear seems to have become a silk purse. There are those who explain the picture in terms of misguided values, who state what the "true" values should be on the assumption that clarity and agreement on values somehow solves the problem of action —an explanation conducive to withdrawal from the larger society and attempts to create a new and better one. This explanation and its consequences are not noted for their rate of production of silk purses. Then there are those who interpret the picture as a necessary consequence of the socio-economic basis of a society which is industrial, capitalistic, and technological and gives primacy to things and not people. The process of production and man's relationship to his work dehumanize him and restrict his consciousness and potentialities. Consequently, the society must be radically overhauled. Where this overhaul has presumably taken place on a national level—where the rate of setting a creation has been phenomenal—the pictures are not discernibly different from what I have described. Finally, there are those who view the picture as very overdrawn and no more than one should expect from naysayers and prophets of doom and gloom, an *argumentum ad hominem* which at least has the virtue of simplicity.

There is an element of truth in each of these explanations. I do not say so because I prefer eclecticism or because collecting elements of truth in itself guarantees a more encompassing truth, but rather to emphasize that the details and processes of the problem we are dealing with cannot be understood by any of these views. I would contend that the present state of our knowledge should restrain us from feeling very secure about the picture we have of the creation of a setting. The Marxist, the rugged individualist, the theorist of bureaucracy, the conceptualizer of institutional dynamics, the myriad leaders—each will see and explain the problem differently, if he sees it at all.

Few factors are as important in understanding the conflicts between the leader and his core group, and among the core members, as their view of the extent of resources available to them. That their view is usually grossly distorted because of unexamined assumptions is the subject of the next chapter.

CHAPTER 5

Myth of Unlimited Resources

The myth of unlimited (or even adequate) resources has its general and specific aspects. The general aspect is seen in the belief that our society is capable of training enough professional people to render the quantity and quality of service that people are considered to require. For example, during World War II planning began for the development of mental health services which were going to be needed by returning veterans. Never before had the government been faced with the planning of personal services on such a vast scale. All kinds of hospitals and clinics would have to be built. It was obvious that mental health professionals would have to be trained in very large numbers and that in order to do so the government would have to underwrite financially the relevant university departments. Several guiding assumptions were basic to the planning. First, psychotherapeutic techniques of various sorts were the most effective means for dealing with the problems of individuals—psychotherapy, so to speak, was the mental aspirin to be dispensed en masse. Second, the chief dispenser of the mental aspirin was the psychiatrist, with the clinical psychologist and social worker performing primarily other, related functions peculiar to their traditions and training. Third, mental health professionals could be trained in numbers sufficient to make a discernible and effective dent in the size of the problem. (I should emphasize that all of this planning was only in relation to the veteran population which, although staggering enough, was insignificant in comparison to the demand which could be anticipated in the general population.) So we had the situation of national resolve and billions of dollars to do justice to the veterans. As important as what did happen is that it was all quite predictable that personnel could not be trained in numbers necessary to meet objectives. Even early on when it became quite clear that viewing psychotherapy as in the medical domain was an inexcusable indulgence of professional preciousness, and clinical psychologists and psychiatric social workers were thrown into the breach, the disparity between defined need and available service was in no way lessened—particularly as the demand for mental health services by nonveterans mushroomed.[1] Other branches of the government got into the well-heeled act in order to ensure that the mental aspirin would become generally available. Crash programs to train psychotherapists sprang up almost monthly. But the programs began to crash in unexpected ways, in part hastened in the late fifties by the reports of the Joint Commission on Mental Health, particularly the work of George Albee (1959, 1968a, 1968b). As he then and since has pointed out (among other things), our resources were far too limited to do the job in the ways the problem was conceived. Disillusionment set in both in the government and in the field. Disillusionment turned into chagrin and guilt when events in the larger

[1] In less than two decades the battle over who "owned" psychotherapy was essentially over, and legal and professional sanction to engage in psychotherapy was given to a variety of professions. This was viewed as a victory for professional freedom and, of course, society. It may have been a victory for professional freedom but not for society, because even by increasing somewhat the number of professionals available to practice psychotherapy it did not (and could not) make much of a dent in servicing the number of people who wanted the service, let alone those for whom the professionals deemed psychotherapy the treatment of choice. Instead of one profession, medicine, claiming expertise in psychotherapy there were now several professions making such claims. The battle having been "won," what still remained effectively obscured was that the problems of people were still being defined in a way so as to require solution by professionals, and as long as this was unquestioned the disparity between the number offering and asking for the service would remain. Those who won the battle were, like the vanquished medical man, no less steeped in the values of professionalism.

society made it quite clear that blacks and poor people were not getting and could not purchase the aspirin. (It was no balm to the blacks and the poor to be told that purchasing a therapist's time was by no means easy even if one were rich and white.)

Let us take another example. One of the most frequent fantasies in which teachers indulge—and it is by no means restricted to teachers—is how enjoyable life in a classroom could be if class size were discernibly decreased. Like the heavens of religions, reduced class size is a teacher's ultimate reward in comparison to which inadequate salaries pale in significance. The reason I label this a fantasy is not only because it is incapable of fulfillment but because those who hold it tend to be unaware that it is unrealistic. Let us put it this way: if Congress in its infinite wisdom were to pass legislation making it financially possible to cut class size in half, the legislation could not be implemented. It is conceivable that over a period of a decade the necessary physical plant could be built—our society has rarely failed in crash programs of a technological nature. What would be impossible would be to train teachers and other educational specialists in the numbers necessary to implement the legislation. Our centers of training simply cannot train discernibly more people than they are now doing. In fact, our centers of training are quite aware that they are not now doing the quality job that is required in terms of selection of students and quality level of faculty. These centers cannot, nor will they, discernibly increase the numbers being trained. In short, the goal of dramatically reducing class size is far from a financial problem.

Essentially, the general belief—general because of the number of people who hold it and because of the number of social problems which give rise to it—is that by an act of national will or resolve, accompanied of course by appropriately sized expenditures, we can train as many people as are necessary to meet a particular problem, if not all problems. Those who assume that there are really no justifiable bars to quantitative expansion also assume that qualitative improvement of existing and future personnel can be accomplished at the same time. The belief characterizes the thinking of many individuals who are starting new settings, particularly when seemingly large sums of money are available. The belief is that by virtue of money one will be able to hire enough people to provide services to eligible people in the best way those services should be rendered. (Another part of this belief is that one will be able to hire people all of whom will be equally competent or effective.) I have never known a setting, old or relatively new, which did not complain that it had inadequate numbers to do the job in the way it was conceived best to do. I have known many individuals who were starting new settings who never entertained the idea that they would not be able to provide services to the number of people eligible for them. The complaint about inadequate number of staff is practically never seen as a possible function of how the setting was conceived but rather as (and only as) the indifference of society. As we shall see later, it is only in very recent years that there is evidence that the issue is at least being raised, and with the consequence of sharp controversy centering on heretofore implicit values and beliefs.

The extent of the discrepancy between intent and accomplishment is in large part a function of how one defines the service and the criteria of its quality. In practice, the higher the criteria of quality, the fewer people who meet them, and the longer the period of their training—a set of correlated factors which automatically limits resources even more. Defining the service in terms of highly specialized training and knowledge is usually viewed as an obvious professional virtue at the same time that its unavailability to most people who need it is viewed as a social sin. The sense of virtue and sin can exist side by side in the same individual because the virtue is seen as a characteristic of the individual while the sin is a reflection of society, that is, society must change by making it possible for many more people to obtain the specialized training, if society will only do so! There is little or no willingness to question how the service is being defined, the validity of the assumed degree of relationship between training and competence, and the justification of a situation which makes a service unavailable to many people. To ask these questions is to ask how one justifies the service (and the setting), and that involves explicating values and confronting the possibility of changing them. The reason that for decades there was little questioning of the adequacy of settings dealing with the poverty and other minority groups was that the values on which these settings rested were accepted and unscrutinized. It was not until the events in the larger society forced the question of values into the open that people began to think differently about resources, services, and settings (Sarason, Levine, Goldenberg, Cherlin, and Bennett, 1966; Levine and Levine, 1970; Goldenberg, 1971).

Most of us are aware that there is a limit to natural resources. "Scarcity of nature" is a fact and concept without which the field of economics would not exist.

Man, not nature, is the source of most of our economic problems, at least above the level of subsistence. To be sure, the economic problem itself—that is, the need to struggle for existence—derives ultimately from the scarcity of nature. If there were no scarcity, goods would be as free as air, and economics—at least in one sense of the word—would cease to exist as a social preoccupation.

And yet if the scarcity of nature sets the stage for the economic problem, it does not impose the only strictures against which men must struggle. For scarcity, as a felt condition, is not solely the fault of nature. If Americans today, for instance, were content to live at the level of Mexican peasants, all our material wants could be fully satisfied with but an hour or two of daily labor. We would experience little or no scarcity, and our economic problems would virtually disappear. Instead, we find in America—and indeed in all industrial societies—that as the ability to increase nature's yield has risen, so has the reach of human wants. In fact, in societies such as ours, where relative social status is importantly connected with the possession of material goods, we often find that "scarcity" as a psychological experience and goad becomes more pronounced as we grow wealthier: our desires to possess the fruits of nature race out ahead of our mounting ability to produce goods.

Thus the "wants" that nature must satisfy are by no means fixed. But for that matter, nature's yield itself is not a constant. It varies over a wide range, depending on the social application of human energy and skill. Scarcity is therefore not attributable to nature alone but to "human nature" as well; and economics is ultimately concerned not merely with the stinginess of the physical environment, but equally with the appetite of the human being and the productive capability of the community [Heilbroner, 1968, p. 5].*

There is no reason to believe that scarcity of human resources is less a fact and problem than that of the scarcity of nature. And yet when one observes the creation of settings devoted to direct human service (schools, hospitals, clinics, colleges, universities, institutions for the so-called mentally ill or the mentally retarded, the aged, and delinquents, new societies, and the plethora of programs for poverty groups) the myth of unlimited or even adequate resources rather than the realities of scarcity dominates thinking. One should not expect it to be otherwise because to face the reality of scarcity forces one to examine alternatives which conflict with cherished values.

Origins

The origins of the myth are no less complex than its contents. The reader will recall that the decision to create a setting usually reflects dissatisfaction with an existing state of affairs which, at times, may best be characterized as scandalous. Hardly a year goes by without the appearance of books, congressional reports, and newspaper articles exposing the horrors of ghetto schools, homes for the aged, institutions for the retarded, reformatories, prisons, state hospitals, city hospitals, and sundry other types of "humane" institutions. The result is indignation and frustration and, not infrequently, a sincere resolve not only to change what exists but to create new settings which will not be contaminated or constricted by a sorry history. The new setting is a response to an inadequacy as well as to a felt need, and it is powered by money, resolve, and hope. Something "bad" exists, sin has been uncovered, everyone wallows in virtue, and something "good" will be created.[2] It is a context of movement and social pressure in which having some, or more, or even a lot of resources (such as money and people) is subtly transformed into the myth that one has enough resources. It is not a context conducive to questioning the assumption that money can purchase the *quantity* of the types of people the setting is deemed to require, or the assumption that what was wrong with the old setting was largely due to too few of the right kind of personnel. Both assumptions are usually grossly invalid. To question these assumptions is to confront the possibility that the task at hand is not solvable in the conventional way—a possibility as upsetting as the conditions giving rise to the new setting.

Some of the clearest examples of the adverse effects of the myth can be seen in those instances where those who were creating something new had something close to unlimited power. I refer again to the Russian and Cuban revolutions and to Lenin's and Castro's explicit descriptions of their mistake in assuming that political power can develop and harness human resources adequate to perform the services they wanted their citizens to have. It is too simple to attribute their admitted mistake to revolutionary fervor and enthusiasm, although there is no doubt that as these revolutionary movements picked up momentum, and as enthusiasm and hope escalated with the achievement of political power, the realities of scarcity (material and human) had no way of coming to the fore. The fact is that when one examines the publications of these and other revolutionaries written

[2] In his bold book *Exodus from Pandemonium*, Blatt (1970) describes the public clamor resulting from the publication of *Christmas in Purgatory* (Blatt and Kaplan, 1966), which was a "photographic essay" detailing the horrors in the back wards of institutions for the mentally retarded. As a result of this clamor Blatt was asked to address the Massachusetts legislature. In his last book, Blatt publishes his address as well as that of Dorothea Dix to the Massachusetts legislature a century before on the same problem and with identical descriptions. The more things change the more they remain the same. See also Biklen (1970).

long before achieving power was a realistic possibility, the problem of
scarcity is hardly discussed.

For our present purposes it is really not necessary that the
reader agree with what I have said about the myth of unlimited or
even adequate resources. I am fully aware how strong the belief is in
all of us that where there is a will there is a way, and I am not advocating that this cliche be completely abandoned or denying that it is
without any validity. But there is a vast difference between viewing it
as a saying and as a law having inevitable consequences. What the
skeptical reader must confront and explain, however, are the following
observations which I shall put in the form of questions.[3] Why is it that
in the earliest phases of the creation of a setting there tends to be little
or no concern with the possibility that known available resources will
not be adequate to rendering the quantity or quality of service to those
who are eligible for it? Why is it that shortly after the setting is functional, concern with the problem markedly increases and becomes one
of its major complaints? Why is competition for available resources
one of the major sources of division among the core group in the setting? Why does each core member proceed as if there is no doubt that
resources are indeed unlimited? These questions require explanation
even if one does not assume that there are always limited resources.

Implicit Factors

The strength and perpetuation of the myth are only partly
comprehensible in terms of the clamor and enthusiasm surrounding
the sense of mission, the desire to right wrongs, and the sense of
superiority stemming in part from the belief that what was wrong in
the past inhered in adequate numbers and quality of personnel.
Precisely because these factors are pretty much out in the open and
accompany or lead to actions deemed socially desirable, they effectively
distract attention away from other factors, implicit but no less part of
the picture.

I can illustrate this point by describing what happened a
decade or so ago when it became clear that the discrepancy between
the numbers who seemed to need psychotherapeutic help and the
number of professionals who could render such a service was growing

[3] I ask and shall discuss these questions in terms of settings explicitly
devoted to direct human service. I am not clear as to what extent the discussion
in this chapter is applicable to other types of settings. When one considers the
phenomenal rate at which settings devoted to direct human service are being
created, the possible restriction in applicability of this discussion is not as great
as it might seem at first blush.

increasingly large and was essentially unsolvable. Within the mental health professions there had been a growing number of individuals urging change, and from without there was even stronger pressure to change the pattern of traditional services so that they were not solely obtainable by the affluent segments of society. Up to this point the federal government had been pouring large sums of money into centers of training, with no discernible effect on the size of the discrepancy that the funding was supposed to reduce. When the federal government changed its emphasis, it was accompanied by a good deal of fanfare and (some thought) by a good deal of money. Let us listen to what President Kennedy said (what some mental health professionals wrote for him) in his special message in 1963 announcing the new comprehensive community mental health center program which meant that many new settings would be created. I present his message in some detail, as well as the enabling legislation, in order to provide the reader a basis independently to judge the extent of the variety of new services the new settings would provide and the increased number of people who would receive them. It also should help the reader judge my opinion that rarely in a situation of recognized scarcity was so much promised to so many.

I propose a national mental health program to assist in the inauguration of a wholly new emphasis and approach to care for the mentally ill. This approach relies primarily upon the new knowledge and new drugs acquired and developed in recent years which make it possible for most of the mentally ill to be successfully and quickly treated in their own communities and returned to a useful place in society.

These breakthroughs have rendered obsolete the traditional methods of treatment which imposed upon the mentally ill a social quarantine, a prolonged or permanent confinement in huge, unhappy mental hospitals where they were out of sight and forgotten. I am not unappreciative of the efforts undertaken by many states to improve conditions in these hospitals, or the dedicated work of many hospital staff members. But their task has been staggering and the results too often dismal, as the comprehensive study by the Joint Commission on Mental Illness and Health pointed out in 1961.

Comprehensive Community Mental Health Centers. Central to a new mental health program is comprehensive community care. Merely pouring federal funds into a continuation of the outmoded type of institutional care which now prevails would make little difference. We need a new type of health facility, one which will return mental health care to the mainstream of American medicine, and at the same time upgrade mental health services. I recommend, therefore, that the Congress (1) authorize grants to the states for the construction of comprehensive community mental health centers, beginning in fiscal year 1965, with the federal government providing 45 to 75 per cent of the project cost; (2)

authorize short-term project grants for the initial staffing costs of comprehensive community mental health centers, with the federal government providing up to 75 per cent of the cost in the early months, on a gradually declining basis, terminating such support for a project within slightly over four years; and (3) to facilitate the preparation of community plans for these new facilities as a necessary preliminary to any construction or staffing assistance, appropriate $4.2 million for planning grants under the National Institute of Mental Health. These planning funds, which would be in addition to a similar amount appropriated for fiscal year 1963, have been included in my proposed 1964 budget.

While the essential concept of the comprehensive community mental health center is new, the separate elements which would be combined in it are presently found in many communities: diagnostic and evaluation services, emergency psychiatric units, outpatient services, inpatient services, day and night care, foster home care, rehabilitation, consultative services to other community agencies, and mental health information and education.

These centers will focus community resources and provide better community facilities for all aspects of mental health care. Prevention as well as treatment will be a major activity. Located in the patient's own environment and community, the center would make possible a better understanding of his needs, a more cordial atmosphere for his recovery, and a continuum of treatment. As his needs change, the patient could move without delay or difficulty to different services—from diagnosis, to cure, to rehabilitation—without need to transfer to different institutions located in different communities.

A comprehensive community mental health center in receipt of federal aid may be sponsored through a variety of local organizational arrangements. Construction can follow the successful Hill-Burton pattern, under which the federal government matches public or voluntary nonprofit funds. Ideally, the center could be located at an appropriate community general hospital, many of which already have psychiatric units. In such instances, additional services and facilities could be added—either all at once or in several stages—to fill out the comprehensive program. In some instances, an existing outpatient psychiatric clinic might form the nucleus of such a center, its work expanded and integrated with other services in the community. Centers could also function effectively under a variety of other auspices: as affiliates of state mental hospitals, under state or local governments, or under voluntary nonprofit sponsorship.

Private physicians, including general practitioners, psychiatrists, and other medical specialists, would all be able to participate directly and cooperatively in the work of the center. For the first time, a large proportion of our private practitioners will have the opportunity to treat their patients in a mental health facility served by an auxiliary professional staff that is directly and quickly available for outpatient and inpatient care.

Research and Manpower. Although we embark on a major national action program for mental health, there is still much more we need to know. We must not relax our effort to push back the frontiers of knowledge in basic and applied research into the mental processes, in therapy, and in other phases of research with a bearing upon mental illness. More needs to be done also to translate research findings into improved practices. I recommend an explanation of clinical, laboratory, and field research in mental illness and mental health.

Availability of trained manpower is a major factor in the determination of how fast we can expand our research and expand our new action program in the mental health field. At present manpower shortages exist in virtually all of the key professional and auxiliary personnel categories—psychiatrists, clinical psychologists, social workers, and psychiatric nurses. To achieve success, the current supply of professional manpower in these fields must be sharply increased—from about 45,000 in 1960 to approximately 85,000 by 1970. To help move toward this goal I recommend the appropriation of $66 million for training of personnel, an increase of $17 million over the current fiscal year.

I have, in addition, directed that the Manpower Development and Training Act be used to assist in the training of psychiatric aids and other auxiliary personnel for employment in mental institutions and community centers.

Success of these specialized training programs, however, requires that they be undergirded by basic training programs. It is essential to the success of our new national mental health program that Congress enact legislation authorizing aid to train more physicians and related health personnel. I will discuss this measure at greater length in the message on health which I will send to Congress shortly.

And now let us read how the Community Mental Health Centers Act of 1963 (Title II, Public Law 88-164) defined adequate services.

(a) Adequate services. The state plan shall provide for the following elements of service which are necessary to provide adequate mental health services for persons residing in the state, which shall constitute the elements of comprehensive mental health services: (1) inpatient services; (2) outpatient services; (3) partial hospitalization services, such as day care, night care, and weekend care; (4) emergency services twenty-four hours per day must be available within at least one of the first three services listed above; (5) consultation and education services available to community agencies and professional personnel; (6) diagnostic services; (7) rehabilitative services, including vocational and educational programs; (8) precare and aftercare services in the community, including foster home placement, home visiting and half-way houses; (9) training; (10) research and evaluation.

(b) Adequate facilities—(1) Provision of services. Based on comprehensive mental health planning, the state plan shall provide for adequate community mental health facilities for the provision of programs of comprehensive mental health services to all persons residing in the state and for furnishing such services to persons unable to pay therefor, taking into account the population necessary to maintain and operate efficient facilities and the financial resources available therefor. (2) Accessibility of services. The state plan shall provide that every community mental health facility shall: (i) serve a population of not less than 75,000 and not more than 200,000 persons, except that the Surgeon General may, in particular cases, permit modifications of this population range if he finds that such modifications will not impair the effectiveness of the services to be provided; (ii) be so located as to be near and readily accessible to the community and population to be served, taking into account both political and geographical boundaries; (iii) provide a community service; and (iv) provide needed services for persons unable to pay therefor.

(c) Personnel administration. A system of personnel administration on a merit basis shall be established and maintained with respect to the personnel employed in the administration of the state plan. Such a system shall include provision for: (1) impartial administration of the merit system; (2) operation on the basis of published rules or regulations; (3) classification of all positions on the basis of duties and responsibilities and establishment of qualifications necessary for the satisfactory performance of such duties and responsibilities; (4) establishment of compensation schedules adjusted to the responsibility and difficulty of the work; (5) selection of permanent appointees on the basis of examinations so constructed as to provide a genuine test of qualifications and so conducted as to afford all qualified applicants opportunity to compete; (6) advancement on the basis of capacity and meritorious service; and (7) tenure of permanent employees.

I am not concerned here that the law is the equivalent of making sure that there is a chicken in every pot and at least one car in every garage. Nor will I elaborate on the fervor, enthusiasm, and excitement which were experienced in certain segments of the mental health professions or on their sense of victory over traditional thinking and patterns of service. And I shall not attempt to describe how these new centers, created as most of them were out of an existing organization of settings (such as departments of psychiatry, hospitals), in every respect confirm what I have already discussed about the creation of settings. The significance of the quotation is in three assumptions. First, the solution of the problem requires certain kinds of personnel. Second, these personnel are specialists. Third, these personnel, already in fantastic short supply, can be trained in numbers adequate to a fantastic increase in range of services. (After all, what seemed to be a lot of money was going to be available.) Yes, new knowledge would be necessary and research was not going to be left out of the picture. But when all is said and done the fact remains that what was most clear was that the problem was being defined in a way which dictated a solution requiring certain kinds and quantity of personnel. It could not be otherwise because the problem and the solution were formulated by these kinds of personnel. It would have been a distinctive page in human history if these professions had formulated the problem and solution in a way which would not have given them the central role.

Some readers will be troubled and will be asking the question: Do not people with "mental health problems" require help from those with very special knowledge and training? Are you suggesting that anyone (such as a surgeon, barber, taxi driver) can render help? These questions effectively obscure the problem of values because they rest on the assumption that adequate specialized resources exist or can be developed. If this assumption is invalid, as has been perfectly clear for a long time, one is confronted with the should and ought kind of question: How should one decide who gets the service? How do we justify providing nothing to those who are deemed to need it? Do we have an obligation to say that the problem is unsolvable as defined? Should we reformulate the problem (are there ways of reformulating it) so that more people will get more help? Does the value we attach to specialization conflict with the value (if one holds it) that health service is a right and not a privilege?

The reader who believes that adequate resources exist or can be developed should consult Albee (1959, 1968a, 1968b) and Matarazzo who, in 1971, summed it up: "The unfolding of this drama for the field of psychology is representative. First there was Albee's 1959 tradition-shattering analysis of the current and projected manpower problem for psychology as well as for psychiatry, social work, and nursing. His perceptive analysis of this country's number of youth and current and projected university resources revealed for the United States Congress, the core professions, and our educational institutions of higher learning that demand would continue to outdistance supply at an accelerated rate. Today, over a decade later, more current analyses of the same problem for psychology and, in some instances, the other three professions by Albee, Arnhoff, Boneau, and others have shown that the worst of Albee's 1959 projections are coming to pass."[4]

As soon as one accepts the limitation of resources two things tend to happen: one confronts the contexts of one's values, and the formulation of the problem and its solutions take on different forms.

Albee eloquently has affirmed and reaffirmed the fact that a shocking number of this country's state mental hospitals and psychiatric clinics did not have even a single psychiatrist on their full-time staff. I

[4] The reader who wishes to examine the issues of resources and values in the larger context of American medicine should consult Ehrenreich and Ehrenreich (1971) and Michaelson (1971). These publications are instructive but not reassuring.

feel certain that most readers, much as I did, momentarily recoiled at this startling revelation by Albee but soon left it to pursue other issues. From hindsight now, it is clear that some of the professional and allied professional persons who worked in these hospitals and clinics, and select individuals in many local communities, did not merely recoil. Rather, impressive evidence is now at hand that although uncoordinated and at first largely unrecognized outside their own community, refreshing, innovative, and highly effective solutions were being employed in a large number of state hospitals, clinics, and other mental health facilities. These local solutions utilized no single manpower group but rather, as available in its own community, took advantage of a surprisingly heterogeneous set of heretofore neglected segments of the manpower pool making up its own local citizenry. . . . It is now becoming clear that beginning a decade ago, the occasional single physician, nurse, psychologist, or social worker practitioner in an isolated state hospital, finding himself solely responsible for a whole hospital, or two or three wards, was freed to a burst of innovative creativity by the concept of the therapeutic community with its key concept that each employee of the mental hospital was potentially a therapeutic agent. Almost overnight, and merely by a change in role definition and assigned responsibilities, such an administrator could transform his hospital from a one-physician or no-physician statistic in Albee's actuarially factual table, to a hospital with dozens of professionally trained, actively working subprofessionals requiring only modest supervision and the barest numbers of hours of additional training. (Matarazzo, 1971, p. 365)

Necessity is sometimes the mother of invention and sometimes the spur to a different set of values. Unfortunately, the federal legislation of 1963 defined necessity in a way which reinvented failure.

Consequences

In choosing education or mental health as illustrative problems it was not my aim to convince the reader that it is axiomatic that human resources are always limited. My aims were more modest and they were to suggest (a) that for the most important problems of society for the solution of which new settings are being created at an ever-accelerating rate, there is a serious limitation of human resources; (b) that the seriousness of the limitation is in part a function of how the problem is defined; (c) that confronting the limitation of resources involves one in the problem of priorities and distribution, that is, the values by which they will be established; and (d) that in the context of creating a new setting the limitation of resources tends not only to be denied but to be replaced by the myth of unlimited or adequate resources.

The consequences of avoiding or denying the problem of resources depend in part on when and how the problem is confronted

—and reality ensures that they will be confronted. It makes a difference whether early on the leader sees the problem, or it is forced on him by the demands of the core group for resources, or, as is increasingly the case, outside groups militantly expose the inadequacies of the setting's resources for the task at hand. In the instance where the leader begins truly to comprehend the nature and extent of the problem he is faced with a number of questions among which are whether or not to inform his core group, how much to inform, how to adapt to the reality, and how much the relevant outside world should be told, and when and how. It is precisely because comprehension of the problem brings in its wake the perception of the possibility of failure (in varying degrees) that the leader has difficulty making the problem public. The phenomenology of the leader will be taken up later in this book, but what needs to be said here is that the usual way in which the problem is experienced and handled by the leader tends to affect negatively his relations with his core group, to exacerbate the competition for resources among the core group, to set the stage for other settings and groups to raise the issue of competence and honesty, and to reinforce the leader's sense of aloneness.

Independent of the leader, the core group members at some point perceive the problem, and the consequences are fairly predictable: each becomes more concerned with the growth of his piece of the action; conflicts stemming from other sources (such as personality) are heightened or created; and not only do members begin to question the purposes of the setting but they become aware of sharp differences in the realm of values—the bases for justifying what is or is not important and how things should be done.

Another consequence of the recognition of the problem is as significant as it is subtle, and that is an increasing emphasis on production or results. The greater the perceived discrepancy between resources and goals, the more the goals of the setting subtly become transformed or reformulated in ways productive of data proving that the setting is a success. The clearest examples of this I have seen over the years have been in newly created direct service settings (public and private schools, clinics, health centers) a major aim of which initially was to individualize service or to create an atmosphere in which the quality of social relationships and social learning were more important than the number of individuals provided service. In the case of schools this took the form of criticizing the value and relevance of measuring children's progress by standardized achievement tests and valuing instead how children learned to live and learn with each other without the pressures of meeting criteria predetermined by others. It all sounded refreshingly different. But then in almost every instance a subtle transformation in the criteria of success began to occur so that what had been criticized became a cherished standard of performance. The word *subtle* has to be qualified because to some people in the settings the transformation was blatant and they left. I am not contending that the transformation of goals was due to the failure to face the problem of limited resources. I am contending that the failure to face the problem realistically was an important ingredient contributing to heightening pressures and conflicts stemming from other sources. What is noteworthy and discouraging about the usual explanation of how these transformations came about is that it does not address itself to how the failure initially to deal with the problem of limited resources interacted with other problems. One of the most important arguments of the usual explanation, formulated after failure (partial or complete), is that forces outside the setting denied it the resources it needed. The implication is that these forces had available unlimited or adequate resources, and so we are back where we started.

Some colleagues and I had the opportunity to witness the creation of what most people considered the most innovative community-action program in this country, a program antedating in certain respects the federal one. We have described in detail the context in which this setting was born, emphasizing its explicit goal of delivering new services in new and controversial ways (Sarason and others, 1966; Goldenberg, 1971). The program had bold and imaginative leadership, strong political support, and several millions of dollars of foundation support. Once federal money became available, this program was, by virtue of experience and ideas, in a position to get a good deal of it, proportionately more than any other such program. Enthusiasm, sense of mission and superiority, and a vision of uninterrupted progress were among its more obvious characteristics. More subtle, however, was the impression its reports and news releases created that this truly exciting setting was adequate to meet its goals. Although in one part of their heads the leaders knew otherwise, this was never reflected in any central way in their messages to the community. In our description and evaluation of the setting, published in 1966 but written in 1964–1965, two years after its beginnings, we emphasized the possible adverse consequences of the failure to deal realistically with the obvious fact that it did not, nor would it have, the resources to achieve its goals. At that time our concern was less for the sensibilities of the community than for what was beginning to happen in the setting itself. What was happening was no less than an emphasis on numbers as a criterion of success. How many clients were entered into new job-training programs began to be more important than whether or not the programs were adequate or appropriate. How many young people were returned to high school was given more play than the number who subsequently dropped out or the number who never should have been returned. The multiplication of new programs (and in those days they multiplied) took on far greater significance than concern for the inadequacies of existing ones. Whereas the ethos initially was to avoid the mistakes and dilemmas of the traditional social agency—its emphasis on professionalism and "psychologizing," as well as its timidity in relation to social action—in subtle ways it began to resemble what it wanted to avoid. Many within the setting were quite aware of what was happening and the departure of the leader accelerated the transformation.

I repeat: I am not saying that what happened was caused by the failure to confront the realities of limited resources. It was far more complicated than that. But there is no doubt that as the leaders became aware of the problem the pressure to do and get more mounted, the *basis* for justifying doing and getting more resulted increasingly in a game of numbers, morale plummeted, and competition within the setting for available resources skyrocketed. It was only as the war on poverty deescalated into a skirmish that the leaders of the setting could state publicly in the most unequivocal way that the resources originally available to them had been woefully inadequate and that even if funding had been maintained on the previous level its goals could not have been reached. And this brings us to still another myth which interacts with and is related to the myth of unlimited or adequate resources and that is that one can count on the future as both untroubled and predictable—just like in the literary utopias. Avoiding the problem of limited resources and holding to the belief in a predictable future are among the most potent factors influencing the creation and development of a setting, and their potency is increased in proportion to the extent that they are implicit or unverbalized.

The choice and use of human resources always partially rest on value judgments which, for the most part, are confused with the dictates of reality. It usually requires some drastic social events and changes for us to become aware that the usual ways in which human resources have been viewed and allocated were based on "shoulds" and "oughts" not contained in nature or given by divine revelation. The great economic depression of the thirties is a particularly clear example of how a social catastrophe brought into question the nature and appropriateness of values heretofore viewed as natural and good. Before the Depression it was unthinkable to most people that an unemployed person *should* be provided with some means of support, or that a person *should* be protected against dependence in old age, or that the government *should* in any formal way assume any responsibility for resolving conflicts between labor and management. Obviously, these were not unthinkable ideas; rather it was that they were seen as socially and morally *wrong*. "Separate but equal" schools were accepted for a long time, as were child labor and discrimination on religious, ethnic, and sexual grounds. The conflicts surrounding changes in these practices had several sources, and deeply held values were certainly not the least of them. When with Ciceronian regularity the American Medical Association would sanctify the concept of the unregulated, private practitioner, it was a mistake to view it only as a reflection of economic self-interest and to fail to see that beyond economics was a set of values about what was good or bad in medical care. Professional imperialism, like the national variety, has economic underpinnings but its rallying points are almost always sincerely held statements of unalloyed virtue. The disbeliever may see connections between the economic and value structures, but that is no secure basis for assuming that the believer does.

Choosing and allocating human resources are some of the earliest and most important tasks in the creation of a setting. How these tasks inevitably reflect certain values, how the definition of the purposes of a setting illuminates these values, and how bypassing these issues helps defeat the purposes of a setting will become more clear in the next chapter where case material will be presented.

CHAPTER 6

Resources and Values

In this chapter I shall describe and discuss several settings in order to clarify further the relationships among the setting's definition of its task, its view of resources, and underlying values. The recognition that there is a need and the decision to create a setting to meet that need usually assume that the shape of the solution is known and in a way so that issues of values and resources need not be posed and clarified. That is why settings serving the same kinds of populations are amazingly similar. Their underlying values and view of resources are so similar that despite differences in rhetoric and architecture their atmosphere and practices are as predictable as those of a supermarket. From one era to another one can see marked changes in some types of settings and this is due as much to the obvious fact that the values of the society have changed as it is to new knowledge, and the latter generally is a function of the former. In one state the statute giving force to its juvenile court says, "As far as practicable, they [children seven to seventeen] shall be treated, not as criminals, but as children in need of aid, encouragement and guidance. Proceedings against children . . . shall not be deemed criminal proceedings." These children were not always viewed in this way. In earlier times their actions were judged by a different scale of values that dictated a different kind of solution. Whereas in earlier times it was considered "good and right" to hold these children responsible for their actions and to utilize punishment as the chief ingredient of the solution, these same actions today are viewed quite differently, with the result that the solution (aid, encouragement, and guidance) is of a different order and requires different kinds of human resources (such as psychiatrists, social workers, psychologists). Different theories of human behavior are involved but, as Levine and Levine (1970) so beautifully describe, these different theories are not unrelated to changing forces and values in the larger society. The current definition of the problem requires types and quantities of resources that were, are, and will be in shortest supply, which goes a long way to explaining why juvenile courts have been failures.[1]

In describing those settings I shall be emphasizing how the process of defining a setting's task or goals is related to one's view of resources and at the same time that all of this reflects some basic values. This emphasis inevitably distorts the picture one gains of these settings but in each instance much fuller descriptions are available elsewhere.

Maximum Use of Resources

The reasons for starting the Yale Psycho-Educational Clinic were no less varied and complex than any other instance of motivation and action, but several things were quite clear and they are contained in the following propositions. (1) The mental health professions were oriented primarily to dealing with individuals who presented themselves (or in the case of children were presented by others) as having personal problems. (2) These problems were conceptualized in ways that required "treatment" by highly trained specialists. (3) The disparity between the number rendering and needing service was of a magnitude that was unresolvable. (4) Those who obtained service were almost exclusively white and middle class, and they represented a small fraction of white, middle-class people who wanted the service.

---

[1] The reader who wishes to comprehend different facets of the problem of limited resources should consult the book by the Levines (1970). I know of no other book which has described so well, and in regard to so many areas of human service, how the process of professionalizing a service previously performed by lay people not only changed the nature of the service but also guaranteed that resources would become increasingly limited. Their chapter on the history of child guidance clinics would be amusing if it were not so socially tragic. And all of this took place with the best of intentions and the expectations that the appropriate resources could be developed.

(5) The most notable exception to all of this was our public "mental hospitals," where treatment as an individual human being was notable by its absence.

Today, it is hard for anyone to read these statements without spontaneously and unreflectively passing judgment: the situation is bad, sad, and wrong. Although these statements are and have always been true (in modern times), they did not always elicit strong negative feelings, within or without the professions. That the reaction is different today is due to the fact that both within and without the professions there has been growing awareness of the inequities in the distribution of services, an awareness that is explainable only on the basis of the value that color and money should not determine eligibility for service. In the previous chapter I described the actions and programs that were spurred by considerations of equity. Simply put: the problem continued to be defined in a way that required dependence on certain kinds of human resources which, given the increased scope of the proposed services, could only increase the disparity between the numbers rendering and needing service—and all of this was taking place before the dimensions of the drug problem were recognized.[2]

What conclusions did we draw and how did they influence the shape of the clinic? There were six conclusions:

(1) The clinic should not define its task in terms of service to individuals because if it did it would in short order have a waiting list. Although working with individuals was our area of training and expertise, and it was expected of us to capitalize on our strengths, we felt it was our obligation to explore new ways of thinking and acting. Our primary responsibility was to ourselves in the sense that we had to learn new things. We were going to judge ourselves only secondarily by how helpful we were to others. Conceivably we would not be very helpful, and conceivably we could even be harmful and yet be successful in terms of our personal learning and growth.

(2) Anyone who spent his life helping individuals with their personal problems did not have to justify his existence, to us at least. However, if such a professional person was not acutely sensitive to the fact that many people could not obtain his kind of service, and if he did not support and justify some radically different ways of thinking about service, we considered him socially irresponsible. In the face of

---

[2] Note the value judgment implied in the phrase *drug problem*. There are those who contend that a person has a right to live his life the way he wishes and if that includes hard or soft drugs, so be it, laws and society to the contrary notwithstanding. Paradoxically, many who hold this contention are not willing to extend the principle to a professional person who wishes to restrict his service only to those who can afford his high fees.

overwhelming need one should feel a responsibility to give as much service to as many people as possible without unduly diluting the quality of the service. To define a service according to the highest standards puts one on the side of the angels, but when this means that some will get all and most will get none of it one is making decisions that seem to lack divine guidance or inspiration. What is "unduly diluting" is a question of fact *and* value.

(3) The clinic's focus would be on any kind of setting devoted to children and young adults—schools, reformatories, neighborhood centers, and a variety of other institutions. The goal would be to understand each setting so that we would have a basis for helping the setting better to cope with its problems, regardless of whether the problems stem from within or without the setting. Defining a setting as our object of understanding and change would have one immediate consequence: no one would be clamoring for our service because each of them would see its problems as primarily those of individuals and not as reflections, in part at least, of the culture of the setting.

(4) If we were ever faced with the problem of choosing between working with an ongoing setting or putting our energies into creating a new service setting, we would choose the latter and for two reasons. First, we placed a higher value on prevention than on repair, and second, *we* would learn more. Of course, in the best of all possible worlds one should not have to decide or make these kinds of choices but this is not the best of all possible worlds. The creation of the clinic was facilitated and shaped by our willingness to help create a state institution. We were quite aware that in creating our own setting and in helping to create another (and more complicated) one we were novices secure only in the belief that what we were doing needed to be done. We did it *for ourselves* and not because we were convinced that we were going to be all that helpful. If we were not helpful, it would be *our* fault and our primary responsibility would be to understand wherein we made our errors.

(5) Being a member of the clinic would not be decided on the basis of professional title, paper credentials, or amount of education. The correlation between education and wisdom, or between training and competence, was sufficiently far from perfect to justify choosing personnel on other grounds. One of our major tasks was to locate people who, for whatever reasons of background and experience, seemed to have the talent which, under appropriate conditions, could be developed to a productive level of service. We had to be a talent-seeking setting, and this would make available to us a far larger pool of human resources than if we proceeded by more conventional cri-

teria of selection. The problems we would be dealing with were not conceived or defined in ways that required personnel with certain titles and formal experiences. Of course, we were not antiprofessional. And we were not glorifying the untrained and the nonprofessional as possessing a special kind of superior folk wisdom, a sentiment no less shortsighted or stupid than that which makes for professional preciousness.

(6) To an undetermined extent every member of the clinic would be doing what every other member was doing. There would be no departments or specialized functions. Obviously, people would have or develop special interests, but that could not be a basis for compartmentalization. To the extent that we would become a hierarchically organized setting, and members could be readily differentiated from each other in terms of what they did, we would have failed; the clinic would have become another item in the supermarket of professional settings.

These statements, formulated between 1961 and 1963 and implemented with the opening of the clinic in 1963, did not (locally) meet with a mixed reception. From all sides the reaction was at best skeptical and at worst damning, and it all centered on how we were organized (there seemed to be no organization) and who was performing services. It was incomprehensible to some that we did not have social workers or psychiatrists and that we had personnel who had no relevant professional training. We had people who had been classroom teachers but they were not teaching. We had recent college graduates who had important service responsibilities. We were all doing things we had never done before. What each of us had done before was respectable and definable; what we were now doing was ambiguous and held suspect. I point this out because these reactions clearly suggested that we were successful in that we were perceived as being different in a way consistent with our ideas and values. If we were perceived like other helping settings, we would have had good reason to be skeptical about any judgment of success based on our own perceptions and opinions.

If the clinic were to be created today, a decade after it was, the reaction would be rather different and far more positive, and therein lies the point of this chapter. In almost all spheres of human service there has been, *even* within the professional communities, a recognition of and reorientation to the fact of limited resources, with the result that many settings now contain individuals undreamed of a decade ago and give them responsibilities heretofore considered performable only by highly trained professionals. This has not happened because of choice or theory but because of the developments in the larger society which literally forced these settings to confront the disparity in numbers between those who received and those who needed service. For example, in the *New York Times* of May 12, 1971, there appeared the following news item:

A bill creating the state-regulated positions of physician's and specialist's assistants was passed overwhelmingly by the Senate here today.

The bill, which passed by a vote of 46 to 8 after almost three hours of debate, provides that persons with limited medical training, such as medical corpsmen, could assist doctors in aiding sick people and could relieve doctors from some of the more arduous routine tasks which did not require extensive training.

Opponents of the paramedical bill argued that it was creating second-class medical services for the people of the state and would allow untrained persons to "practice medicine." They argued that the bill did not spell out what the qualifications or educational requirements were for the positions but left them up to the commissioners of education and health.

Proponents of the measure argued that there was a severe shortage of medical personnel in the state and that some counties had virtually no doctors available to treat the sick. They said the bill would allow persons licensed by the state and under the supervision of a doctor to relieve some of the problems in providing at least some medical care.

Ralph J. Marino, Nassau Republican and a former army medical corpsman, opposed the bill and said that it would be "encouraging doctors to turn over the patients to assistants who are not qualified."

"We're going to pad the wallets of the doctors," he said. "We're approving legal mayhem on an unsuspecting public."

Senator Paul P. E. Bookson, Democrat of Manhattan, said the use of medical corpsmen was an acknowledgement that health care was a "battlefield." He said the bill would create "two classes of medicine," with the poor having the paramedics foisted on them, while those people with money would continue to receive first-rate care.

Senator Seymour R. Thaler, Democrat-Liberal of Queens, a sponsor of the measure, said that he had visited hospitals in New York City—including Bellevue—where there were only licensed practical nurses to handle large numbers of patients.

He said that in Bedford-Stuyvesant there were only four doctors to treat the thousands of poor in the area and that the bill would allow medical corpsmen to help relieve the doctors so they could treat more patients.

Senator Waldaba H. Stewert, Democrat of Brooklyn, whose district includes Bedford-Stuyvesant, voted for the bill and said that the area did not have four doctors on weekends and that one of the doctors had stated that he would be unable to continue to treat Medicare patients.

Senator Robert Garcia, Democrat-Liberal of the Bronx, termed the bill "one of the most important pieces of legislation before us this year." He said that his experience in the army with medical corpsmen showed that many of them were highly qualified and that their help in battle conditions was greatly appreciated.

"The same situation prevails in my area," he said. "People are in desperate need of medical care."

The comparison between the view and utilization of resources in war and peace is instructive indeed because it demonstrates so clearly how in one situation the fact of limited resources was realistically faced, only to be ignored when the stress of that situation was over. Whereas in the war situation attention was given to an individual's formal education, training experience, and paper credentials, his placement was by no means automatically decided on such grounds. Thousands of professionals found themselves doing things they would never have dreamed of doing, or would never have been allowed to do, in civilian life. Similarly, many nonprofessionals were performing tasks which in civilian life could only be done after a good deal of formal training and only with the sanction of the law. It is no exaggeration to say that in the war the problem of human service was so faced and defined that its solution obviously and automatically ruled out any solution based on the civilian traditions of prolonged training and specialization. And yet, irony of ironies, during the war when governmental groups were already planning for the care of veterans after the war and it was obvious that over the years the discrepancy between the numbers needing and receiving service was alarmingly great, the problem was defined so that the solution required people with prolonged training and ever-increasing specialization. It is not my purpose here to delve into the different factors which brought this about. Certainly economic considerations, the weight of tradition, and professional imperialism played their roles. Equally important, and paradoxically so, was a view based on what should be and not what could be, and therefore the problem was defined so as to be incapable of solution.

In creating the clinic we placed a good deal of significance on the different ways in which human resources were used in peace and war because the difference had helped us answer three related questions long troubling us: Why did service settings remain much the same over long periods of time? Why was it not troubling them that so many people were not getting the services they were considered to need? Why did they not see that the time would or might come when they would be forced to define the problem and its solutions differently? One part of the answer was in the overlearned tendency to think of solutions exclusively in terms of professionalism and specialization;

the other part was the lack of a historical perspective or knowledge of
social history which would not allow bypassing the fact that the major
stimulus for changes in settings and professions have come from outside forces.[3] In war these changes are made far more willingly and
graciously than in peace.

The view of human resources which influenced the creation
and organization of the clinic in no way reflected a penchant for a
democratic ethos, or a belief in the universal equality in ability, or a
view of organization tantamount to anarchy. It was rather that we
defined our task in a way which discernibly increased the pool of
human resources available to us—in much the same way and for the
same reasons as was done in war times. That settings devoted to human service are created and developed differently in times of war and
peace says far less about differences in need than it does about the
self-defeating aspects of narrow professionalism. It also underlines the
obvious fact that one's view of resources is very much a function of
time and social forces. But when other factors becloud the obvious—
when one proceeds as if past and future history are not variables to be
reckoned with—one of the necessary conditions is met for continuing
to do what one has done because that is only what one knows to do,
however socially irresponsible this may be.

The necessity of integrating history into the matrix of one's
thoughts and practices is not a new theme in this book. The reader
will recall that in earlier chapters when I was discussing the before-the-
beginning and the beginning phases of the creation of a setting I
placed great emphasis on confronting the past. In those discussions I
was, of course, talking about "local" history, whereas in the present
chapter I am talking about a broader social history. At best, professional training may alert the student to the history of certain aspects
of his field, usually a token gesture to scholarliness. As to the history
of the intimate and changing relationships between a field (not only a
piece of it) and the larger society, the student gets nothing. It is not
surprising, therefore, that professionals think that their ideas, theories,
and practices are the descendants of the thinking of those who came
before them—a lineage unrelated to social forces and changes. It is

---

[3] In the short run specialization appears to have productive consequences in terms of new knowledge and practice, but in the long run it seems to
render the individual, or field, or agency increasingly unable to assimilate and
adapt to changes in surrounding social events and processes. Worse yet, the
forces (individual and social) which generate specialization unwittingly increase
the extent of ignorance of the larger social picture so that assimilation and
adaptation are not even perceived as problems. The dialectical consequences of
specialization are pithily and amusingly discussed by Fuller (1969).

no wonder that when professionals have the opportunity to create a setting a historical perspective, local or otherwise, is almost always absent. Of the numerous times I have observed the creation of a setting and have heard the phrase *tooling up*—that phrase meant to give the impression of an engineering efficiency—it never reflected a historical stance.[4]

The negative reaction to the clinic's view of resources and organization contained the implication that it was most unlikely that such a setting could render valuable service. Again and again we would be asked the question: How do you know you are being helpful? This was a troubling and, of course, a legitimate question. It was a troubling question not because we had no ways to answer it but because the question assumed agreement on a *primary* value: justifying one's existence in terms of what one does for others. The true answer to the question was: "You are asking a legitimate question, but if we answer only that question we would be misleading you into believing that help to others is the primary basis upon which we want to be judged. The fact is that our primary value concerns our need to help ourselves change and learn, for us to feel that we are growing in our understanding of where we have been, where we are, and what we are about, and that we are enjoying what we are doing. We are not here because we have solutions, and we do not believe that there is *a* solution. By accepting this value we are not likely to blame failure on others (*we* know the score but *they* don't even know the game) but instead would view it as a stimulus to change. To help others to change without this being preceded *and* accompanied by an exquisite awareness of the process in ourselves is "delivering a product or service" which truly has little or no significance for our personal and intellectual growth. If in the coming years we are thinking and doing the same things—that is, acting as if we have discovered the truth and know how to deliver it—we will have failed even though others might say we were helpful. When toward the end of his life Freud (1964)

---

[4] In his excellent introductory statement to *The Professions In America* (1965) Lynn puts the matter very well: "As for the books that professional practitioners themselves have written about their callings, they have tended to concentrate on the philosophical and technical issues of a particular intellectual discipline at the expense of discussing the organic relationships of that discipline to the community at large. . . . And the books . . . which do display an interest in society have more often than not been behind the times in their conception of ever changing needs. Consequently they have prescribed social roles for the professions which are more or less out of date. If we knew as much about the professions as we ought, then we would undoubtedly be more conscious of the crisis that now confronts them as well as the threat that crisis poses to the whole course of our national development."

recommended that psychoanalysts should be reanalyzed every five years, it was not because he thought analysts were not being helpful but because he did not like what he saw happening to analysts in the role of helpers: *they* had stopped growing and that was fatal for them, for psychoanalysis in general, and ultimately for those who would be seeking help.

On those occasions when we gave this answer, the reactions varied, not surprisingly, from staring disbelief, to implicit accusations of narcissism and callousness, to a benevolence which seemed to view the answer as a kind of pious idealism which would not stand up in the real world. (There is, I know, a fine line between selfishness and a concern for one's self-development.) These reactions really reflect the heart of the matter because they reflect values and a way of thinking implicit in the creation of almost all settings. I use the word *implicit* advisedly because they are rarely verbalized. That is the way it *should* be, and what is there to say and think about? There is a good deal to say and think about, and I will use our schools as a case in point. Nobody would disagree with the statement that schools are primarily for the education of children. People may disagree about what education is but they would all agree that the primary purpose of schools is to do something for and with children. (This becomes quite clear when one has had the opportunity to observe or participate in the creation of a new school.) What children should be taught, what experiences children should have, how much progress children should make—these questions reveal who is center stage. I have spent thousands of hours in schools and one of the first things I sensed was that the longer the person had been a teacher the less excited, or alive, or stimulated he seemed to be about his role. It was not that they were uninterested, or felt that what they were doing was unimportant, or that they were not being helpful to their students, but simply that being a teacher was on the boring side.[5] Generally speaking, these teachers were not as helpful to children as they might have been or as frequently as the teachers themselves would have liked to have been. It took me a long time to realize that what would be inexplicable would be if things turned out otherwise, because schools are not created to foster the intellectual and professional growth of teachers. The assumption that teachers can

[5] The factors contributing to this are more complex than I can reflect here. They are taken up in my book *The Culture of the School and the Problem of Change* (1971). One of the chapters in that book describes the school which John Dewey created at the University of Chicago at the end of the last century, a school *not* based on the value that schools are primarily for the education of children.

create and maintain those conditions which make school learning and school living stimulating for children, without those same conditions existing for teachers, has no warrant in the history of man. That the different efforts to improve the education of children have been remarkably short of their mark is in part a consequence of the implicit value that schools are primarily for children, a value which gives rise to ways of thinking, to a view of technology, to ways of training, and to modes of organization which make for one grand error of misplaced emphasis.

Dewey knew all of this well, as the book by Mayhew and Edwards (1966) demonstrates. Dewey created the conditions for his teachers which he wanted them to create for their students. When Dewey recommended that an elementary school teacher should receive the same salary as a university professor, it was because he expected of the teacher what he expected of the professor: to investigate, to learn, and to change, and to continue to do so. The error that Dewey made in trying to influence the public schools, the same error made by those eager to implement his ideas, was the failure to recognize that the public schools and those responsible for them were operating on the basis of a value that schools exist primarily for children. As a colleague once remarked: "It is hard to help people find their way when you have lost your own way."

The question about the success of the clinic breaks down into two questions. Did *we* feel we were successful according to our primary value? Did those we sought to help feel they were helped? To the first question I can only talk for myself, although I have no reason to believe that others who helped create and maintain that setting would answer the question differently. I had an intellectual and interpersonal ball, such as I had never had before or am likely to have again in another setting. As for the second question (and in part the first) I must refer the reader to other publications (Sarason, Levine, Goldenberg, Cherlin, and Bennett, 1966; Kaplan and Sarason, 1970; Levine and Levine, 1970; Goldenberg, 1971; and Kaplan, 1972).

I must remind the reader that in this chapter it is my purpose to discuss certain settings in order to clarify the relationships among a setting's definition of its task, its view of resources, and underlying values. Although these relationships are the most important about which people must be aware in creating a setting, they receive the least amount of critical scrutiny, and sometimes they receive no scrutiny at all. The consequences are many and usually adverse: rigidity in function, insularity from changes in the larger society, increased competitiveness for resources within and among settings, decreasing satisfaction in work with a concomitant increase in the need for professional status and money, and the steady loss of the sense of community within the setting. The story, as later chapters will suggest, is more complicated than this but enough has been given the reader for him to begin to understand that creating a setting involves problems of values and resources which, although almost always viewed in individual, or local, or professional terms, turn out to be in large part a function of a particular society at a particular time. The failure to understand this, a direct consequence of an ahistorical stance and theories which pay no attention to social history, is what gives undue weight to tradition and makes it likely that changes in values and view of resources will come about more as a result, so to speak, of being hit on the head than as a consequence of using what is inside of it. To the extent that these problems are bypassed or, in the case of resources, are based on a myth, creating a setting is akin to engineering a building, and like so many of these products some settings are seen as obsolete or inappropriate soon after they are operational.

In the next section the issues of values and resources will be further discussed in terms of the creation of a setting quite different from the clinic. It is, perhaps, the best description we have of a setting from the standpoint of why and how it was created. The fact that the leader of that setting was a member of our clinic is noteworthy only because it may help explain how self-conscious he was of the process he engaged in and the need to describe it. Goldenberg's book (1971) was of inestimable value in clarifying for me the significance of the prehistory and beginning phases of the creation of a setting, and I urge the reader skeptical of the fateful dynamics of the before-the-beginning context to consult his detailed account. I must again remind the reader that in the next section I shall not (cannot) attempt to describe and discuss the creation of the setting except in terms of how its character and organization reflected certain values and view of resources. That even this is possible is a consequence of the fact that these issues were explicitly confronted. That is to say, from the earliest point these were seen as problems and not, as is usually the case, implicit "givens."

Residential Youth Center

The Residential Youth Center (RYC) in New Haven is a house in which twenty or so inner-city male youth (ages sixteen to twenty-one) live while they are learning about or adjusting or readjusting to the world of work and social living. The bulk of the residents are black, have disorganized or disorganizing homes, are school dropouts, and have prison records or many skirmishes with the law. The label *hard core* is quite appropriate. For the first six months of its existence the staff members with one exception (Goldenberg) were nonprofessionals, some of whom had histories not much different from those of the residents. After the first six months all of the staff were indigenous nonprofessionals.

The RYC was created within the context of an existing organization of settings: Community Progess Incorporated (CPI), the local community action agency. As I indicated in earlier chapters, and as Goldenberg makes abundantly clear in his book, a setting created within the context of an existing organization of settings sets processes going (for example, for resources, direction, and control) which can change the character of the setting and usually in ways that transform innovative into traditional goals. This, however, was not something of which Goldenberg was much aware, as he forthrightly states:

> It was clearly understood by all those concerned (e.g., CPI, the Department of Labor, and the Psycho-Educational Clinic) that the RYC's first director, a member of the Yale faculty, would return to his academic responsibilities on January 1, 1967, after having spent six months with the program on a full-time basis. After January 1, 1967, he was to be involved in the RYC program as a consultant. The reason for this type of arrangement was that one of the goals of the program was to prove that you did not need a "professional" to run a program—clinically oriented though it was—like the RYC. Another consequence of this arrangement—a consequence we only became aware of with the passage of time—was that the very fact that the first director of the RYC was not a full-time employee of CPI and, hence, was relatively immune to the social and political pressures of the "mother" organization, was an asset in the development and implementation of the program. It provided the director with the kind of leverage (i.e., that he did not "need" the job of directing the RYC) that enabled the RYC to function with a degree of latitude and freedom that might not have been possible were the director totally dependent upon CPI for his livelihood [p. 131].

Goldenberg learned, and very fast, that the process of creating a setting within the context of an existing organization of settings makes naivete a gross liability. I cannot resist quoting him on this same point but this time in relation to an existing organization of settings in Washington:

> There is also the situation in which the decision to create a new institution carries with it little or no pretense that the new institution will even try to coordinate the efforts of other agencies involved in similar areas of concern. This does not mean, however, that the new institution

will not seek or need the help of agencies that already exist. All it means is that the new institution will function independently of, and will not try to coordinate in any formal sense, the efforts of existing agencies that are, and have been for a long time, trying to meet certain human needs in the same area. What is usually overlooked in this decision, however, is that the rise of the new organization is in many ways an indictment of the ways in which the more traditional agencies have been meeting (or, in reality, not meeting) the needs they were originally intended to serve. What often results, regardless of public protestations to the contrary, is that the new institution is perceived both as a condemnation of previous attempts to render service and as a distinct threat to the future existence of the more established agencies. Under these conditions, cooperation of any sort, formal or informal, is highly unlikely. More important, the overlapping and duplication of functions that inevitably result once the new agency begins operations guarantee the development and perpetuation of greater conflicts—the kind of interagency conflicts that are, in the long run, not only harmful to all the agencies involved but cruelly detrimental to the clients who hope to receive service. It is, in the final analysis, a situation in which "cooperation" becomes little more than a slogan to be used for purposes of public consumption, and political maneuvering and under-mining become the accepted order of the day.

There is little doubt (at least now and in our own minds) that the creation of the Office of Economic Opportunity (OEO) was as much a reaction against the ways in which existing agencies were waging their "undeclared" War on Poverty as it was a response to the newly grasped needs of the poor. The implied indictment was a simple and clear one: had the existing agencies (e.g., the Office of Education, the Department of Health, Education and Welfare, the Department of Labor) met their responsibilities and obligations to the poor in an appropriate and relevant manner, there would have been much less need for the launching of the War on Poverty in general, and for the creation of a new super poverty agency (OEO) in particular. From the very beginning, then, one might say that the War on Poverty, at least in terms of those already engaged in efforts to provide services to the poor, could have been perceived as a criticism of existing programs and agencies. Again, this may seem to be a glimpse of the obvious, but what is less apparent are the ways in which these perceptions can influence the development of new programs and the motivations behind them.

The reader will recall that . . . we described as "decidedly cool" our reception at Job Corps headquarters (OEO) in Washington when, in the process of developing the initial proposal for the Residential Youth Center, we visited them seeking information and assistance. In actuality, we now feel we were being rather gracious in describing our reception as "decidedly cool." In point of fact we were treated more as interlopers, meddlers, even spies, rather than as people who were genuinely interested in the problem and wanted to be of some help. But this reception was almost "warm" compared to the one we received some two months later when we returned to OEO to ask them to fund the RYC, which was now in proposal form. This time we received no reception at all. We were told, in no uncertain terms, that our proposal would not be considered, that the idea for the RYC was at variance with Job Corps philosophy, and that we should "go elsewhere to peddle the project." Somewhat shaken, we did just that. We walked two blocks to the Department of Labor (Office of Manpower, Policy, Evaluation and Research), where we recounted our experiences and presented our proposal. Within twenty minutes we found, to our utter amazement, that our proposal not only was being listened to with much enthusiasm and delight but also was almost guaranteed its funds. We left the Department of Labor feeling, quite naively we now believe, that at least someone understood our program, shared our belief in its values, and was willing to support it all the way. Only later were we to realize that there may have been many other reasons for the speed with which we were funded by the Department of Labor, reasons having at least as much to do with the relationship and conflicts between OEO and the Department of Labor as with the particular merits of the RYC proposal. On the basis of this kind of experience, as well as a variety of others to be described in later portions of this book, one wonders—or at least has a right to speculate—about the motivations that lie behind the funding of a variety of antipoverty programs [p. 47–49].

The immediate stimulus to the concept of a RYC was the failure of the Job Corps program, a failure Goldenberg and his colleagues in the community action program recognized within a few weeks after the first Job Corps camp was opened. They had sent some New Haven inner-city youth to one of these camps, they started to receive from them some disquieting letters, they went down to the camp, and the idiocy of it all became clear.[6]

Creating the RYC was a direct consequence of some critical observations of and conclusions about resources, professionalism, history, and how labels and the definition of problems subtly undermine efforts at change. "A second aspect of the problem has to do with the ways in which nonprofessionals are perceived. Here, too, the situation is a somewhat curious one, for no sooner did the nonprofessional, via the Community Action Program, get into the "business" of delivering what for all intents and purposes were mental health services—and begin to show that he could do the job—than great pains began to be

[6] The creation of the Job Corps, like most programs created under the umbrella of the war on poverty, has never been described and is not likely to be. Moynihan (1969, p. 167) discloses the remarkable and discouraging fact that "in the early planning of the Youth Employment Act, the main provisions of which became the Job Corps and the Neighborhood Youth Corps, the Department of Labor library searched in vain for a decent account of the Great Civilian Conservation Corps of the New Deal." About many of these war-on-poverty programs Moynihan (1969, p. 129) says: "The history of these programs has not been written. It must be." It won't.

taken to indicate that he was, indeed, ill-equipped to perform that function with any high degree of competence" (p. 68).

Goldenberg's conclusions are not those of someone who is anti-professional or a glorifier of the virtues of human ignorance or a partisan of the view that sheer experience in mystical ways produces skill and wisdom. They are not the comments of someone who views and defines problems in ways that make it seem "natural" that his training, special theories, and techniques contain the appropriate and best solution. They are the comments of one who believes that whatever the virtues of professionalism may be (and there are many), they cannot obscure the defect of the tendency to transform unfamiliar into familiar problems at the expense of relevance. This is like the joke of the patient who after being examined by his physician was told to go home, open up a window, stand in front of it and breathe deeply, several times a day. Said the patient: "But, doctor, it is midwinter and if I do that I will get pneumonia." Replied the doctor: "But for that I know what to do."

Goldenberg goes on to point out that the traditional ways of thinking about service lead directly to the pyramidal type of organization. The RYC was organized horizontally and not pyramidally.

The horizontal structure came to mean many things. On a clinical or service level it meant that each staff member, regardless of his position in the organization or formal "job description," would carry a case load. Carrying a case load was defined as assuming the total responsibility for all decisions and interventions involving a resident and his family. No staff member, regardless of his status in or out of the organization, would presume to make clinical decisions involving another staff member's cases. Staff meetings were clearly to be utilized for purposes of trying to influence the decisions people made, but it was left completely up to the individual staff member to make the final determination in his case.

The rationale behind the "horizontal" sharing of clinical responsibilities was a simple one: that no one be spared the experience of dealing with a client and his family. This was undertaken in the hope that under such conditions people would begin to participate in one another's problems, could share and work through the anxiety that such responsibilities inevitably create, and would eventually come to view one another as sources of knowledge, help, and support. We wanted to make it as difficult as possible for people inhabiting positions of differential status and power to look at one another and say: "You don't understand my problems. You sit up there and tell me what to do but you don't know what I'm feeling. You haven't been through it yourself." Clinical "horizontality" was designed to put everyone "on the line" in the hope that it would enable people of different backgrounds and experiences to learn from one another in an atmosphere of mutual trust and respect [p. 128].

It is truly beside the point that these words were put into deeds and with a remarkable degree of success, despite anticipated and unanticipated problems. The RYC could have been early on a dismal failure without disproving the validity of its conception and the utilization and organization of resources. Similarly, the fact that it was successful does not permit one to claim that it was because of its basic views. The individual case can be seminal but not conclusive. The fact this RYC gave rise to another in New Haven and many more around the country, fathered by those who started the first RYC, is suggestive, but we will have to await on each the kind of detailed report Goldenberg has given us. In the quest for validity we should not overlook that the rationale which Goldenberg has so clearly spelled out, and which shaped the organizational character of this setting, is not new and was present in almost all of the viable communes created in this country in the nineteenth century. Its similarity to the Israeli kibbutz is also noteworthy. The principle of interchangeability of roles, external need as the major determinant of the utilization and organization of human resources, and the importance of interchangeability as a way of preventing barriers against mutual understanding—these similarities emerge when one cuts through the differences in language in which these rationales are couched. Here, for example, are two statements from the *Circular,* the regular publication of the Oneida Community. The first is from the issue of October 8, 1853, and the second from August 29, 1854 (Robertson, 1970):

We feel roused to new earnestness to favor the mingling of the sexes in labor. We find that the spirit of the world is deadly opposed to this innovation, and would make it very easy to slip back into the old routine of separate employments for men and women. But the leaven of heavenly principles about labor, resists, from time to time, this backward tendency, and brings forth a new endorsement of the truths contained in the Bible argument on this subject. We believe that the great secret of securing enthusiasm in labor and producing a free, healthy, social equilibrium, is contained in the proposition, "loving companionship and labor, and especially the mingling of the sexes, makes labor attractive" [p. 58].

Certainly we could not wish for better surroundings for a child, to make him—not indeed a distorted professional, or a hard-faced speculator—but to make him a gentle, thoughtful man of use and improvement. I hope he will be ever kept from the mercenary idea of doing things for pay, or making riches for himself. I am not afraid of its leading him to poverty. On the other hand, let him remain free from the absurd notion that one kind of employment is more honorable than another, which causes so much mischief in the world. He will be taught in the Community that it is not the kind of work that dignifies a man but that by good spirit and good manners the man dignifies every kind of work; and that he is the truest gentleman who is capable of doing the most useful things [pp. 59-60].

The RYC, its rationale and rhetoric bearing the stamp of the 1960s, the war on poverty, and race, is in distinguished company. The Oneida Community later had as one of its outstanding, indeed amazing, characteristics that which we also find in the RYC as an explicit value: the purpose of the setting was quite self-consciously the development and growth of its members.

One would expect that when those who are creating a setting have never engaged in such a venture before, they would assign primary value to their own development. This is far from the case, although I have seen numerous instances where this was recognized on a verbal level. Sometimes this has meant that individuals in the new setting will seek further knowledge and training. Rarely, if ever, will this be viewed as the collective responsibility of all who are creating the setting because in the pyramidal type of organization not everyone is seen as equally important or necessary. What I have seen with increasing frequency is the attempt to build in from the start "openness in communication," and this is done by bringing in an expert in group dynamics who employs procedures (usually over a very few days) intended to accomplish three things: for each member of the core group to see how he "comes across" to others, to make clear how the avoidance of "straight talk" leads to problems of communication, and to instill in the setting a tradition of candidness. In no instance that I observed, or I have been told about, were the desired effects lasting; in at least three instances the results were disastrous; and in one instance it began a tradition of group decision-making that effectively prevented most people from ever doing anything. It could hardly be otherwise because even where straight talk culminates in understanding and even agreement about how to live with each other, it may never reach or question the basic values and purposes of the setting. Straight talk about *feelings* is no substitute for clarity about values. More important yet, the very fact that an outsider is brought in already suggests a failure to take responsibility for one's collective growth and development, that is, to assign primacy to the value of the development of those in the setting.[7] In no instance, either before or after the group procedures,

---

[7] These comments should not be construed as generally calling into question these procedures. They have their time, place, and usefulness, although

was the possible primacy of this value raised, let alone its consequences explored. In all the instances I have observed or known about, all of them in the area of direct human service, there was never any question that the justification for the setting was only in terms of what one did for others. It is ironical that all of these settings wanted "to do good," although in regard to lay or nonprofessional people who would want "to do good," those same people would be the first to point out the real dangers involved in justifying action on that basis. They would rightly point out that to do good for others requires knowledge and experience by means of which one becomes changed or becomes a different kind of thinker. The point is well taken, of course, but what is not well taken is the implicit suggestion that learning and changing are not a continuous obligation and, therefore, always the primary value especially in the case of a new setting which almost never intends merely to replicate already existing settings. Most professionals stop learning and changing fairly early in their careers. I am raising the question of the nature of work, but more of this later.[8]

Goldenberg has stated the primary value and its significances in a lucid and compelling way:

It would be highly demoralizing, to say the least, for an institution to view itself as a potential candidate for the kinds of services it wishes to offer to others. From almost the very moment of conception, most institutions accept as fact the assumption that they are, and will continue to be, "healthier" than the clients whose needs they were created to serve. . . .

By far the most important consequence of the assumption that the institution need not overly concern itself with its own mental health is that the institution rarely attempts to develop or build into itself any viable mechanisms for preventing or dealing with its own problems. By "viable mechanisms" we mean any processes that would enable the insti-

---

their current faddishness will undoubtedly result in their disrepute and obscure what merits they have. The single point I have tried to make is that they are not designed to get at and question the basic, and usually implicit, values on which a setting rests.

[8] Everybody would agree that most jobs do not lend themselves to the feeling of continuous growth and development. Rarely does this statement refer to professional work. It is my opinion that what is true in general is true, to a lesser extent, of many professionals, not because the work is uninteresting but because the challenge has been mastered, diversity of stimulation is discernibly decreased, and the setting of which they are a part locks them into their professional niche. The feeling of being locked in is isomorphic to the way in which most settings are organized. These professionals would be aghast if they recognized their degree of kinship with industrial workers. The myth of the professional is that by virtue of being a professional he is saved from the feelings of stagnation and boredom, regardless of what setting he may be in. Professionals tend not to view or study professionals the way they do the rest of humanity.

tution systematically and regularly to take a long, hard look at its functioning, its growth, and its conflicts. The fact that few institutions or institution-builders ever develop such vehicles for self-scrutiny should not be taken as evidence of bad faith, poor judgment, or questionable motives. It is the inevitable result of a situation in which an organization does not view itself, its staff, and its problems as legitimate and important areas of concern. Once the assumption has been made that there is something inherently different between its own life and the lives of its clients (between its own needs and the needs of those it wishes to serve), a pattern of thinking is born which inhibits or stamps as irrelevant the development of vehicles for self-study and self-correction. In short, once the institution accepts as fact the alleged dichotomy between its own existence and those of its clients—a dichotomy which then allows the institution to rationalize and justify its being solely in terms of "helping others"—the institution need no longer "trouble" itself with questions of internal self-actualization or problems of self-confrontation. . . .

The tendency of an institution to avoid looking at itself and to refrain from the often agonizing search to develop internal mechanisms for dealing with its own problems does not bring with it any guarantee that serious problems will not occur. All it does is guarantee that when such problems arise they will be dealt with haphazardly, instinctively, and reflexively; in short, they will be dealt with in precisely the kinds of ways that the institution would never condone or allow to happen were it dealing with a problem of any of its clients [pp. 97–99].

From the beginning this value was explicit at the RYC and one can say that it was part of its "constitution." It determined the development of its horizontal organizational structure and it also was the basis for allowing and encouraging each staff member "to pursue and develop these work-related areas of his life in which he, and he alone, had an abiding and personal interest. We assumed that such personal fulfillment would result in activities that would be exciting and helpful to our clients." What this meant, for example, was that each member was responsible for an evening program, growing out of his own interests, training, and experiences, that was available to all RYC residents and their families. But what was a most distinctive consequence of its primary value were the procedures that were explicitly developed and regularly employed to cope with two facts: the RYC would *always* have problems—and how people dealt with them would be a function of how they defined the problems—and it was imperative for an individual to understand how others are seeing the problems; these facts were a kind of preamble to its constitution which no one was allowed to forget. The staff gave a good deal of thought to how to deal with this issue but there was never any doubt that it was *their* issue and not one for which any outsider could be given responsibility.

Goldenberg's book contains verbatim transcripts of the differ-

ent types of meetings and the reader is urged to consult them in order
to judge for himself the degree to which they reflect the primacy given
to the personal, interpersonal, and conceptual development of participants.[9] It is not the practice of settings to transcribe their meetings in
order to use them as a basis for reflection and change. Meetings are
for the purpose of understanding and making decisions about "others"
and only secondarily, if at all, as a means of self-scrutiny. For a setting
to take self-scrutiny seriously, in the sense that its vehicles for discussion
regularly have this as an explicit goal, requires, at the very least, agreement on the value that that is what the setting is for. The failure to
confront this issue and the seductive and "self-evident" quality of do-
goodism go a long way to explaining why over time most settings
change little or not at all and why those who create and populate them
only rarely experience the sense of change, growth, and accomplishment. On the level of settings we have yet to take seriously what Freud
and Dewey knew so well: it is nonsense to think and act as if helper
and helped, teacher and pupil, are different kinds of people and that
the one can change or help the other in desired ways without experiencing change in himself.

What about the boys at the RYC? Were they helped? Did it
pay off for *them?* By the requirements of its funding the RYC had to
study and answer these questions. Needless to say, the source of funding was not interested in discussions of values and horizontality. They
were interested in two questions. Did the boys at the center (the experimental group) do better after they left than a control group of
boys who by random selection happened not to be chosen? Could the
RYC remain viable after the first six months when Goldenberg left
and no professionals were running the center? Goldenberg gives impressive evidence that the answers to both questions were affirmative.

Goldenberg leaves no doubt in his readers' minds that for those
who created and maintained the RYC the experience was one that
wrought great changes in them. They learned, developed, and changed.

[9] The procedures employed at the RYC are highly similar, and in certain ways identical, to those employed by the most successful communes of the
nineteenth century. I gather that a similar orientation characterizes many of the
communes of today but they are so ill described, or not described at all, that
I cannot judge either its use or value. If I had to judge on the basis of available poor description and discussions with several people who helped create
communes, I would have to conclude that there is utter confusion between
self-indulgence and self-development, and between talk and action. One of the
root causes of this—more cautious.*;*, a concomitant characteristic—is either the
denial of the necessity and prerogatives of leadership or abrogation by the
leader of the obligation to lead. There is a difference between being a moderator
and a leader.

Such words, however, are far from clear as to their meaning and the values they are intended to reflect. When I use these words (as would Goldenberg, I am sure) they are meant to convey a complicated process during which an individual willingly accepts a challenge requiring him to think and act in unaccustomed ways and roles that, if the challenge is successfully met, change his perception of his capabilities and increase the range of new challenges—all of this being accompanied by a sense of satisfaction and an obligation to help others to have similar experiences. Those who created and maintained the RYC approximated this ideal to an extent I rarely have seen. For an individual or group to approximate this ideal requires certain internal conditions in the setting, coping with external factors stemming from these conditions, and overcoming in oneself the weight of tradition and previous training.[10] The last characteristic is well illustrated in the next section where I shall discuss a different type of setting distinguished by its values and nontraditional view of human resources.

What happened to the staff and boys at the RYC is not "explained" by any combination of a particular value and a view of resources, because far more was involved than I have discussed here—for example, leadership. But certainly among the mix of ingredients present the two factors I have been stressing were alone and in combination distinctive.

Ward H

The book *Ward H* (Colarelli and Siegel, 1966) was discussed in an earlier chapter in connection with the various aspects of the prehistory, before-the-beginning, and beginning phases in the creation of a setting, and our focus was on the implications of the fact that this new setting in a state hospital lasted four years. Ward H is another good example of the dynamics set in motion when a new setting is created out of, or within the context of, an existing organization of settings.

The authors describe well the usual living arrangements on the ward for these kinds of patients, the absence of anything that might

---

[10] A very good example of coping with external factors stemming from the RYC's values and view of resources, essentially its horizontal structure, was the tendency of those in the parent organization (CPI) as well as in other agencies to refuse to discuss questions, issues, and problems with anyone other than the leader. This was true even when it involved a boy or some issue about which another staff member had responsibility and the most knowledge. Psychologically speaking, this was not easy for the members to take. They wanted to be respected for what they did and not for what others perceived their job titles to be. A modest expectation!

be dignified as "treatment," and the rarity of professional attention. They also point out how the needs of the patients were secondary to those of the hospital's professional training program.

> One consequence of the residency training program is a regularly scheduled change of residents on a ward every six, nine, or twelve months. As in every hospital, above all the psychiatric hospital, changes in assignment are essential for a well-rounded training program. Many patients, especially the acute and newly admitted ones, benefit from these changes in personnel, where new ideas and personalities are constantly focused on problems and the ever-changing environment generated makes lapsing into a chronic role difficult. One negative aspect of this changing environment, however, is the frequent disruption of the therapeutic relationship built up between the patient and the resident, often resulting in a setback or regression in the patient's recovery. A patient suffering a regression every six months as a result of the rotation of the ward physician may learn to resist therapy, by avoiding deep personal relationships with the physician [p. 3].

"Life on such a ward takes on a terrifying anonymity" (p. 12).

Ward H was created to implement a set of conceptions about etiological factors in schizophrenia, the ways in which the usual hospital setting maintains and even exacerbates the condition, and the kind of social setting which would have more rehabilitative effects on the hospitalized, chronic schizophrenic patient. These conceptions were based on values and a view of human resources quite different from those of the usual ward. (See especially the authors' prefatory statement.) Three principles are enunciated, and their underlying similarity to those of the RYC and the Yale Psycho-Educational Clinic will be apparent:

> The first principle developed from the inconsistency evident in the fact that chronic schizophrenics are seen as non-responsible; they are brought to the hospital to become responsible, but there is no one near them behaving in a responsible way whom they can use as a model. The aides, though present, are the end point of a hierarchy; they receive and carry out orders but are not intended to make responsible decisions. The project altered the structure so that the aides might become models for the patients. It was believed that if these patients could be directly cared for by persons who are in the position of formulating policy and making decisions, then the possibility of the patients developing responsibility themselves would be greatly enhanced.
>
> The second principle guiding this project was the overwhelming importance of commitment, devotion, and above all, spontaneity in the care and treatment of these patients; the nature of their illness made these three qualities absolutely essential. Under the usual system many opportu-

nities for treatment were missed because of the inevitable delay involved in several personnel observing, reporting, and studying a patient's bizarre behavior pattern; when the prescribed response was finally relayed back to the patient the opportune moment for a therapeutic intervention was past. The reaction to these patients must be immediate and spontaneous. But spontaneity and devotion cannot be expected of treatment personnel who in themselves do not feel the responsibility for the treatment of patients nor in any real sense have it. You cannot prescribe devotion and spontaneity, you can only provide the opportunity for its development. In giving the aides the responsibility for treatment, the project permitted them to be spontaneous as well as committed to these patients.

A third guiding principle cannot really be separated from the above but does have other implications. This principle is the belief that one of the greatest resources we have to offer patients is ourselves. There is not sufficient difference between any two people, regardless of the amount of education, the degrees they have, the formal trappings of their status and prestige in society, to differentiate them basically in terms of their capacity to help one another. The inference of this principle is that with a certain amount of guidance and support there is no reason why a psychiatric aide who is on the lowest salary and prestige level of the institution cannot be given the opportunity and does not have the resources to do as much as the person at the other extreme of the status and financial hierarchy of the institution. The potential for development and growth in the aide is as great as that of any other human being and merely requires an optimal structure in order to develop. The project was structured to provide opportunities for development and growth in the psychiatric aide group which would then make new abilities available for the treatment of the patient [p. 19–20].

This way of defining the problem does not lead to impossible solutions. On the contrary, it discernibly expands the pool of human resources that are available at the same time that it exposes the inhumanity of the armor protecting professional preciousness. Reading between the lines (and sometimes on them) it is no wonder that Ward H encountered the obstacles it did in its four years of existence.

The authors were quite aware that at least two processes had to be initiated and successfully carried out if Ward H stood a chance of meeting its objectives. The first was that the professional staff connected with the ward would have to undergo changes in their ways of thinking and in their attitudes toward their roles. The second was that the aides would have to change their accustomed ways of thinking and conception of their roles. The second could not occur without the first and neither could occur with ease, expectations that were amply confirmed. What makes *Ward H* such a moving and dramatic document is the way in which these struggles are described. It is easy (but not all that easy) for professionals to say that they will regard aides, patients, and themselves differently. When the game begins and the cards are on the table the realities one confronts can be quite upsetting, particularly when the game is being played before a variety of hostile kibbitzers. The rest of the hospital was not exactly a cheering section for their colleagues on Ward H. However eager the aides were to participate in this "adventure in innovation" they did not (could not) anticipate what they would confront and experience when they accepted new roles and responsibilities. The stakes were higher, the game far more significant, but shades of Pygmalion are discernible. In Shaw's play we *know* how Eliza Doolittle changed; at the end we are intrigued and tantalized by how much Professor Higgins has changed. On Ward H the struggle was never ending and always uphill but the increments of desired change in the actors were marked and gratifying.

But what happened to the chronic, schizophrenic patients? Colarelli and Siegel present a variety of comparative data demonstrating that their patients did significantly better than other comparable groups in the hospital. "The comparative data apear to confirm the observational data on the Ward H patients. Ward H, as a whole, had a discharge rate equivalent to that of the whole hospital for chronic schizophrenic patients from the same cohort. For patients who were institutionalized less than five years, this rate was somewhat higher than for the rest of the hospital, and the readmission rate to date has been dramatically lower. These results were especially remarkable in view of the fact that the Ward H population was generally assumed not to be amenable to treatment. At the same time, the personnel cost of the Ward H program was equivalent to that of the least expensive ward in the hospital" (pp. 168–169).

It would be, of course, nonsensical to say that the Yale Psycho-Educational Clinic, the RYC, and Ward H were not absorbed with the importance of helping others. It would be equally nonsensical to say that these settings were created for the sole purpose of the personal and intellectual development of their members. What these settings were based on was the conception that a setting that wished to help others to learn and change had to learn and change itself. Indeed, these changes had to be reflected in all phases of the creation of the setting and this was a continuous process; that is, it was not a problem which was ever "solved." The task of these settings was not "out there" (in schools, the ghetto, the minds of people) but "in here" *and* "out there." Creating a setting based on this conception makes an enormous difference in the character of the setting and is in dramatic contrast to the creation of other help-oriented settings. Most settings are created as if they know what needs to be done and their members are what they need to be. There is usually, of course, some basis for these assumptions. I do not wish to create the impression that knowledge is meagre and that those engaged in the task of helping others are generally incompetent or personally inadequate. But I do maintain that most settings early on lose whatever innovative spirit they had, spontaneously change their services and thinking little or not at all, get caught up in internal struggles for status and resources, reflexively resist new ideas or practices, begin to change only when external conditions force them to question their basic values or obligations, and in the process of attempting to change transform the substance of the new challenge into the familiar rhethoric of an outworn tradition. Settings, like an individual, have an almost infinite capacity to treasure their "symptoms" at the same time they proclaim their desire to change. All of this is in part a consequence of justifying a setting's existence and purpose primarily in terms of what one does for others, a value which makes a productive self-consciousness either a luxury or a burden but never a necessity.

What significance can be attached to the fact that the three settings (and undoubtedly others) were created around the same time? There can be no doubt that the stress that each of the settings placed on the inequities of the distribution of services, and the obvious and scandalous consequences of the limitations of professional resources, reflected what the larger society was beginning to realize and to be disturbed about. The problems of race and poverty were catalysts for bringing out into the open what had long been true but obscured by unrealistic attitudes toward professionalism and resources. It is no exaggeration to say that the past two decades have witnessed an increasing antiprofessionalism, and among the most articulate critics have been professional people. Educators, physicians, social workers, mental health personnel, and others are on the defensive, and although the substance of the attack is not always clear, or rational, or justified, it in one way or another implicates the values and attitudes underneath the limitations of resources. The three settings reflected changes in the larger society. However, in contrast to many new and old settings which have attempted to reflect changes in society, the three settings did not fall into the trap of defining their task in terms of solving problems "out there" but rather in terms of drastic changes in their thinking that had to precede and accompany whatever they did for others. It is a difference that makes an enormous difference.

Although these settings were created on the bases they were, a fact which eliminated many wearying and disillusioning issues confronting a setting, one should not underestimate the difficulty of their task. One set of problems was substituted for another. Leaving aside the skeptical, hostile (and even subverting) reactions which they encountered from external sources, these settings were faced with four critical issues, any one of which could have effectively killed the setting if not handled well. The first was in selecting nonprofessionals who could learn to do what only professionals heretofore were considered capable of doing. None of these settings considered the lack of professional knowledge and training a good indicator of courage, wisdom, and the capacity to learn.[11] Just as possessing professional credentials is not, ipso facto, a defect, being a nonprofessional was not, ipso facto, a virtue. The second issue, confined to the professionals in the setting, was the degree to which they could really share responsibilities with the nonprofessionals consistent with the basic conception and not with noblesse oblige. The third issue was the degree to which the setting could support the nonprofessional in his difficulty with and anxiety about his new role. And the fourth was how to keep the enterprise "honest." A major factor which worked against succumbing to the challenge, and this is best poignantly described in the accounts of the RYC and Ward H, was the early recognition that these issues are never solved, that they will come up again and again in varying strengths and guises, and that the temptation to prevent their occurrence or to obscure them by administrative changes is the beginning of the end.

Review: Creation and Self-Development

Before going on with the life of a setting, it is appropriate to review the highlights of its earliest phases, literally the most creative aspects in that they concern the evolving of planned structure and form reflecting the thinking, attitudes, and energies of people confronted with a problem they willingly attempt to solve. As in all creative endeavors the structure and form may be rather different from the original conception but there is always a relationship between the two, and the inevitable discrepancy between original intent and actual result gives rise to varying degrees of discontent and frustration. Unlike the creative artist who, for example, can throw away his canvas and try again to solve his artistic problem, those who create human settings

[11] The Aristotlean way of thinking, as Kurt Lewin pointed out in a classic paper (1935), is in all of us and extremely hard to recognize and overcome. For example, there are those who truly believe that only blacks can understand blacks; that is, there is a class of people who are black, this person is black, this person has the characteristics of the class, therefore he understands others in the class. Those who think this way never bother to pursue the implications of the fact that white people frequently do not understand white people.

rarely have this option. The most notable exception is marriage. The more complicated settings are rarely dissolved even when they are obvious failures, but, as we shall see later in this chapter, the equivalent of divorce is quite frequent within the setting and for much the same reasons.

The creation of a setting is rooted in local and social history, and, as a consequence, it almost always reflects more or less conventional values and styles of thinking. Although the setting is always intended to be different from or better than existing ones, there are several factors which drastically limit the success of this intent. First is a lack of the sense of importance of local history which could allow for knowledge of and confrontation with the conflicting and often contradictory ideas and forces at work in the prehistory of the setting. The second factor is a dulled sensitivity to the historical relationships between settings and social forces, as a consequence of which there is a *belated* recognition of social changes, a tendency frantically to react, and an uncritical emphasis on quantity and numbers as the basis for solving the problem. The third factor (related to the second) is the tendency to define the problem in a way so as to contain a solution requiring those kinds of professional groups which heretofore had been inadequate in meeting the problem and which exist (and will exist) in numbers too small to meet the problem as defined. The final factor has to do with the consequences of a value which is almost always implicit because it is seen as so obviously "true": the primary justification of a new setting is what it does to help others. The failure to view as a coequal value what it must do for itself results over time in rigidity in thought and action, resistance to ideas requiring change, and a parochialism which insulates it from the changing needs of the society it purports to serve.

From a purely internal standpoint the major problems of creating a setting center on two related tasks: growth and differentiation, on the one hand, and the forging of a "constitution" by which the setting will be governed. The usual way in which the leader organizes his core group—the arrangements he makes with each, and the relationships of each with the others—usually reflects several assumptions held by the leader and each of the core group members. The first is that the appropriate kind and degree of motivation will overcome any and all obstacles, including those encountered by the leader and the core group in their precious settings. The second is that there is agreement on values and goals, perhaps the first assumption which in point of time is invalidated. The third assumption is that there are sufficient resources, or the promise of them, which will allow each of the core group members to realize his goals. The ambiguities inherent in the usual way of selecting and organizing the core group, ambiguities only later realized as such, are a consequence of the failure to view the creation of a setting as a constitutional problem among the most important aspects of which are the anticipation of problems and the ways they will be handled and the surfacing of differences in values among the participants. The failure to think in constitutional terms maximizes ambiguities which usually lead to informal, unambiguous, and individual kinds of resolutions, such as heightened competitiveness and individual empires. The process tends to be repeated as each core member organizes and develops his core group. What I have just summarized has less to do with the fact and problem of growth (and even size) than it does with the lack of a set of conceptions which would mirror the realities and complexities of the creation of a setting, and not, as is presently the case, the wish-fulfilling propensities of the human mind.

Much that I have summarized is not readily apparent to an observer viewing the creation of the setting. It is somewhat more apparent to the participants that there are powerful forces which prevent them from early recognition of what has happened and why. For one thing, in its earliest phases the setting is suffused with hope, enthusiasm, a sense of mission, and unity which maximizes selective perception. The dynamics of love have never been noted for their positive effects on the assessment of reality. Marriage, the smallest but most frequent instance of the creation of a setting, illustrates these dynamics best. Courtship, marriage, honeymoon, and the next year or so are times when the heart is dominant over the head. I do not say this with cynicism but, if anything, with despair because the feelings and fantasies experienced in the early phases of the creation of a setting are part of what is best in man; that they have the defects of their virtues is a fact which says a good deal about the dialectical character of man and his works. Another factor which prevents a realistic assessment of what is happening and why, and this is especially true of settings devoted to human service, is that they usually do help others. They do perform functions which others need and value. This result alone has tremendous "reward value," particularly because such a result is the basis for justifying the setting's existence. But there is a more subtle factor: in the early stages of the setting's existence the process of helping others is usually accompanied by a personal sense of growth. The service is not experienced as a routine without personal challenge and intellectual excitement. In other words, in these early phases it is *as if* the value of self-development were operative. However, precisely because this value is not viewed as equal to, or more important than, the value of help to others, over time the sense of challenge and change diminishes and routinization of thinking and action takes place—a process taking place in, and mutually interacting with, the other negative features of the setting's development I described earlier. With the passage of time the members of the setting feel locked in to their particular function and increasingly experience the disruptive discrepancy between a desire to learn and change (a need for novelty and stimulation) and the perception that this may not be satisfied. The exclusive focus on doing for others has been maintained at a very high personal price.

Earlier I used the preparation of a dramatic production for the commercial theatre to illustrate some aspects of the creation of a setting. It has additional relevance for the present discussion. Not unlike the discussion in this chapter, there has been a long-standing argument about the type and degree of formal training and knowledge an individual must have to become an actor. There are those who are partisans of certain schools of acting and those who claim that formal training is vastly overrated. There is agreement, however, on several factors. The first is that there must not be conveyed to the audience any distinction between the actor as a person and the actor in his particular role; he must not remain himself but he must change himself so that he is the role. He must become other than what he ordinarily is and feels; he must transform himself. Laurence Olivier (Cole and Chinoy, 1970, p. 410) says: "If somebody asked me to put in one sentence what acting was, I should say that acting was the art of persuasion. The actor persuades himself, first, and through himself, the audience." John Gielgud (p. 398) put it this way:

Of course, all acting should be character-acting, but in those days I did not realize this. When I played a part of my own age I was acutely aware of my own graces and defects. I could not imagine a young man unless he was like myself. My own personality kept interfering, and I began to consider how I was looking, whether my walk was bad, how I was standing; my attention was continually distracted and I could not keep inside the character I was trying to represent. In Trofimov for the first time I looked in the glass and thought, 'I know how this man would speak and move and behave'; and to my great surprise I found I was able to keep that picture in my mind throughout the action, without my imagination deserting me for a moment, and to lose myself completely as my appearance and the circumstances of the play seemed to demand. I suppose the truth of the matter was that I was relaxed for the first time. The finest producers I have worked with since have told me that this relaxation is the secret of all good acting. But we were never taught it at the dramatic schools. One's instinct in trying to work oneself into an emotional state is to tighten up. When one is young and nervous one tightens the moment one attempts to act at all, and this violent nervous tension, if it is passionately sincere, can sometimes be effective on the stage. But it is utterly exhausting to the actor and only impresses the audience for a very short space of time.

What Olivier and Gielgud are saying the individual actor needs to do in principle is precisely what I have said a setting needs to value and do—to look into itself and to create the conditions whereby it changes. The actor who cannot do this is seen as an unconvincing routinizer. There are actors who despite different times and roles never change their style or get outside of themselves. They are the hacks who never experience change—like many settings. To carry the analogy one step further: there are actors who will change only when they are forced to change, and the account of the first English production of *Pygmalion* is a case in point. A second point of agreement is that over time the actor's performance in a particular role should deepen and even change. Even when his first performance has been greeted with critical acclaim, the actor's obligation is self-consciously to pursue his role, to continue to study the character. The third point, related to the second, is that performing the role several times a week over a period of months runs the risk of routinization and mechanical acting which may still satisfy the audience at the same time that the actor has lost interest and is bored. It is not unusual for an actor to be unaware that his performance has deteriorated and that he has lost his audience. To avoid this is the actor's primary responsibility. Some actor's limit the time they will stay with the production. Another control is the director or his designate who regularly observes performances in order to detect the symptoms of the passionless performance.

Regarding the obligation of a setting to itself as co-equal with, and even more important than, its obligations to others has the sound of virtue but it has only the faintest echo in the creation of settings.

CHAPTER 7

Symptoms of Decline

Although the focus of this book is the creation of a setting and its earliest phases of growth and differentiation, it is illuminating of the problems and processes we have discussed to look briefly at some later events or turning points. Essentially they are in part a continuation or consequence of earlier dynamics. I do not maintain that these later happenings are an inevitable consequence of earlier processes, as if what men have created they are powerless to change. Far from feeling powerless, my observations indicate that not long after a setting has been in operation, a good deal of time and energy are devoted to efforts to change the setting in order to eliminate or dilute recognized problems. The feeling of powerlessness and despair are later phenomena which can only be understood in light of the recognition by participants that earlier efforts were of no avail. The important question is what gives rise to these early efforts to change the still fledgling setting and why are these efforts usually unsuccessful?

Equivalents of Divorce

In a young setting the most clear-cut indication that things are not going well is the departure of the leader, and most frequently this takes place when the setting is an outgrowth and part of a larger organization of settings; the leaving primarily reflects conflicts which arose between the leader and those who chose him. This comes about in a number of ways but rarely is the conflict only between the leader and those who chose him. On the contrary, it is usually conflict between the leader and members of his setting, or "outsiders" who had or have a vested interest in the setting, that antedates and sets the stage for the conflict between the leader and those who chose him. It is the unusual case where the sources and nature of the different conflicts leading to leaving are made public. The explanation given is usually the small tip of the covered iceberg. It is like the substance of the legal brief in most divorce proceedings: they are either contrived, or misleadingly incomplete, or both.

In the instances I have observed or known about the most common characteristic is that each of the participants in the drama ending in the leader's leaving agrees that the way things are is not the way they expected (or were told to expect) things would be. Each describes the setting as something which started as a pleasant dream and then was transformed into a nightmare. The implicit assumption is that at the beginning there was peace and agreement and then something happened; there was a "golden age" from which the setting declined.

The leader's leaving almost always has been preceded by conflict around his powers, policy, and personal style, and which of these interrelated aspects is important varies considerably, depending upon with whom one talks. There are those who are disposed to see personality and style as the etiological factors without which the conflict would have been avoided or diluted; others tend to see it as a familiar power struggle; relatively few (in my experience) couch their diagnosis in terms of contrasting ideas, goals, and values. The diagnoses which departing leaders give are basically the same. What is often overlooked, however, is that the participants by no means agree about the diagnosis, and why the leader has left is usually the subject of endless discussions and analyses, which at some point shade into a related question: who will be the new leader and why was *he* chosen. The fact that there is usually a lack of agreement about diagnosis is rarely, if ever, seen as but the latest instance in a history of differing perceptions about the purposes of the setting, and that the basis for that history was in an initial assumption which was too quickly accepted, rarely examined, and effectively blocked a realistic view of the future and how to think about it in the present. That assumption was that in fact the leader and the core group were in complete agreement about values, goals, and resources; power and conflict were never issues in the beginning.

On several occasions I have had the opportunity to meet with the staff after the leader had left the setting, and I asked three questions: How was it at the beginning? When did the craziness start? Was it predictable? In the beginning it was sweetness and light. It was, as some put it, the honeymoon phase when everyone seemed to be thinking in the same ways about the same things; it was all onward and upward.[1] As to when the craziness began there was a variety of answers with two underlying themes. One was purely internal and involved unkept promises, inadequate resources, chaotic or arbitrary or contradictory decision-making, failure to adhere to the original goals, and of course "poor communication." The second theme was more external in that powerful individuals or groups outside the setting, but who had an interest in or were affected by it, were perceived as the subversive force.

Was it predictable? No one ever said it was predictable, but this answer had little or no conceptual substance. After all, as one individual said, "Do you think I would have come here if I had thought things would turn out this way?" What needed to be done? Communication had to become clear, people had to work together, and responsibilities needed to be clearly defined and allocated. Their answers were essentially the same as those which determined how the setting was created in the first place. If only the honeymoon phase could be reinstated and reexperienced.

My experience has been such that by this time I am no longer surprised that people do not conceive of the creation of a setting as a set of internal and external problems which are fairly predictable if one views man and our society as they are and not as what one fantasies they are or would like them to be. That history is always a variable; that people represent different values, interests, and ambitions; that the uses and allocation of powers are best not left solely to the ambiguities of motivation; that the individual and the general welfare are not always perceived as synonymous; that conflict is neither bad nor avoidable but ignoring it is calamitous; that checks and balances are necessities and not luxuries; that growth is a double-edged sword and the problem is how to manage it consistent with first principles—far

[1] In earlier chapters I have pointed out similarities between the creation of the marital and other settings. These similarities are frequently and spontaneously perceived by many people. The phrase "honeymoon period or phase" as applied to the creation of nonmarital settings is the most clear and frequent reflection of the perception of the similarities.

from being cynicisms these are the "amnesias" which contribute to later trauma. These are the predictable needs, problems, and issues around which the constitution of the setting has to be forged; they are the realities that take some of the joy out of the honeymoon but make it more likely that a viable setting is being created. As I indicated in Chapter One, it took several months for the Constitutional Convention of 1787 to forge a constitution, and the word *forge* is used advisedly because the temperature of the mixture of ideas and controversy within the convention at times rivaled that of the torrid Philadelphia summer. The participants were amazingly conscious of the nature of their task and they rarely allowed themselves to confuse sentiment with reality, the aura of the present with the possibilities of an ambiguous future, ignoring or avoiding problems with the necessity to compromise, and confronting the past with enslavement to tradition. They were anticipators and problems-solvers, and their devotion to the rhetoric of brotherhood and freedom powered but did not produce the final product.[2]

There is at least one major type of new setting in which leaders frequently have to leave but where there is no earlier golden age. In fact, power as an issue was always central. I refer to the revolutionary situation which usually consists of a tentative amalgam of diverse groups differing significantly in values and ultimate goals and agreeing only on the need for radical changes in the society. Whatever agreement they have holds only for the immediate present and very near future. Far from the amalgam having a long-term sense of mission based on shared values and a devotion to mutuality, there is usually an acute awareness of differences, a sense of tentativeness, and a radar-like acuity to the issue of power. The explicit agenda centers around the need for "collective security"; the hidden agenda in one way or another centers on the jockeying for power. Frequently, what is true of the amalgam is true for each of the groups comprising it. Basically

[2] Settings which are created in the absence of love, devotion, or enthusiasm can suffer the same fate as those based exclusively on them—witness the results of marriages which used to be arranged purely for reasons of state. They tended to be cold-blooded affairs based on a formal contract describing future contingencies and the ways they would be handled. The only thing they did not deal with (the absence of love) was the very thing on which many of these marriages foundered and contributed to large and small wars. Settings based strictly on "business" or primarily on love tend to have similar fates.

The fact that I regard what went on at the American Constitutional Convention as among the most impressive processes and achievements in the history of man should not be interpreted as a claim for perfection, a claim at which its participants would have jeered. They were quite unrealistic about avoiding parties and partisan politics, and we are still dealing with the consequences of how the slavery issue was "resolved."

there is no constitution but rather an acknowledged transient treaty. When the leader leaves or is deposed or removed his departure almost always is the culmination of the not so dormant power struggle which was always there. There can be a succession of leaders and the elimination of groups which comprised the amalgam. In marked contrast to the situation I described earlier, where the troubled setting looks back nostalgically to a golden age and the proffered solution to the present difficulty is essentially the same as the basis on which the setting was created, the falling apart of the revolutionary amalgam is always seen retrospectively as a consequence of how it all began; the end of the amalgam was built into the beginning. Particularly for those leaders and groups who end up on the outside looking in (assuming they are alive to look in), the function of retrospection is to distinguish between perceiving the original amalgam as necessity and as naivete. Necessity told them what the game was; naivete prevented them from knowing the score—and the name of the game was power.

What is true of the revolutionary situation from the start, the concern and jockeying for power, is in my experience precisely that which gets crystalized when the leader leaves in the smaller and more conventional setting I have been discussing. Cliquishness increases, self-interest dominates, power is consolidated in different ways in and between different groups, and some individuals may even seek to be chosen as leader. The golden age has been forgotten in the obsessive concern for power and survival in the era of the cold war. Organizational craziness has become the norm. It is no wonder that we have a flourishing consultant industry—for those who can afford it. It is also no wonder that marriage counseling is a fast-growing field—for those who can afford it.

The turnover of leaders in relatively new settings is less frequent, of course, than that of other personnel who are more numerous. I am not aware of any data that would answer the question whether among all leaders of relatively new settings (one or two years of existence) the percentage who leave differs from that of other types of personnel (core groups). My impression is that the difference on a percentage basis would not be very great. Whatever the numbers may be they would be an underestimate of the "true figures" because leaving the setting is no easy personal affair, depending as it does on financial and family considerations as well as on pride and the availability of comparable or better opportunities. The desire and inability to move elsewhere is a combination which can only have adverse effects on the setting. The feeling that one has little or no freedom of movement is not one with which it is easy to live, accompanied as it is by the feeling that one *must* compromise and that what one is doing violates one's own standards. One hangs in because one cannot drop out. This is all the more poignant and shattering in relatively new settings which were able to attract people precisely because they held out the inspiring possibility that life would be different. Matters are not helped any by the fact that many of those who help create the new setting are frequently in positions "superior" to those they held before; they got what they wanted only to find that they got more than they bargained for.

The most clear-cut criterion of the failure of a setting would seem to be when it goes out of existence shortly after it has been created. There is a question, however, about the criteria of death. There is no problem when the setting is terminated, its members scatter, and there is no sign of continuity as that may be reflected in name and function. How frequent this is I do not know because I have not been able to locate the relevant statistical data. (For example, in any one year there are several thousand bankruptcies but not all of them are relatively new settings, not all of them go out of existence, and certainly not all of them are due to the kinds of developmental factors I have been describing.) In the case of settings devoted to human service, death of a setting is very infrequent. More frequent, particularly when the leader leaves, is a deliberate and discernible change in the scope and purposes of the setting so that even though there is continuity of personnel, name, and place one is justified in asking if the setting still exists.

I am not maintaining that the early death of a setting or marked changes in its goals and scope shortly after its creation are inherently bad or unwarranted. I have drawn attention to them because so often they are the culmination of dynamics which, so to speak, were built into the setting, and when they occur the tendency is to see them within a very restricted time perspective and on the basis of events and personalities which, although important, obscure the implicit values and assumptions which set the stage for what happened. Precisely because events and personalities so easily compel our attention and precisely because they are important they divert attention away from the interrelationships among categories of thought, values, and history. We see symptoms and confuse them with etiology, and as a consequence, the solutions we employ make it likely that the more things change the more they remain the same, as I have pointed out in relation to schools (Sarason, 1971).

Organizational Charts as Symptom and Cause

Almost all settings are set up on a pyramidal basis in contrast to a horizontal one. In fact, one of the major preoccupations of the leader, and later of the core group, is devising an organization chart which, by clearly spelling out tasks and responsibilities will make for efficient functioning. The functions of the organizational chart are highly similar to those of the architectural blueprint: they both go through various transformations, they are both visual, and they are both intended to allow for a certain way of living. They are supposed to reflect and permit implementation of the needs and tasks of those who will inhabit the setting. They both structure the future, and it is this knowledge which gives the process its importance. Those who develop the organizational chart (as with architectural plans) are aware, at least at the beginning, that planning for the future is not the same as controlling or predicting it and that there will be a discrepancy between present planning and the future reality. Consequently, the need for being tentative—and flexible—is recognized, at least at the beginning.

In the case of the organizational chart the need for tentativeness runs afoul of several obstacles, not the least of which is the difficulty many people have in tolerating ambiguity. This is not wholly due to personality factors because very frequently the sources of funding require a table of organization that is specific and deemed appropriate to the setting's task. But this is not always seen as a serious obstacle because many leaders assume (or know) that there are many ways one can get around or change organizational structure. This knowledge or hidden agenda or tentativeness may be in the leader's head and that is where it remains; it is usually not shared or discussed in the process of attracting his core group. On the contrary, the basis on which he attracts core members emphasizes definiteness rather than tentativeness of structure. The leader and the prospective core member both accept the concept of specialization of function and this works against rather than for a commitment to tentativeness of function and role. The prospective core member wants to know "where he will be and what he can do," and so does the leader; in making an agreement, definiteness rather than tentativeness of organizational structure is one of the bases of agreement.

The process and consequences of developing an organizational chart cannot be understood without recognizing an underlying assumption: that efficiency, responsibility, and motivation can be legislated. The organizational chart is the visual picture of the legislation; the expectation is that if everybody follows the chart everything will come out all right. The organizational chart is based on the same assumption as that for a football play: if everyone carries out his assignment in the way he is supposed to—if the tackles throw the right block, if the guards pull out and provide the right interference, if the linebackers are taken care of, and so on—we have a touchdown. Football coaches are infinitely more realistic than people who create settings because they know that the great bulk of plays will not work; they indulge hope, but they plan realistically. In my experience those who create settings tend to come to regard the organizational chart as having a special power to compel people to do what they are supposed to do. As the leader becomes increasingly enamored with the chart as a "rational" statement of how to achieve a smooth-functioning setting he is no longer aware of something he once knew (but which football coaches never forget) : the chances are that it will not work. And the chances are *very* high that it will not work. The extent to which it does not work is not the issue. The important fact is that the setting is created as if it will function the way planned and there is no discussion of, or vehicles developed for, how to think about, become sensitive to, and be prepared for the necessity to change. That change will be necessary is not even agreed upon, but lack of agreement is less serious than the more usual situation in which the imperfections of planning and their implications are not allowed to becloud a rosy view of the future. The situation is not unlike that of new parents who see themselves and their newborn as launched on a conflict-free voyage through time, marked only by delights and pleasures, wish-fulfilling accomplishments, and a cooperative, unchanging world.[3]

I have seen instances where the organizational chart was viewed as if it were akin to a mathematical solution to a problem. The leader and the core members sit around and struggle with anticipated problems, change the chart to "solve" the problems, and sometimes the "solution" is accompanied by shouts of glee as if "Eureka! We have the solution." There is relief and satisfaction because the proof is iron-tight. It would be amusing if it were not so discouraging to see grown people play the chart game so completely seriously that they are un-

---

[3] Rodgers and Hammerstein capture this beautifully in the song "My Boy Bill" in their musical *Carousel*. The would-be father, an engaging but irresponsible person, fantasies what his boy will be like and, needless to say, the boy will be the epitome of masculinity and a close pal to his father. Neither in the music nor words is their a troubled note in this view of the future. But what if it is a girl and not a boy? There is momentary consternation but he recovers; the music becomes delicate and the words poignant as he now weaves a picture of the girl's unrivaled beauty and accomplishments. Suddenly he is thrown into a panic as he recognizes what *he* is and what this bodes for the future, particularly if his child is a girl. The reality frightens him and the song ends with what is obviously a doomed determination to change and to ensure that the fantasy becomes a reality.

able to see that what they are doing can only be the first of many similar steps whereby an ever-changing collection of people is trying to accommodate to an ever-changing complex of problems. Unlike the football coach who has a game plan which he is prepared to scrap if it does not work, those who create settings tend to act as if all they need is one good play.

There are, then, two potentially dangerous sources of trouble in the usual way in which organizational charts are thought about and developed. The first is that the leader and each of his core members reach an agreement which far from being based on a tentative view of structure (and the future) is characterized by a degree of definiteness presumed to endure. The second, a variant of the first, is the view that the organizational chart, having been an outgrowth of an attempt to anticipate problems which can interfere with smooth functioning, has "solved" these problems—relationships are clear, the future has been predicted, the world will be stable, and all will go well if the participants will follow the letter and spirit of the chart. As a consequence, the participants are unprepared for the inevitable. There is a third and less frequent source of difficulty and that is when the leader knows that changes will be necessary, he has the power and is prepared to make the changes, but he does not share this with others—he is tentative, the others are definite.

In most fledgling settings there comes a time of "administrative reorganization" which is almost always a symptom that there is and has been trouble. The sources of difficulty can be many, as I have attempted to demonstrate in previous chapters. The reorganization is always presented (internally and publicly) as a rational and an expected happening; such euphemisms as *streamlining, normal adjustments,* and *increasing efficiency* are part of the rhetoric. The participants know otherwise, and those whose responsibilities and power have been decreased (the losers) know best that the reorganization is the culmination of a long train of events. Some leave the setting, not infrequently one of the hoped for results of the reorganization. The reorganization is almost always a result of trouble, and somewhat less frequently it is the cause of more. Unlike the process which gave rise to the original organizational structure, the reorganization is far less deliberate and preventive in orientation and unaccompanied by anything resembling enthusiasm. It takes place in an atmosphere of tension and conflict. The golden age has become more golden in face of a future already tarnished by a demoralizing present. There are instances where within the first two years the leader and several core members have left, and memories of a golden age have been effectively removed from the perceived history of the setting.

Quiet Symptoms: Boredom and Decline

The leader's leaving, the departure of some core members, and administrative reorganization are "noisy" symptoms of difficulty in a young setting. They are more dramatic but less frequent than the "quiet" symptoms of boredom and the feeling of a walled isolation. These are not easy symptoms for an outsider to observe or an insider to talk about; when they are experienced or discernible varies considerably with a variety of factors. For example, the younger the person the longer it seems to take for the challenge of the new setting to wear off, and this is not only because of the brevity of previous experience or a perspective toward the future which is relatively unbounded and full of options, but also because he is more likely to feel he is learning, developing, and changing. That the setting may be in trouble and that he may be embroiled in the organizational craziness do not necessarily preclude the possibility that the younger person will feel that he is developing intellectually and cognitively, as is his feeling of technical competence. Even though the setting does not have its members' development as a primary value, or as a value equal to that of helping others, the consequences of that value may nevertheless be experienced by the younger person. The chances are greater for the younger than for the older person—at least for a time.

The ingredients of job satisfaction (like those of organizational craziness) are many and interacting, but there is one which tends to have devastating effects, and that is when one's work is no longer challenging, or interesting, or unpredictable; one knows from one day to the next, from one month to the next, what one will be doing and this stretches into an indefinite future. It matters little if what one does is valuable to others or even if others regard it as interesting and even fascinating. If one has mastered one's task, if that mastery does not lead to new challenges, if one's job no longer is *experienced* as interesting, if one feels one has learned as much as one will in that job, one is in trouble and it compounds difficulties from any other sources. I am talking about not only so-called lower-level jobs but higher ones as well. I have seen too many professionals who are bored by their work to exempt them from those generalizations. Conflicts within a setting around power, status, and money are in some measure a consequence of the fact that people no longer find their jobs intrinsically interesting.

The dynamics of the creation of a setting work against recognition by the outsider or insider of the vague feelings of boredom, of being trapped, and of a strong desire for diversity and stimulation.[4] It is not easy to face the fact that the setting qua setting is not meeting one's expectations and that one's position is not meeting the criteria of onward and upward. In a dim way the individual realizes that there is a discrepancy between what he is expected to give to the setting and what he knows he can get from it. As I pointed out in the previous chapter, it would be surprising if it worked out otherwise because most settings are not based on the value that the growth of their members is equal to any other value. The nature of work and the conditions which make it interesting are not issues taken up and confronted in the creation of a setting.

There is an old joke which contains a truth quite instructive for the problem of boredom in work, all the more interesting because it is not about people on the assembly line but about highly sophisticated professionals whose work is regarded by others as endlessly fascinating. Two psychoanalysts had offices in the same building; one had just started his practice while the other was much older and with an established reputation. They had never formally met although they had seen each other a number of times in the elevator at the end of the day. On this particular day they were alone on the descending elevator; the older analyst was whistling gaily and, to the younger analyst, he appeared alert and eager.

Younger analyst: Excuse me, Dr. X., I know you, of course, but you don't know me. My name is Dr. Y. I am also an analyst. I have long wanted to meet and talk with you.

Older analyst: Why don't we get together some time?

Younger analyst: That would be wonderful. But I do have one question I would like to ask you now, if I may.

Older analyst: Go ahead.

Younger analyst: I know you have a full practice, as I do. We see one patient after another, and we spend almost all day listening,

---

[4] Those who like to look into the future when prolonged travel in space will become possible and frequent had better confront the problem of boredom. Space travel in the future will require the creation of settings, involving people in new and sustained relationships in order to achieve certain goals, and boredom is only one of the many problems that will be encountered. I would assume, for example, that organizing the expeditions in terms of specialized functions and knowledge (the bureaucratic-pyramidal way of thinking) would be to extend lunacy from earth to space. In our earthly settings we can opt out, an option not available to the space traveler. Adapting man to machine and vice versa will be nothing compared to the difficulties of anticipating and dealing with the problems of social living. Of course, if the problem is being viewed as one of human engineering, so that the issues of value and constitution-making are either glossed over or typically oversimplified, the problem is not all that difficult—even though the price will be disaster.

and listening, and listening. At the end of the day I feel tired, sometimes even depressed, and wilted. And yet when I see you in the elevator at the end of the day you usually are whistling or humming, you
look eager and springy, while I feel quite the opposite. How can you
feel like that at the end of a day of listening, listening, listening?

Older analyst: Who listens?[5]

The conditions in which an interesting job becomes boring and
routine, and one no longer feels that his intellectual and personal
powers are being productively used, are not too well understood in the
case of the professional people. That they hardly have been studied is
in part due to a reluctance of professional people to face the issue in
themselves; it is so much easier to study the problem in others (such
as those in an obviously nonchallenging job). This is not true of professional actors in the commercial theatre who have long been aware
of a conflict between a lucrative income and maintaining interest in a
role in which one has performed over and over again. The actor who
is in a hit looks forward to a steady income at the same time that he
knows that performing well in a role several times a week over months
(and sometimes years) may run afoul of lagging interest, routinization
of performance, and even boredom. As a group, actors do not want to
be typed, to be seen as capable of performing only one kind of role in
one kind of medium; they tend to see themselves as needing to be
tested in a diversity of roles. They are one of the few professional
groups who give explicit primacy to the value of their own development. Not only will many actors limit the period of time they will stay
in a role but they will also seek to engage in other roles in other media,
and this is not explainable only by financial need. It is also standard
practice in a production to hire a stage manager, one of whose major
functions is to see that the dulling effects of repetition are avoided.

There are two issues: creating a setting which allows people to
experience growth, differentiation, and diversity; and consistently
maintaining this value over time. Most settings bypass the first issue
and never have to confront the second one. The quiet and unverbalized symptom of boredom is one of the most frequent and devastating

---

[5] I assume (although it is not really essential) that this joke originated
in psychoanalytic circles. I subscribe to the psychoanalytic notion that many jokes
serve the function of dealing with an anxiety. The truth in this case is that
there is anxiety that reality cannot be depended on to satisfy some important
personal needs. Over the years I have seen scores of people begin the full-time
practice of psychotherapy. What has impressed me is how many of them after
two or three years seek to cut down on their office practice and to engage in
other activities in other professional settings.

reflections of a troubled setting. Boredom is the last word that comes to mind in reading the accounts of Ward H and the RYC.

From a different set of considerations Bennis and Slater (1968) come up with observations and suggestions relevant to this discussion. Beginning with the problem of how to integrate individual needs and organizational goals, Bennis begins by describing the bureaucratic-pyramidal type of organization structure.

> Bureaucracy, as I refer to it here, is a useful social invention that was perfected during the industrial revolution to organize and direct the activities of a business firm. Most students of organizations would say that its anatomy consists of the following components: a well-defined chain of command; a system of procedures and rules for dealing with all contingencies relating to work activities; a division of labor based on specialization; promotion and selection based on technical competence; impersonality in human relations. It is the pyramid arrangement we see on most organizational charts.
>
> The bureaucratic "machine model" was developed as a reaction against the personal subjugation, nepotism, cruelty, and the capricious and subjective judgments which passed for managerial practices during the early days of the industrial revolution. Bureaucracy emerged out of the organizations' need for order and precision and the workers' demands for impartial treatment. It was an organization ideally suited to the values and demands of the Victorian era. And just as bureaucracy emerged as a creative response to a radically new age, so today new organizational shapes are surfacing before our eyes [pp. 54–55].

Bennis then goes on to list four threats to this type of structure.

> (1) Rapid and unexpected change. (2) Growth in size where the volume of an organization's traditional activities is not enough to sustain growth. (A number of factors are included here, among them: bureaucratic overhead; tighter controls and impersonality due to bureaucratic sprawls; outmoded rules and organization structures.) (3) Complexity of modern technology where integration between activities and persons of very diverse, highly specialized competence is required. (4) A basically psychological threat springing from a change in managerial behavior [pp. 55–56].

He then points out that these threats are real and picking up momentum. "Bureaucracy with its nicely defined chain of command, its rules, and its rigidities is ill-adapted to the rapid change the environment now demands." In light of this, and projecting some budding trends into the future, Bennis comes up with the concept of "temporary systems."

But in the new adaptive organizations I am talking about, work groups will be temporary systems, which means that people will have to learn to develop quick and intense relationships on the job and learn to bear the absence of more enduring work relationships. Thus we should expect to experience a concentration of emotional energy in forming relationships quickly and intensely and then a dissolution and rapid relocation of personal attachments. . . . From an organizational point of view we can expect that more time and energy will have to be spent on continual rediscovery of the appropriate mix of people, competencies, and tasks within an ambiguous and unstructured existence [pp. 75–76].

Following Bennis' chapter Slater examines some social consequences of temporary systems, and what emerges is that "work will become more meaningful" and that it will be necessary to obliterate differences among people, that is, to break down the compartments into which people are put or into which they put themselves. In fact, Slater emphasizes, people will need to be interchangeable in work. Professional lines and preciousness will no longer have adaptation value. "I am merely saying that insofar as uniformity is sought, specialization and incompleteness must be eschewed. Less variety from person to person requires more variety within each person. The individual will be more changeable, less predictable from moment to moment and from situation to situation, less able to play the same tune all his life long. Wardrobes, taken as a whole, may be more similar, but each one will be far more diversified, and the variety of dress in any given social situation much greater than today" (p. 82).

In effect, Bennis and Slater's analysis and recommendations rest on (among other things) one empirical fact and one explicit value. The empirical fact is that work is not very meaningful—a lot of people are bored with what they are doing. (It should be pointed out that Bennis and Slater talk primarily about highly trained, professional people.) The explicit value—which is equal to any other organizational value—is that conditions should exist that allow an individual to experience change, growth, and diversity. The significance of the explicit value resides in the empirical fact that most people in most settings do not find their work intrinsically challenging and interesting, regardless of education, training, status.

Bennis and Slater are far more optimistic than I about the future use of temporary systems and the support for the values underlying them. They seem to regard them as necessities that organizations will recognize as having survival value. To be optimistic requires that we know how existing settings can change in the desired direction and that we know how to create and maintain settings consistent with the new values. In neither case am I impressed with our knowledge and capabilities. I shall return to these issues in later chapters where, as I hope to show, the issue is less optimism or pessimism than it is one's conception of social change and its consequences for one's time perspective.

CHAPTER 8

Buildings as
Distractions

This chapter is based on my experience with new settings in new buildings, and all of this experience has been with settings devoted to the residential help of handicapped people of one kind or another. There are two purposes to this chapter: first, to discuss why the process of putting up buildings to house a new setting is so frequently disruptive of the achievement of goals; and second, to describe a concrete instance illustrating the point that the unexamined assumption that buildings are necessary is a bar to the recognition of the relationships between values, resources, and public policy. Put in another way: in the area of human service putting up new buildings tends to perpetuate the problem of limited resources, contributes to the inadequate services they ordinarily provide, and separates the setting from the larger society. If this seems strange, the reader should ponder the fact that the history of helping services, especially those created by federal, state, or local government, is part of the history of human misery. And part of the explanation is the assumption that in the best of all possible worlds a new human setting should have new buildings.

In trying to reconstruct the history of a relatively new but troubled setting it has never happened that people paid attention to the fact that physical structures were built to house the human setting. My experience leaves no doubt that having to plan and oversee construction at the same time that one is attracting staff and planning programs is at best a dubious opportunity and at worst a catastrophe. It need not work out this way but it usually does and the reasons are sometimes quite subtle.

It is alleged that most actors (and some actresses) dream of playing Hamlet. Few get the opportunity, and even fewer succeed. Similarly, most professional people dream of building their own facility, few receive the opportunity, and even fewer succeed. The opportunity to create a new setting in new quarters is a temptation that few can resist. Among the few who receive the opportunity are some for whom the new buildings are more of a temptation than the creating of the human setting. It is not within the scope of this discussion to "hell-dive" into the different conscious and unconscious motivations that make building an almost irresistible temptation. Suffice it to say that it is usually a deeply personal affair (literally and symbolically), and therein lies the source of a major problem, because creating the physical structure can become such an absorbing, challenging, time-consuming process that one is distracted from other and more important issues. It *is*, for a time at least, a task of creation, self-fulfillment, and a never-ending source of learning and growth. Making a pleasurable dream into a reality gives a humdrum quality to other tasks. The danger is, of course, that building can become an end itself rather than a means to certain ends; it can become the tail that wags the dog. The danger is compounded if the individual or small group planning the building perceive themselves as having artistic souls, in which case the process becomes increasingly isolated from consideration of the values and purposes of the setting. Needless to say, the planners always see themselves as exquisitely sensitive to the problem of form and function, of individual and environment, of intent and reality, of change and flexibility. The well-intentioned rhetoric rarely reflects the reality.

One of the most subtle and important consequences of all this for the planners is the strength given to the implicit view that they own the setting; that is, psychologically it is *their* setting, *their* creation, *their* monument. Whatever the base rate or the normal amount of man's narcissism may be, planning for buildings at the same time one is creating a human setting tends to raise it markedly. The dynamics are such that seeking and responding reflectively to criticism and alternative possibilities are neither frequent nor easy. Matters are not helped any by the fact that building involves certain steps (preliminary plans, final plans, estimates, bids, timetables) that cannot be skipped and are extremely difficult, and at some points impossible, to retrace. In short, there are points of no return, and one does not take kindly to suggestions about what might have been done.

These individual dynamics do not take place in an organizational vacuum. However, in seizing the opportunity to plan buildings the leader, particularly if this is his first venture of this kind, holds to the fantasy that there will be few constraints on what he can plan and do. Beyond knowing that the money is limited, although the absolute amount may seem on the astronomical or luxurious side, he tends not to recognize the scores of restraints he will encounter in transforming dream into reality. From the very beginning he is accountable to those who chose him and they in turn are usually responsible to other bodies. If this takes place in the context of federal, state or city organization the restraints are numerous. If, as is increasingly the case, all three organizations are involved it is hard for the leader to escape feelings of persecution—and Kafka's *The Castle* takes on personal significance. Zoning restrictions, fire laws, building codes, access roads, parking space—these are some of the factors that for the leader become obstacles obviously devised by ignoramuses to prevent innovation and progress. And then, of course, there are the architects, many of whom have little patience with amateurs (defined as all those who are not architects). Architects do not like to be viewed as high-level bricklayers who run to the drawing boards when someone has a new idea. Architects are becoming increasingly specialized and if their specialty coincides with that of the leader (such as a psychiatric facility or a residential institution for handicapped children) it can be a mutually rewarding or a catastrophic experience. In the public sector, at least, the choice of architect is usually a purely political manner over which the leader has little or no influence, and this simple fact of life is not lost on the architect who *knows* what will be approved and how to maneuver the building plans and process through the winding road leading to the castle.[1]

---

[1] In some states (like Connecticut) the hiring of an architect is the only state purchase not subject to competitive bidding, and this is not an oversight. One of the most illuminating conversations I have ever had was with an architect who explained to me the tie-ins among architects, contractors, and

In recent years another specter haunts the scene and that is an aroused local citizenry who for one or another reason "want in" on what is being planned. In some cases they want in to make sure the setting "gets out." The leader who has started with *his* hopes and dreams, who has weaved on paper *his* pattern of people, program, and architecture, cannot be expected to view these lay people as other than professional intruders.

Creating a physical environment is under the best of circumstances a formidable intellectual task. Unlike the administrative chart, a brand-new structure cannot be changed, and this knowledge is a stimulus both to anxiety and creativity—under the best of circumstances (which I have never yet had a chance to observe).[2] As one gets further from the best of circumstances, anxiety, impulsiveness, and rigidity come to the fore, and the planning for the physical structures and the human setting become increasingly isolated from each other. The intrinsic difficulty of the task, exacerbated as it is by the factors I have described, leads to the situation where the planners cannot wait until the setting is opened. Somehow, the feeling is, when it is opened things will simmer down, present problems and conflicts will disappear, and the "real" work will begin. It is less that the future is so attractive than that the present and past have not been all that rewarding.

My description is highly similar to what was so well delineated in the movie the *Father of the Bride* in which what was supposed to be a beautiful, happy, and joyous process and occasion, the planning for and occurrence of the marriage of a daughter, becomes an anxious, debilitating, neurosis-producing affair the termination of which is equated with release from hell. It all ends happily, of course, and that is where the similarity to what I have described ends. Creating concurrently a physical and human setting is a profoundly serious affair because it has such deep personal significance for those responsible for it and (too easily forgotten) because it is supposed to serve people.

---

politics. He concluded the discussion by pointing out that the major justification for these realities was that the buildings would be constructed, a result he doubted would obtain with any procedure I could devise.

[2] I have never engaged in planning for new physical structures to house a new setting. In one instance I became part of the planning for the new setting after the architectural plans were approved and construction had begun. Later in this chapter I relate another instance where I was in on the ground floor, so to speak, and where the first order of business was how to avoid constructing buildings for which the legislature had appropriated money. Over the years, as my fascination with the problem of the creation of settings increased, I made it my business to get to know and interview those who were engaging in the process. Perhaps the most frequent phrase appearing in these discussions was "I never realized that."

The situation is usually more complicated than I have indicated because my description has been only in terms of *a* leader or a leader and those who have chosen him. At some point the leader begins to form his core group, and personnel keep getting added as opening day approaches. There is a personnel population explosion! From a leader and his core group the setting may contain scores of people when it opens. Most people do not know each other or the plans and programs or the physical structures. Whereas the leader and the core group earlier concerned themselves with how the program should go *and* why, the population explosion relegates the why question to the background. How things should work becomes the central and all absorbing question. These are not times for extended discussion of underlying values and philosophy or anticipation of problems other than those in the very near future. These are not times for thinking but for action, for organizational "law and order." Any thought anyone had of staying organizationally loose and flexible is forgotten. "Things will shake down once we have opened and we see the problems and iron out the wrinkles"—a hope far more understandable than it is fulfilled.

But my description in no way takes into account any or all of the sources of pitfalls I discussed in earlier chapters, such as ignoring prehistory, how the core group is chosen, and the myth of unlimited resources. When these are part of the picture, and they are always part of the earlier picture, the sudden and uncontrolled growth exacerbates the already existing organizational craziness.

I had the opportunity to observe the creation of a mental health center built by the state and to be run by a university department of psychiatry. A leader and a core group from the university department were to be responsible for planning the structure and program. This took place before I had ever conceptualized the creation of settings as a process and problem, and my foreknowledge of what would happen reflected no conceptual wisdom but rather knowledge of certain facts derived from firsthand experience. The first fact derived from the several years of experience I had as full-time employee of that state. The fact, simply stated, was that any agency which enters into intimate financial and joint arrangement with that state should have its collective head examined and trepanned *unless* it understood precisely how the state organization functions, unless it had the appropriate contacts and wrote a contract (constitution) in which all the *i*s were dotted and all the *t*s crossed, preferably in at least six different languages.[3] The second fact was that the leader and the core group,

[3] What did not become clear to me until several years later when I had

far from having any knowledge of what lay ahead, actually believed that they would be unfettered in realizing their plans. I am not being unfair when I say that they believed they were, noblesse oblige, doing the state a favor. The third fact was that the existing setting was not noted for its interpersonal peace and quiet, in no way different from a lot of other departments. But not all such departments are given the opportunity of designing their own buildings. Every existing conflict was exacerbated as they began the process of creating and opening the new setting. The subsequent history was quite stormy and many lives were adversely affected. In almost all respects it duplicated what I had observed in at least two other instances of the creation of a setting. These are all troubled settings and many people have spent many hours diagnosing the problem. I never heard (or hear) anyone implicate the decision to build and its consequences as an important piece of history still "living" in the here and now. Personality conflicts, power plays, poor communication, broken contracts and promises— these are the most frequently given diagnostic ingredients. This type of diagnosis is only in part explained by the fact that in each instance the turnover of leaders, core group, and other personnel was so large that not many who are there now know what a comprehensive case history would demonstrate.

A case history is not a collection of facts, if only because facts do not necessarily tell the truth, but rather a description of events which are considered important according to some conception or theory about how things work and develop. The contents of a case history are determined by a priori considerations that may be right, wrong, or misleading—which of these it is will be determined over time by competing considerations subjected to study. The justification for a case history is that it tells us what we might do to change or prevent certain conditions. In the case of the problem of the creation of settings (and why so many of them misfire) we do not possess adequate case histories, less because of faulty conceptions than because it has hardly been conceptualized as a problem. Once it is conceptualized as a problem a number of things become obvious and important, such as creating a physical environment to house the human setting. But as we shall see in the next section the need or desire to build are

---

begun conceptualizing the problem was that the state would have been equally well advised to view an arrangement with a university as an invitation to masochistic pleasure, a view it subsequently arrived at. The point is that neither of the two parties possessed a way of thinking that could direct them to the implications of two facts: they represented different traditions and purposes, and yet the internal dynamics and organization of each were quite similar.

frequently "facts" that have no compelling rationale. The values which give rise to settings are usually perceived as so self-evident as to require no critical reflection.

They Shall Be, Therefore They Should Be

To illustrate several points I shall discuss a concrete instance of the creation of a setting in which I and some colleagues participated and to which we are still committed.[4] We had the opportunity to help create one of a dozen state regional centers for the mentally retarded. A decade earlier, because of some farseeing leadership, the state of Connecticut decided never to build another giant institution but rather to divide the state into small regions each of which would have a center with relatively few beds but with facilities for day care programs and related community activities. It is not necessary for the reader to be knowledgeable about mental retardation to grasp the points to be discussed in the following pages. They are equally applicable to other patient populations for the "care" of which billions of state and federal dollars have been spent in the past decade to put up buildings. Unfortunately, the kind of thinking which permitted this, indeed cloaked it with the appearance of obvious humanness, guarantees that the trend will continue well into the foreseeable future.[5]

In approaching the creation of the Central Connecticut Regional Center (CCRC) we were quite aware of a set of related ideas and experiences which dominated our thinking and plans. The first of these was that living and working in the typical state institution devoted to residential care, either for the mentally retarded or the so-called mentally ill individual, were intellectually confining, interpersonally conflictful, and socially isolating. Living and working in and around the institution circumscribed one's world and involved one in a seemingly endless series of struggles to which one accommodated or from which one fled. What we are saying explicitly is that this institutional world was as confining, physically and intellectually, for the employees as it was for the residents in their care. Much more has been written about the maladaptive consequences for the residents than for

[4] The remainder of this chapter was written long before Sarata (1972) undertook an independent study to evaluate some of the basic conceptions which gave shape to the setting I shall be describing. Sarata's study has not yet been completed but systematic analyses of his data give substantial support to these conceptions.
[5] Most of what follows is taken from a chapter in a book, "The Creation of A Community Setting" (Sarason, Zitnay, and Grossman, 1971). Reprinted with the permission of the Division of Special Education and Rehabilitation, Syracuse University.

the staff. I am not saying that these consequences are inevitable but rather that they are the rule rather than the exception. The variations which exist among institutions have hardly been described or studied (Klaber, 1959; Blatt and Kaplan, 1966; Blatt, 1970).

A related idea which dominated our thinking had to do with the tendency for state institutions, however small they may be to start with, to grow slowly but steadily and in ways which guarantee that both residents and employees grasp less and less of the total picture and, in the case of the employee, which increase the strength of the feeling that one is impotent to effect what is going on. Whereas at the beginning employees know each other as well as the residents, the need to accommodate more residents—which has almost always been viewed as a necessity for which there was no alternative except to build another institution—ultimately produces the situation in which the opportunity for meaningful face-to-face contact has decreased drastically. But the aspect I wish to stress is that this steady growth tends to occur without any self-conscious and deliberate attempt to anticipate and to dilute the effects of these negative consequences. What permeates the institution is the attitude that one is facing a losing battle in which the consideration of choices and planning for the attainment of what is considered desirable employee relationships are seen as either luxuries or activities best left to the realm of fantasy. The end results are employees who do not experience a sense of growth or challenge or satisfying working relationships with others.

It has often been said that the classroom teacher whose thinking and activities have become routinized and who no longer experiences any challenge in his work or the desire to learn and grow cannot make the classroom an interesting and stimulating one for children. This is precisely what I am saying tends to happen over time to employees in our institutions, in part as a result of growth and the way it is perceived and managed.

The idea about the usual quality of institutional life which guided and dominated our thinking in relation to the CCRC stemmed from our personal experiences as well as from countless discussions with and observations of employees in a variety of state institutions for the mentally retarded. Beyond such sources, however, was our acquaintance with the pioneering work of Klaber (1959) and Blatt (1970). Although Klaber's studies had as a primary focus mentally retarded children in different state institutions, it is hard to avoid concluding from his data and discussion that these institutions, despite variations among them, were not fulfilling their stated objectives. At the very least, his data should dispel the notion, if anyone still holds to it, that the modal state institution is in practice an educational one. His brief discussion of the difficulty that these institutions have in attracting and keeping employees, when taken in conjunction with his data on the children, presents a somewhat grim picture. If to gain this picture one has to infer from, or read between the lines of, his report, this is not necessary with Blatt's publications.

In light of what I have said it should be clear that we approached the creation of the CCRC with a decidedly negative view about the modal state institution. It was not that we believed that institutions are inherently evil but rather that they seem to become evil. It was not that we felt that children were being shortchanged but that employees as well were victims.[6] It was not that the conditions were due to individual perversity or that they could be rectified or avoided by atypically heroic individuals, but rather that assumptions absolutely fundamental for their existence remained unverbalized or unexamined. One such assumption, for example, is that the state institution is a part and reflection of the community in which it is located or the communities it serves. Every institution states explicitly that it is a community facility, it exists because of and for the citizens of a particular geographical area. In reality, of course, the institution is usually physically and psychologically removed from the community (or communities), it is frequently viewed as an "alien body" in the community, and there is no basis for asserting that the citizens of the community in any way have any feeling of responsibility for and involvement in the institution.

I shall attempt to indicate how all of the foregoing considerations became crystallized in our minds in terms of two goals: to avoid a building program, and to avoid either having beds or using them in the usual custodial manner.

Avoiding a Building Program

Perhaps nothing was as revealing of our thinking, or as fateful for what happened, as our attempt to avoid spending the large sum of

---

[6] It cannot be otherwise because these institutions are always set up for "others" (variously called patients, children, clients, inmates) and there is no consideration of the idea that the quality of the conditions of employee learning and growth in large part determines what these "others" will experience. Every superintendent ritualistically reminds his employees that "we are here to serve others." And it sounds so reasonable and good. It is like in the anecdote about a young lawyer who was arguing his first case before the Supreme Court and he kept reminding the justices that it was his and the justices' duty to serve the cause of justice. And how much more reasonable could one be? Except that Justice Oliver Wendell Holmes reminded him that "we are here to serve the law," and that is not always the same as serving justice. Our "humane" institutions should be set up to serve the law *and* to do justice to all those within them.

money which the legislature appropriated for buildings. From the day
we knew who the director of the new facility would be—and this was
six months before he would actually be in office—he and several members of the Psycho-Educational Clinic devoted a number of meetings
to what we thought was the fantasy of how nice it would be if we did
not have to be concerned with designing and putting up buildings.

Each of us had already had the experience of developing and
opening a new institution and we were well acquainted with the enormous (if not insuperable) difficulty of keeping attention focused on
the community at the same time that one was forced to attend to the
myriad details and problems attendant to designing, developing, and
opening a new institution. In theory this difficulty is not an insuperable one; in practice it almost always is, especially with institutions
supported by state governments which allow one to hire new personnel
only when the new institution is open. As a consequence, and despite
the best of intentions, the opening of the institution makes it impossible
to pay attention other than to matters of internal policy and programs.
Under these conditions, thinking and finding out about as well as interacting and programming with community settings become luxuries,
whereas initially they were necessities.

The presence of a new institution in the community facilitates
the unfortunate process whereby the community looks to the institution
as the place to which all relevant problems are or should be sent,
thereby weakening or eliminating whatever community tendencies
may have existed to accept responsibility for these problems. Weakening such community tendencies is bad enough but what is far worse is
that it obscures the fact the new institution will never be adequate for,
or appropriate to, all or even most problems. Obscuring this fact sets
the stage for the community disillusionment which inevitably occurs
when it is finally made clear that there are no more beds, programs
are full, and staff time is completely filled.

If the proposed regional center were built to service the region,
it seemed apparent that even though it was a small geographical unit
it would be far from easy to transport children to the center so that
they could take advantage of its different programs and services. To
check on this we got in a car and, starting from a proposed central
site for the center, clocked the time and mileage between different
points of the region and the central site. It soon became obvious that
given the traffic and routes, some children would be spending as much
as one and a half hours traveling—this in a small region in a small
state. But this estimate was based on the use of an ordinary passenger
car. If one used a school bus, meaning that there would be many stops
and the speed of travel much reduced, the amount of travel time for

many children would be unconscionably high. In short, a single center would have difficulty making its services available in a serviceable way.

There were three major population centers in the region: Meriden, Middletown, and New Britain. Although the proposed site was to be in Meriden, the largest concentration of population by far was in New Britain. Each of these cities had parent associations which looked forward to the building of the regional center, and needless to say, each of them could justify placing the center in their city. It did not require any special wisdom to anticipate that placing the regional center in any one of these cities would bring in its wake a whole host of policital-diplomatic problems with various groups in the other two cities. We thought it legitimate to assume that whichever city had the regional center would get most of the services.

Accepting as we did the value that a community should assume major responsibility for its mentally retarded children, we viewed the role of the regional center as one which would help the community do this. This could mean providing individuals and agencies in the community with regional center money and staff to strengthen, expand, and improve existing programs or to help them start new ones, that is, to start *their* programs, not ours. It was our hope that regional center staff would be working *in* other agencies for a good part of their working week. Our past experience taught us that this way of thinking conflicted with professional training programs in which the student assumes without questioning that one works in one's office in one's own setting to which problems are brought. The fact that one's setting has a specific geographical locale and that it contains a number of people whose primary loyalty is to that setting—its inhabitants see themselves as more related to each other, and as owing each other more allegiance, than to anyone outside the setting—are obstacles to venturing out and becoming part of other community settings. A building (particularly a new one) represents a physical and psychological barrier to becoming part of the community.

These, then, were the major considerations, experiences, and facts which motivated us to seek ways of subverting a building program.

At the end of the first three years of its formal existence no buildings had been constructed and none was planned. Initially, and it was thought temporarily, the CCRC secured offices in a wing of a building containing a day care program run by a local parent association. This building was one of several of what had been a state sanitorium but which was in the process of becoming a community mental health center. Two years later another building was given to the

CCRC. These two buildings were renovated and, aside from offices, will house three programs.[7] The first is the day care program which is still under the aegis of the parent association but with financial and personnel support from the CCRC. This had been a small and struggling program with no supportive services to speak of. It was understandable to us that the parent association would view the fledgling CCRC in a very ambivalent way. On the one hand, we anticipated the parents would view us as a savior inasmuch as we would have financial resources which presumably they would have some call on. On the other hand, we also expected that the parents, who were justly proud of the program they had developed on their own, would fear that the CCRC would "take over" and that there would no longer be a role for the parents. Although from the very beginning of our relationship with the parents' association we said in a variety of ways that the CCRC would not take over the program but rather would make money and personnel available to help make *their* program what they always hoped it would become, we did not deceive ourselves that our words were viewed as more than words and that our intent was probably seen being at variance with our words. They clearly were dubious about our statements that we wanted more involvement from parents. As matters turned out, however, the major problem in our relationship was how to get more parents of the children to be more involved and to accept greater responsibility for the program. Even before the CCRC appeared on the scene, increased involvement of parents had been the most thorny problem confronting the handful of parents who had taken the initiative in starting and maintaining the program. If we had taken over the program, it would have simplified our lives at the same time that most of the parents would have been provided with grounds for remaining passive and taking little responsibility for their child's program. It has taken three years of discussion and controversy to reach the point where almost all parents are actively participating in some way in the overall program.

The second program (started in the third year of the CCRC) is the Independent Living Unit which ultimately will involve a dozen retarded individuals selected on the basis that they can learn to work in the community at the same time that they live in the unit, the aim being that after a relatively short period of time they can live and work in the community with some supervision both from family and the

[7] The costs of renovations were paltry compared to those of comparable new buildings. Besides, the renovations took several months whereas new buildings would have taken several years.

CCRC. In the modal case the individual will have previously lived at home where it seemed unlikely that he could learn to work and live in the community. This program is for the five working days; weekends he continues to live at home. The third program (started near the end of the third year of the CCRC) is the Family Involvement Program which can accommodate, again on a five-day week, six younger children whose family situations seem to be maintaining patterns of interaction self-defeating of the purposes of everyone. Before a child is accepted in this program, a written and signed agreement is entered into between the parents and the CCRC, specifying the length of time the child will be in the program and obligating the parents and other members of the family to spend time in the unit observing the child's behavior and how he is handled and interacting under guidance with him. The children are selected on the basis that their problems and family situations would be amenable to a behavior modification approach.

The reader will note that the Independent Living Unit and the Family Involvement Program are not "total" programs in the sense that they commit the CCRC to seven-days-a-week care for an indefinite period of time. There were a number of reasons against such a policy of total care, but chief among them was the opinion that as soon as the CCRC assumed total responsibility for the individual it made its task of getting the community to accept some responsibility difficult, if not impossible. Our experience was quite clear in demonstrating that, however understandable it may be, many parents very much desire to have someone else take over complete responsibility for their child, and if this desire is satisfied the possibility of shared responsibility and programming reduces close to zero. Parents are not alone in this matter; there are social agencies which take the same view. Put most simply: *a program which purports to be community oriented is not consistent with its purposes if it accepts cases in ways which absolve the community of continuing concrete responsibility.*

But, someone can ask, are there not instances where total care is required? Would it not be cruel to deny total and long-term residential care in those instances in which, regardless of past history, the life, unity, and stability of a family are at stake? The answer to both questions is, of course, in the affirmative, but in so answering the questions one does not have to commit oneself to the typically large institutional building or, more important, to putting up new buildings at all (Sarason, 1969). The fact of the matter is that in the three years of its existence the CCRC has helped to place forty children in full-time residential care in existing state facilities. More important, however, is the fact (which we do not pretend fully to understand) that we have not had very many requests for full-time placement.[8] This in part may be due to our publicly stated and restated policy that it would be a long time before we had any beds for full-time care and that at that time it was our hope to care for such cases either through foster homes or small group homes in various neighborhoods of the community. Our policy has not met, of course, with universal acceptance. This is not surprising when one recognizes how deeply ingrained it is in all of us to think of an institution for the retarded as acreage dotted with buildings. Elsewhere (Sarason, 1969) I have discussed this ingrained tendency to think in *a* way, and only in *a* way, about residential care:

> It is appropriate at this point to ask a deceptively simple question: How do we understand why, in this country, at least, the pattern of residential care has been so consistent, namely, a relatively large number of children are housed in a place staffed by a wide variety of professional and nonprofessional personnel? This is even true in a state like Connecticut where they have decentralized the state into regions in each of which there is a regional center. In each regional center there are residential facilities, and although the number of residents is far fewer than in the usual monstrous institutions, it is still true that the residents are in that regional center. It seems, unfortunately, to be the case that a large part of the answer to the question involves the failure explicitly and systematically to list and evaluate the universe of alternatives in regard to residential care.
>
> There is more involved here than the weight of tradition, although that is an important factor. What I have been impressed by is that even in instances where the conditions for innovation were ripe those who were responsible for creating the settings did not examine the alternative ways one could view and implement residential care. It is ironic that in planning buildings these same people can spend vast amounts of time creatively examining the alternatives for design and allocation of space, but fail to act and think similarly in regard to the alternatives to housing the children in one locale. Let me illustrate my point by relating the following experiences: On four occasions I had the opportunity to ask the following question of a group of individuals who either had or would have responsibility for creating an institution for mentally retarded children: "What if you were given the responsibility to develop residential facilities with the

---

[8] When later we started to develop a satellite program in the largest city in the region we had several meetings with parents and other community groups. What we found out was that a weekend placement facility was the top priority with group homes next. Institutionalization in the traditional sense was a poor third or the last. Frankly, we were amazed at the priorities. Within a year after these meetings the satellite office had helped different community groups in planning and creating a group home which could also be used for weekend placements.

restrictions that they could not be on "institutional land," no one of them could house more than twelve individuals, and no new buildings could be erected?" The following, in chronological order, were the major reactions of the different groups.

(1) Initially the groups responded with consternation, puzzlement, and curiosity. For some members of each of the groups, the question seemed to produce a blank mind, but for others it seemed as if the question quickly brought to the surface all their dissatisfactions with the usual mode of residential care and stimulated consideration of alternatives. (2) In the early stages of discussion, the chief stumbling block was the restriction that "no new buildings could be erected." I should say that throughout the discussions I adopted a relatively nondirective approach and tried only to answer directly questions which would clarify the meaning of the initial question. For example, when asked if one could remodel existing structures, I indicated that this was, of course, permissible. When I was asked if there was any restriction as to where these houses or small buildings could be bought and rented, I said there were no such restrictions. The point deserving emphasis is that many individuals struggled for some time until they realized that there was no one way to act and think but rather that there was a potentially large universe of alternatives for action from which they could choose. In addition, as some individuals came to see, there was no necessity to choose only one alternative, i.e., one could and should proceed in different ways at the same time. (3) Midway in the meeting the behavior of the members began to change in rather dramatic ways. Whereas before most were hesitant, deliberate, and cautious in their remarks, they now seemed to respond as if they were engaged in an exciting intellectual game in which one possibility led to thinking about other possibilities, and what at first seemed to be unrelated was then seen as crucially related. Faced with the task of creating settings they truly began to think and talk creatively. (4) In two of the groups—and for reasons I cannot wholly account for—a plan for residential care evolved which brought together the renovation of substandard housing, training programs for nonprofessional personnel, volunteer services, and neighborhood involvement and responsibility. In short, these two groups were no longer dealing with mental retardation in its narrow aspects but in terms of what has been termed the urban crisis.

One of the more experienced superintendents pointed out to his group that in the plan they had discussed "we are meeting more social problems, and providing more meaningful service to children and their families, at far less money than we are now spending." It was indeed remarkable how intellectually fertile the discussions in these two groups were. For example, one of the group members made the point that if these small housing units were strategically placed around our high schools they could be used by the schools in at least three ways: for educating these youngsters about mental retardation, for purposes of training child-care workers, and for enlisting volunteers for recreational and other purposes. Another group member, in the context of a discussion about food preparation in these small units, maintained that if neighborhood participation and responsibility were taken seriously, food preparation and feeding could be handled on a volunteer basis, besides which the food would probably taste better. In my opinion, the creative thinking and planning that went on in these two groups were, in part, a consequence of a process which permitted the members to think not only in terms of the retarded child but in the context of pressing urban problems which ordinarily are not viewed in relation to the field of mental retardation.

It is, of course, significant that the members could come up with approaches to residential care which they had not considered before and which deserve the most serious consideration. But what I consider of greater general significance is the fact that in the usual ways in which such settings are created the universe of alternatives is never described or thought through. It is my opinion that research on how settings are created will ultimately have a more beneficial impact on the quality and varieties of residential care than any other single thing we might do. Up to now we have focused research on the recipients of residential care. I am suggesting that we will learn a great deal about the recipients by turning our attention to the values, assumptions, and thought processes of those who plan for the recipients.[9]

The issue is not simply residential care but rather the different ways in which this can be provided and the relationship of each of these ways to one's values and purposes. But there is more to this than one's values and purposes and it is contained in the fact that the CCRC was a public facility; that is, it was not our private domain but rather an instrumentality of its citizens. I turn now to the significance of this obvious fact for the problem of residential care.

An Implication of Public Policy

In most instances it is the intent of the law establishing a state institution that its services and programs will be equally available to all those in a defined geographical area who are eligible. It is expected that the institution will serve as many eligible individuals as possible without unduly affecting the quality of those services. I say *unduly* because the fact that there is and will continue to be a discrepancy between the number of eligible cases and the extent of services automatically sets a limit to what can be done or justified in an individual

---

[9] There are children who are so profoundly retarded that they are not ambulatory or very responsive to their surroundings. When people concede that most children in our institutions do not have to be there, they *always* go on to say that the profoundly retarded are, of course, best cared for in the existing type of institution. What they mean is that they cannot conceive of caring for these children in other settings, such as, small homes in the community housing several such children. There *are* alternatives, but they cannot be conceived of as long as we think in terms which separate what is best for children and what is best for those who care for them and which effectively isolate both from the community.

case. The problem facing the institution is how to utilize its resources
so that it can give meaningful and discernible help to as many cases
as possible. As the work of Klaber and Blatt indicates, it is often the
case that the institution services a great number of cases through programs which seem to benefit very few individuals—the quality of service is unduly diluted.

It is not unusual to find a state institution that solves the problem by restricting the kinds of cases it will serve with the consequence
that some eligible individuals get no meaningful help. It is in these
instances that one sometimes gets the impression from its leaders that
the institution is their private preserve rather han a public instrumentality.

If an institution for the mentally retarded is sincerely to discharge its obligation to render as much service as possible to as many
people as possible without unduly diluting quality of service, one of
the first questions it must ask is how it can justify seven-days-a-week
care in those cases where a residential program seems advisable.[10] If
there is anything that is predictable about a new institution it is that
in short order all beds will be filled and many children who need or
will need such care will receive none. In the real world assigning *a*
child to *a* bed means that some children will have no beds. Why not
five-days-a-week or four-days-a-week care so that more children have
some access to the program? Does reducing the amount of residential
care per child unduly dilute the beneficial effects of the program? Is
there any evidence that the bulk of the children who are *continuously*
separated from their families (and vice versa) derive undiluted benefits thereby? Are not many of our state institutions primarily custodial
in part because they require the child to adapt to a culture drastically
different from the family in the natural community? In other words,
full-time residential care is in no obvious way consistent with public
responsibility or the long-range interests of individual children. It
would be more correct to say that whatever data are available strongly
suggest that full-time residential care tends to defeat the thrust of
public policy and the opportunity for many children to experience a

---

[10] The thrust of this question is appropriate to any residential setting.
Let us listen to some comments of a physician (Waisbren, 1971) writing about
the creation of a new general hospital: "I challenge any of you to go to your
hospital and look at each patient as an intelligent layman and ask yourseslf, the
patient, the nurse, and his doctor why he could not be sleeping at home that
night. I feel over half of the patients could do this each night and should. This
obvious overuse of beds at night has to be considered in planning, since, if I
am correct, the hospital will be planned to take over twice as many patients
during the day as at night" (pp. 7–8).

more humane existence, and by *humane* we mean providing the individual with opportunities to develop and utilize his potential in typical social contexts. The institution is not a typical social context.

These issues are usually not a focus of thinking of those who create institutions, and in large part this reflects still another aspect notable by its absence. We refer here to the fact that an institution usually operates on the implicit assumption that it, and only it, has primary responsibility for the type of person it serves. Insofar as it makes this assumption it communicates to those outside the institution that "we handle these problems, we are the experts, you have little or no role to play." Such communications, particularly if the community pleads ignorance or has shown no special interest, result in very willing agreement by those outside the institution. As a result, the institution is in but not of the community; it may serve the community but it cannot be served by it; it may be for but it cannot be with the community; beds are in an institution, they are not in the community; services are in buildings of the institution, they are not in buildings in the community.

The institution which purports to be a community facility cannot be organized or present itself as a self-contained facility prepared to render services to, but not to receive them from, the community—in typical noblesse oblige fashion. A community facility should refuse to adopt primary or sole responsibility for action and service. A community facility explicitly shares responsibility not because "sharing" is inherently a virtue but rather because to go it alone inordinately restricts the range of human and physical resources which exist or can be developed in the community; it perpetuates the invalid assumption that relevant intellectual or personal talents do not exist, or cannot (or worse yet, should not) be developed, in the members of the wider community.

These considerations, in addition to those discussed earlier in this chapter, led us from the very beginning, and in a most self-conscious way, to commit ourselves to several objects. First, if at all possible, to avoid a building program which would in effect be saying to the community: "Here is where the action and beds are." Instead, we wanted to proceed so as to be able to say: "Beds can be all over the community." Second, if we had to, or decided to, have beds, we would avoid full-time residential care. Third, we would refuse to present ourselves, and would resist others who saw us, as having sole or primary responsibility for those eligible for service.

These objects were far from being determined by some vague or abstract conception of democracy or by commitment to values about how people should live and work together. We would not deny that these were factors. But these factors paled in significance before the obvious fact that the usual way of creating an institution almost guaranted that the quantity of service would be far less than necessary and that the quality of service would be unduly diluted. Put more simply and bluntly: residential care in this country generally has been a failure, and in many instances, now and in the past, it has been scandalous.

Per Capita Cost and Gross National Product

In examining an aspect of public policy in relation to residential care we were in a direct way maintaining that one cannot avoid issues of right and wrong, consistency and inconsistency. Put most simply: the quantity of beds, indeed the amounts of money being expended to maintain these beds, are in themselves no index of how well certain values or purposes are being realized. In fact, these amounts of money, particularly when they represent dramatic increases over previous expenditures, may convey the impression that more money means more "good." If the weekly per capita cost of a bed was, for example, five dollars per week and if after public clamor stimulated by exposure of scandalous conditions it is raised to seven-fifty or even ten dollars per week, the public tends to conclude that the quantitative increase means a corresponding qualitative gain. This is identical to the tendency of the public and some economists to interpret increases in gross national product as signs of human progress, that is, as reflecting an unmixed blessing. Lekachman (1970) has shown incisively how naive is this tendency to equate quantitative with qualitative gains.

The gross national product . . . is the total market value of the goods and services produced by our economy for a specified period of time, usually a year. This quite representative definition is notable for its utter neutrality. An unassuming man, the economist makes no value judgments of his fellow citizens' tastes. Whether the customers prefer the Beatles to Bach, football to ballet, *Reader's Digest* to *Commentary,* or *Oh! Calcutta!* to *Othello* is absolutely none of the national-income analyst's professional business. Nor does his private opinion gain force from his professional skills. But this apparently harmless and even ingratiating (scholars ought to be humble!) posture can be shown to sanction some very odd and even ridiculous consequences. Thus, if cigarette smoking were to double, the increase would naturally show up as an expansion of the consumer component of the Gross National Product. And if the corollary were a parallel rise in medical expenditure for the treatment of lung cancer, tuberculosis, heart ailments, and emphysema, this too would be solemnly added to the GNP. If a new pulp mill discharges chemical wastes into a hitherto clean stream, the GNP will go up, not only because of the mill's valuable output but also because other enterprises and municipalities located downstream from the polluter will be compelled to invest in cleansing devices required to return the water to usable condition. Similarly, the GNP rises both with automobile sales and with the increased consumer expenditure for the cleaning of furniture, clothes, lungs, and bodies, necessitated by such purchases.

In residential care the index of per capita cost of maintaining a bed is used and viewed in precisely the same ways as the gross national product as an index of quantitative and qualitative progress. No better device has been devised for the health of those people who require simple explanations, or simple indices of very complex phenomena, or indices which indulge the need to avoid coping with the problem of human costs and values.

In this and previous chapters I have described and discussed developmental aspects and problems of the creation of a setting. If I have made the process seem as if it is an ingeniously planned obstacle course, I have achieved one of my goals. Some settings die early; most continue as legal-administrative entities having quite early lost their capacity to continue to galvanize their participants or to nurture the belief that their superior mission is still achievable. The reasons for this grim picture are many and far more complex than has been recognized. Indeed, the creation of settings as a general problem has hardly been formulated. This has not been a matter of neglect because that would suggest that the problem had been formulated but simply was not regarded as an interesting or important one. It has not been because the creation of settings is an infrequent social phenomenon. Quite the contrary, it is very frequent and involves countless people. We have to look elsewhere for an explanation, and not surprisingly, we look to the nature of tradition that lulls us into confusing what is with what is natural, that routinizes thought and practice, and that constricts the universe of alternatives in thinking and action of which we can become aware. And in the usual way in which tradition opposes new ways of thinking and acting it exposes the unverbalized assumptions without which the tradition would disintegrate. At the same time that tradition serves as a conserving and cautionary influence, a kind of protection both against shifting fashions of the moment and centrifugal volatile social forces, it is also the source of a social vision which defines the future by the shape of the present, and the former turns out to be the mirror image of the latter. Nothing illustrates this as well as our tendency to put up new buildings to house new settings, a tendency which truly ensures that the future will be like the present. We know how to put up buildings and that reinforces the thought that we should put them up. (Because we *can* go to the moon we *should* go there, a leap from capability to action that effectively excludes awareness of the universe of "shoulds.") That they may not be necessary, that they may be disruptive of the creation of the new human setting, that there *are* alternative solutions—these are possibilities tradition makes it hard for us to recognize.

The next section of this book is devoted to an attempt to understand the thinking and actions of leaders of new settings. Here, too, we shall see how tradition and social history are part of the soil out of which the leader's personality and cognitions are formed and through which continuity in the structure and quality of settings is made likely.

CHAPTER 9

Socialization of
the Leader

How one describes and understands the creation of a setting depends on one's relationship to it. One can interview a couple before, during, and after their marriage and the picture that will emerge will differ in certain respects from that given by parents or friends. It is not a question of the validity of the different reports but rather that different vantage points inevitably produce different emphases and reflect different interests, motivations, and goals. The picture one gets of a revolution from its leader or leaders—why and how it was brought about, the forging of new political instrumentalities, the setting of new priorities, the sources of problems—is not the same one obtained from other individual or groups participating in or affected by the events. This was as true in the case of the American Revolution as it was in the French, Russian, Chinese, and Cuban ones. There is no one picture, but there are many related and overlapping ones, and one of the serious consequences of

narrow partisanship is that it is conducive to the belief that there is
one picture, one truth, and all else is heresy.

Just as we do not get identical pictures from those who are
involved in creating a setting, the passage of time permits one to see
the differing pictures in new patterns. Over long periods of time
different generations of historians will tend to see the original pictures
differently. Society does change and these changes provide new ways
of viewing the past. New conceptions lead one to look at previously
overlooked or ignored data and a new picture emerges. From the
smallest to the largest instance of the creation of a setting the picture
changes with vantage point and time. We resist this obvious fact
because of a need to be reassured that the way we have seen and
experienced events is the truth, complete and eternal. We do not
tolerate the mortality of ideas much better than that of life itself,
especially when they are *our* ideas and experience.

In previous chapters I presented a set of ideas stemming from
personal experiences in different roles in different instances of the
creation of a setting. These experiences and ideas led me to seek the
experiences and descriptions of others, less to prove and more to explore some conclusions at which I had arrived. To have attempted to
establish the validity or generality of these ideas would have required
descriptions of a depth and scope that hardly exist. Their relative
scarcity undoubtedly reflects several factors. The first is that those who
create settings are usually people of action for whom the process is a
personal, or a political, or a social affair far more than it is a conception one. That is to say, they do not engage themselves in the
process except in a literally wholehearted way, leaving little or no dispassionate or semidispassionate part of themselves the task of critical
review or conceptualization. These people tend not to write, and when
they do they tend to confuse their picture with the whole picture, their
truth with the whole truth. This confusion, however understandable
it may be, has the effect of obscuring some of the most salient aspects
of the problem—the hidden assumptions remain hidden, the obvious
is not perceived, and the universe of alternative explanations is barely
recognized. Creating a setting is antithetical to productive, dispassionate conceptualizing. Review and reconstruction of the process *for
the sake of learning* is our best hope, and that is extraordinarily difficult for anyone, let alone people of action.[1]

---

[1] Instructive here is the contrast between the reconstructed descriptions
of revolutions by those who participated in them or carried them out and the
characteristics of revolutions as seen by someone who has searchingly examined
and reconstructed the history of many of them. It is not that one description is

The second factor contributing to the scarcity of relevant description and conceptualization is, so to speak, the other side of the coin. Those who are at home in the world of ideas and social theory usually have never experienced the creation of a setting. (They may be married, sometimes several times, but they do not conceive of marriage as the smallest instance of the creation of a setting having certain similarities to the settings they study and about which they theorize.) They are interested in what is, has been, and should be but they themselves have rarely, if ever, put themselves in a situation where the center of action has moved to the creation of what should be, where they will experience the problems as participants rather than as observers, and where theory and practice take on new relationships. The artist and the art critic, the man of action and the man of theory, the participant and the observer—they stand in different relationships to the process and the outcomes. In the case of the creation of settings the men of action know that it is a fantastically complicated affair, more complicated than they ever imagined for reasons they never anticipated, and that the men of ideas and theory know neither the game nor the score. The men of ideas and theory know that most settings go seriously astray, that men of action are devoid of the "right" ideas, and that the major task is how to wed practice to theory. There is some truth to both pictures but neither group can understand this, perhaps because the men of action know they will have to think differently and the men of theory know they will have to act differently.

Perspective at the Top

All of this is by way of approaching a view of the creation of setting that is as unique as it is important--the standpoint of the leader. This is no easy matter to approach or write about because far more is involved than personality characteristics, degree of power, style, and scores of other variables on which leaders differ from other groups as well as among themselves. Most of what we think we know about leaders comes from people who are not leaders. This is not an *argumentum ad hominem* but a caveat that what we think we know may well be every incomplete and misleading. I have had numerous physicians tell me that they did not really comprehend what it meant to be a hospital patient until they themselves had experienced the role.

---

wrong and the other right, although this may be the case in regard to details, but that two are based on different perspectives and data. Edwards' *The Natural History of Revolution* (1970) is most illuminating on this point.

I have known scores of people who considered themselves sophisticated about the theory and practice of psychotherapy until they themselves became patients. I have no doubt that one can learn a good deal about a role one has not experienced but that does not permit us to conclude that what we know is the whole story. This is the case with leaders. Furthermore, we must not assume that the leader who is creating a new setting is, from a purely psychological point of view, in a situation the same as or similar to that of the leader of a chronologically mature setting. The literature in this field almost exclusively concerns leaders in relation to chronologically mature settings. Besides, as Bennis and Slater (1968) put it after stating the major generalizations coming from this literature, they are "majestically useless."

What *is* the standpoint of the leader and how do we determine it? We cannot answer the question without the leader and yet, ironically, what the leader can tell us is both partial and misleading. I am not referring only to the imperfections of memory and the capacity for self-deception (characteristics not peculiar to leaders) but rather to the tendency of leaders to present themselves in socially acceptable ways, in ways that fit with perceived social norms. The issue is identical to that in the matter of how one does scientific research. In the public mind the scientific researcher in his work is a dispassionate, logical, careful, dedicated, lonely individual motivated only by his desire to solve problems, gain new knowledge, and to understand the world better. He "pushes back the frontiers," "is guided only by the canons of his science," and willingly and selflessly gives his life for the greater glory and welfare of man. And where did the public mind get this picture? From the scientists, of course. That the picture is not and has not been true has long been known in the scientific world, so that it came as no surprise when Watson (1968) told it the way it is. As Merton (1969) so well put it:

The stories detailed in *The Double Helix* have evidently gone far to dispel a popular mythology about the complex behavior of scientists. That this response should have occurred among the public at large is not surprising. Embodying as they do some of the prime values of world civilization, scientists have long been placed on pedestals where they may have no wish to be perched—not, at least, the more thoughtful among them. This is not the result of a conspiracy, not even a conspiracy of good will. It is only that men and women of science have long been pictured, through collective acts of piety, as though they were more than human, being deprived in their work of the passions, attitudes, and social ties given to ordinary men. As a result, scientists have been dehumanized in the public mind by being idealized and, on occasion, idolized. Contributing greatly to this centuries-long process of distortion are the pious biographers who, in sapless prose, convert indubitably great men of science into what Augustus de Morgan once described as "monsters of perfection."

In part, too, the imagery of scientists moving coolly, methodically, and unerringly to the results they report may stem from the etiquette that governs the writing of scientific papers. This etiquette, as we know, requires them to be works of vast expurgation, stripping the complex events and behaviors that culminated in the report of everything except their cognitive substance. Compare only the lean, taut, almost laconic, nine-hundred-word article that appeared in *Nature* that momentous April in 1953 with the tangled web of events reported in Watson's forty-thousand-word account of the same discovery [pp. 198–199].[2]

Leaders, like the bulk of humanity, do not find it easy to make their experience public, and what they tend to omit is crucial for understanding the creation of settings. That we understand as well as we do what happened in Nazi Germany is in no small measure due to the fact that Hitler wrote *Mein Kampf,* in which he left no doubt about what his standpoint was. Far from being "majestically useless," what Hitler wrote was a sample of his phenomenology to which, unfortunately, the world paid little heed because its substance was so atypically evil and because so many people possess a stereotype of a political leader that so many political leaders have helped to inculcate —that is, they are astute, knowledgeable, rational individuals who, albeit partisan, strive selflessly for the general welfare and who make decisions in ways and on bases uncontaminated by the personal foibles characteristic of lesser souls. We are not accustomed to political leaders telling us of their hates, prejudices, and private ambitions. Just as children will deny that their parents are sexual beings, we do not like to know that our political leaders are no less human than we are. We know *our* phenomenology and we do not want to believe that those to whom we have entrusted our political fortunes have a similar one.

I hope I do not have to elaborate on the statement that I do not equate leaders in general with Hitler and his standpoint. The point is that Hitler revealed his standpoint to a degree that few leaders reveal theirs. For the most part, when leaders talk of the experience of leadership they talk far more about the role than the person, far more about duties and responsibilities than about the maelstrom of feelings, fantasies, ambitions, conflicts, guilts, and joys (small and large) that are always in the picture. Leaders tell us more about what is denied them than how they indulge themselves and are indulged by others. They give us a job description and not a personal experience. They talk about the importance and pressures of decisions

[2] Merton goes on to give instance after instance illustrating that what Watson described has been true in science for several hundred years.

as if they were engaged in a chess game, and there are some similarities, but they neglect to mention or are ignorant of the phenomenology of the chess player—how he experiences the game, how the experience changes within a game, how it changes over longer periods of time, and what keeps him going and why he sometimes stops.

In *The Last Hurrah* O'Connor tells us more about the phenomenology of a leader than can be found in the bulk of the research literature. Schlessinger (1969) makes the interesting observation that when O'Connor's novel came out a number of critics disparaged it because he had made Skeffington (a seemingly unethical, shrewd, Boss-Tweedish political leader) an attractive, understandable, and even lovable person. We truly like to believe that the phenomenology of our leaders does not reflect the dominant personal themes characteristic of the society. They are supposed to be above self-aggrandizement, lust for power, overweening ambition, hubris, pettiness, anxiety, religious and racial conflicts and prejudice, and even the transient neglect of principle. In part we believe this because this is what leaders tell us, and it is not until we get their unauthorized biographies that we (or later generations) learn otherwise. Then we learn what one sage meant when he said "my God, they do go to the toilet like the rest of us!"

The way we view leaders is the way so many people view psychoanalysts—as qualitatively different people who have overcome the foibles of ordinary people and who possess a degree of reason and control far exceeding that of Olympian Gods (who were *quite* human). Through their own analysis they have been purged and cleansed, at best, and, at worst, given the means permanently to protect them against the dangers of regression, that is, against the fall from a state of grace. That they know better and yet enjoy and reinforce the way they are perceived indicates that the fall has begun, as Freud so well knew. However understandable it may be, the fact remains that analysts (like leaders) do not write about *their* phenomenology, only that of their patients. The omission is neither fortuitous nor justified.

In the minds of most people the name Machiavelli stands for an evil, immoral philosophy and mode of action. This is a view which can be held only by those who have never read his works or by those who pay attention only to those aspects confirming the position with which they started. It is a view by no means generally shared by those who have devoted their scholarly lives to the study of the life and works of Machiavelli (1964). There is no doubt that the disparagement of Machiavelli (the adjective Machiavellian is always used pejoratively) stems primarily from his book *The Prince* in which he describes how a leader should think, feel, and act. (That is, a leader in an Italy torn by internal strife and foreign domination.) Essentially, Machiavelli's descriptions approach the problem of what the phenomenology of a leader is and should be, and it is to his credit that he does not simplify the issues or resort to "majestically useless" generalizations. One may not agree with all that he says or advocates but this should not prevent us from recognizing that he exposed for us the dilemmas, opportunities, and dangers of leadership. He understood, as too few understand today, that leaders are all too human and that unless possessed of certain principles rooted in history their humanity would defeat them and their people. What Freud did for sex Machiavelli did for leadership and there are those who still resent both men for what they did. Freud pioneered in exposing the mind of the child, and the developing picture seemed to some to describe a little monster. Machiavelli addressed himself to the standpoint of the leader and it did not and has not set well with most people. A master novelist such as Edwin O'Connor can make his Skeffington attractive and even lovable. Machiavelli, the founder of political science, could not indulge the luxury of creative fantasy. The novelist can distort reality in order to help us see it better. For Machiavelli there was too much at stake to distort reality as he perceived it.

The creation of a setting looks different from the standpoint of the leader and it is a fateful difference, both for the setting and the leader. Why and how this is so will be the main focus of the remainder of this chapter. Whereas in earlier chapters I described the creation of a setting in terms of developmental "stages" and problems more or less from the standpoint of the outside observer, I shall here retrace some of these steps from the standpoint of leader. The reader may be assured that I am both conscious of and somewhat intimidated by the task of describing the phenomenology of the leader. Although I draw upon my own experiences as well as those of others about their experience of leadership (most of whom never considered making *that* experience public in its complexity and subjectivity), I make no strong claim about the validity of the emerging picture for all situations of leadership. Intuitively I feel that leadership in the context of the creation of a setting will turn out to be different in certain respects from leadership in a chronologically mature setting.

Some readers of this book will not have been in positions of leadership and, hopefully, they will remain aware of this fact because it inevitably sets constraints on how much they can comprehend or agree with. This does not mean, of course, that if the reader should disagree with some of what I shall describe he is wrong and I am right, or that his experience is far more limited than mine. What I do mean is that the awareness that one has not experienced the role of leader should prepare one to be "surprised" when one experiences the role or reads about its phenomenological aspects. For such a reader the task is one of interspersing a set for creative understanding between my words and his prepotent tendency to judge. This will be no less difficult for the reader than it is for the leader in relation to his followers and for them in relation to the leader. The generation gap is only one of the gaps that isolate people from each other.

Before the Beginning

In scores of ways in our society the fantasy that one is a leader is constantly being stimulated and this is much more true for younger than for older people. Books, television, schooling, parents, play—through these media the individual's capacity to fantasy is directed to the role of leader. We are accustomed to saying that ours is a society in which success is too often defined in terms of material gain, but it is easy to overlook how often this gain is seen as achievable by "being on top," by being a leader of people. To the young child, however, the benefits of material gain are secondary to the imagined good he can do for others by virtue of the power that comes with leadership. The sheriff leading his posse to catch the lawbreakers, the conquering general vanquishing his nation's enemies, the chief astronaut leading his group through the dangers of outer space, the quarterback directing his team to a last-second touchdown and victory, the noted scientist working with his colleagues to solve a problem threatening the existence of the human race, the black person who Moses-like leads his people to true freedom and equality—these are but a small sample of heroes who, whatever other characteristics they may possess, are leaders of people. Not only do we allow the child to say he wants someday to be a leader so that he can do great and wonderful things for his fellowman, we reward him for saying it; leadership is synonymous with power and both are "good." The fantasy is uncluttered by any consideration of self-aggrandizement, unwarranted competitiveness, or any other "bad" motivation. The strength of these fantasies comes not only from their inherent pleasure but also from the fact that society says they are permissible and good. I have never heard of a parent who in any way punished a child because he said he wanted to be president.

Somewhere along the line the public expression of the fantasy that he wants to be a leader no longer is as rewarded as before; the values of modesty and a better grasp of reality, among other things, become inhibitory forces. The fantasy remains but it becomes increasingly private and elaborate and its previously unselfish content is now associated with the more "selfish" themes of material gain, personal aggrandizement, domination, competitiveness, and omnipotence. There is almost always clearly sexual content that gets intimately related to the theme of the victorious leader, and this content is the best indicator that leadership is no longer perceived as a selfless role. Two things have happened long before there is any possibility of realistically becoming a leader. The fantasy has become complex, strongly motivating, and deeply personal; and only a small part of it, that which is perceived as socially acceptable, will receive public expression. In other words, the child or adolescent has learned to talk about leadership in the way we are accustomed to hear leaders talk; that is, they are leaders (or seek leadership) because what they know or can do will benefit others. It is not that the public and private aspects contradict each other; it is rather that the public picture we are given and receive is incomplete and misleadingly so. When our Madison Avenue brethren talk of the importance of an individual's or a corporation's public image they are telling us that there is a private image that is best left private.

Needless to say, the leadership fantasy, developed and nurtured over a period of years, centers primarily on the wish-fulfilling, pleasure-giving aspects. The fantasy does not contain, indeed cannot because it is fantasy, the dilemmas, constraints, difficuties, and any other negative but inevitable feature of leadership. The fantasy not only encapsulates "the power and the glory" but it protects the individual from any information that would allow reality to pierce the fantasy. Fantasy is a refuge from the real world far more often than it is a step toward dealing with it.

If reality is not terribly successful in piercing the content of the leadership fantasy, it nevertheless surrounds it with knowledge and issues that indirectly affect it. It does not take the growing individual long to learn that opportunities for leadership are not provided as gifts and that they require striving in the context of competitiveness. One has only to observe a campaign for class officers in a high school to conclude how strong the desire for leadership is in some people and how early they learn and accommodate to their competitiveness and that of others. It would not take an astute observer to note several things: the strength of the personal need to be a leader, the strength of the need to win, the frequency with which means and ends are separated, and the tendency to divide the world into the good guys and bad guys. Becoming a leader, winning, becomes an end itself that relegates the content of the leadership fantasy to the background. The rhetoric, of course, is that the process of striving and winning is but a means to an end that is obviously and compellingly virtuous and selfless. But even at this age those who seek leadership tend to know otherwise. For some the experience is sufficiently distasteful so as to forever extinguish the desire to engage in similar affairs. For others, winners and losers, the experience of being center stage, tasting the delights of attention and glory however transient, adds strength to the leadership fantasy without its content undergoing much change.

Long before adults have the opportunity to be leaders they have lived with a leadership fantasy stimulated and nurtured in countless ways by an external social reality that favors the public expression of the selfless aspects of the fantasy and helps obscure and keep private the needs and satisfactions that are equally personally rewarding and powerful. Whereas custom requires that the leadership fantasy be expressed as an opportunity to do good for others, phenomenologically the individual does not experience his striving only in such virtuous ways. The split between public rhetoric and private thought produces a guilty tension within the individual, aware as he is that what he says and what he thinks, what he wants for others and what he wants for himself, are by no means identical. This guilty tension is initially exacerbated by experiences in which the desire to become a leader runs afoul of means at variance both with private and public conceptions of virtue. This tension, always private, is reduced or eliminated as time goes on, and the most frequent way this comes about is by identifying private needs with public interest. Earlier there was only the interest in others, then the tension between the needs of self and others, and finally the experienced polarities are dissolved into a "compatible identity." It is a resolution that permits the strongest of strivings, that makes becoming a leader alluring and justifiable, that denies any conflict between narcissism and altruism.

What I have described is a process that begins relatively early in life (in our society) and already has a complicated history by the time adulthood is reached. Although I assume that the leadership fantasy is endemic, I also assume that its vicissitudes are many. Let us now narrow our focus to the vicissitudes of leadership in the context of the creation of a setting.

Beginning Context

Whenever I have asked people to choose between the opportunity to become leader of an existing setting or to create a new one, the choice invariably has been the latter. The chief reason for the choice reveals the strength and attraction of the leadership fantasy because people state that creating a setting allows one to mold and divert it to one's purposes unhindered by any existing tradition or practice. Although this answer always refers to socially acceptable, impersonal purposes, it nonetheless implies the role of the artist who chooses *his* material, fashions and refashions it, and ends up with the concrete embodiment of *his* ideas and efforts. When people explain their choice they seem unaware that they are describing the relationship between the leader and the setting as the same as between the artist and his materials, i.e., the setting is passive, malleable and at the service of the leader. The eagerness with which people seek and seize the opportunity to create their setting is not based on experience but is rather a consequence of a leadership fantasy uninfluenced by reality. In the mind of the leader it will be his setting, an expression of him, a fulfillment of his ideas and dreams. If knowledge and reality were the prime determinants of his thinking, he would be amused at the idea that all one has to do is to select people, give them the right thoughts, and everything and everyone will fall into place precisely according to *his* plans. It may be that, far from being amused, some people might be aghast at the Pygmalionlike quality of his fantasy that the setting will be comprised of people dutifully accommodating themselves to the wishes of the leader. To recognize such negative features, however, is difficult as long as the leader sees an identity between his personal purposes and the setting's impersonal ones.

After World War II when there was pressure on England to give India its independence, Winston Churchill, the Prime Minister, is supposed to have said: "I did not seek to be Prime Minister in order to preside over the dissolution of the British Empire." These words reflect a psychology typical of many leaders who approach the creation of a setting. "I did not seek to be a leader in order to help others create what *they* want and to do what *they* want to do. For me to think otherwise, or for others to expect otherwise, would be to deny the nature of leadership and to rob it of all of its excitement and rewards." Most leaders with whom I have talked readily agreed that this attitude characterized their thinking, particularly the first time they assumed a leadership role.[8] However, they are quick to point out

---

[8] It was in the course of these discussions that I realized that the attitude I described was much more strongly and clearly stated by leaders who created a new setting than by those who became leaders of chronologically mature settings. The former were quite aware that the setting they had created had a deeply personal significance that was qualitatively different from what they had

that this attitude is accompanied by the knowledge that the people the leader chooses are each unique in their backgrounds, ideas, and personality and that it is folly to assume that, like toys, they can be easily adapted to the wishes of the leader. When this point was pursued it often emerged that its significance for the leader was in how to get "his" people to identify with his ideas and goals.

From the standpoint of the leader the projected new setting is viewed and experienced in a truly personal way in which the near and far-future picture contains the fulfillment of his personal and intellectual strivings. It is a happy picture precisely because it is so fulfilling of his individual wishes. It is a picture in which the happiness of others stems from their willing and complete identity with the leader's strivings. It is psychologically quite similar to the way parents fantasy the future of their first-born: he or she will be an independent and a unique individual possessing strivings and characteristics completely in accord with what is in the minds of the parents.

What would truly be surprising would be if the thinking of the leader were otherwise than what I have described, just as it would be surprising if new parents thought of the future of their first-born in other ways. There is, at this point, nothing inherently "wrong" in the leader's way of thinking; this is at a point when there is no setting, the leader is alone with his thoughts, and contemplation about the new setting is heavily influenced by a history of strivings and fantasies. Of course the leader is not living in a fantasy world. A good deal of his planning and initial actions are rooted in reality. The element of fantasy primarily has to do with his picture of a happy organizational family in agreement from the beginning with the leader's values, goals, and styles. In addition, it is a picture based on the assumption that the happiness of his family can be developed and maintained regardless of its relationships with other settings that are not so happy or that feel themselves in competition with or adversely affected by the new setting. The leader can no more envision his people being dissatisfied than he can envision this for himself.

Fateful for the leader and the projected setting is how this attitude changes as the setting is created and he confronts real people and the realities of our society The stronger the attitude the more difficult it is for the leader to accept a compromise between what he and others want and how he and others think. Since the attitude is no

previously experienced as leaders of settings that antedated them. One of these people put it this way: "It's like the difference in experience between writing your own book and translating or editing someone else's. Both can be gratifying, but they are psychologically quite different."

less than the expression of what the leader wants for himself from the setting, the fact that what others· will want for themselves will always be somewhat different, and may frequently be quite different, presents deeply personal issues to the leader. Does the setting exist *only* for the development of the leader or does it also exist for the development of "his" people? The leader does not question the obligation he feels to be consistent with his values and goals. But to what extent, if any, should he limit himself in order to help others in the realization of their goals? The leader is aware of the satisfactions he wants to derive from his activities but can he gain satisfaction from helping others derive satisfaction from their activities, particularly when these activities are in some ways not central to those of the leader? Is the independence which he requires for himself something he can recognize and willingly support in others? Is he like the parent who cannot tolerate, let alone support, his child's strivings for independence, or is he like the parent who exercises control at the same time that he recognizes the dangers and seeks a compromise that would not be self-defeating for all concerned? How these questions are resolved illuminates the socialization process of the leader. No less than the young child the leader is faced with a conflict between internal needs and external demands, and leaders no less than young children vary considerably in how these tensions are experienced and resolved.

Facing Reality

When the new setting will be an outgrowth of and an addition to an existing organization of settings, the socialization of the leader may begin long before he forms his core group. He quickly learns that there are rules, guidelines, and traditions, some of which he comes to feel are not appropriate to his plans. This may happen even though the leader was part of this existing organization of settings and had experienced no conflict with its procedures and their rationale. But as soon as he is chosen as the leader and becomes absorbed in planning *his* setting, there appears in his thinking a dichotomy between I and they, mine and theirs, and my plans and their plans, my needs and their needs. Quite early the leader possesses and "owns" the new setting in a way that implicitly assumes a conflict between it (him) and the "outside" world. This psychological ownership, to some degree at least and frequently to a large degree, changes the perception of the leader of the existing organization. It would be more accurate to say that this psychological ownership *is* a change in the relation of the leader to the existing organization of settings as well as to the world. This psychological process is far from being peculiar to the leader. Frequently, he is given the mission to create something new; he was not chosen to duplicate what exists but rather to do something distinctive and thereby change the way the existing organization of settings is perceived. In fact, he may even be encouraged to depart from the existing organizational rationale in order to fulfill the mission. He may be treated differently and given special privileges, all of which reinforce the leader's sense of separateness, protectiveness, and ownership. But those who have chosen the leader and given him special privileges do not intend that by their actions they will have created problems in the existing organization of settings. They may be truly interested in the new setting and may be eager to eliminate obstacles to its creation and distinctiveness, but they do not ordinarily perceive that the very fact that a new setting is being created is something to which the existing organization is not indifferent—just as the newborn's older sibling is not neutral and for many of the same reasons. With or without special privileges, the leader of a new setting is viewed by others in a variety of ways: with good wishes on the one extreme to death wishes on the other. Either extreme reinforces the leader's tendency to view the new setting in the most personal and protective terms.

Only in fantasy is the world organized so that one can proceed as one wishes. In the real world, as the leader quickly learns, there are obstacles, even before he gets to the point of forming his core group. Some leaders react to the obstacles primarily in moral terms, viewing each obstacle as requiring a compromise inimical to their plans and values. They are so identified with the new setting that each obstacle is not viewed as a problem for compromise but as a moral battle in which the good is pitted against the forces of disillusionment and evil. There are times when such a stance is justified. In my experience, however, the stance usually stems from a pathetic and unjustified ignorance of the nature and history of the existing organization of settings, an ignorance that makes it very easy to divide the world into the good guys and the bad guys. The ignorance can also reflect the view that since the leader is a morally superior person with a superior mission, those who place obstacles in his path do so only with the basest of motives. It would be among the more interesting statistics if we had an estimate of the number of leaders of new settings who leave before the setting is created or, even more interesting, the number who desired to leave at the presetting point. My prediction is that the numer is not small.

If some leaders are victims of fantasy, there are others who are victims of reality. That is to say, there are leaders who deal with obstacles by compromises which will effectively rob the new setting of much of its projected distinctiveness. This, of course, is not done deliberately. How this comes about long intrigued me and my understanding of the process was helped when I found myself asking a question about an individual who had just been chosen as leader to create a new setting within the context of an existing organization of settings. The question was: Why did he cry when he was chosen?[4] This person's explanation was that for years he had dreamed of and strived for this kind of opportunity and that being chosen was an overwhelming experience reflected in the tears of joy. What became clear as time went on was that having reached the top, he tended to view each obstacle presented by the existing organization of settings in a way that avoided conflict and produced compromises that were far more in keeping with the goals of others than with his own. It was as if he was afraid that if he fought vigorously for his ideas he would alienate those who chose him, namely, those who could remove him. He was so understanding of and accommodating to those who chose him—he was *so* realistic—that long before the setting was created it had been robbed of much of whatever chance it had of being innovative. When I discussed this with him several years later, he said forthrightly: "Between the time I was offered and accepted the position, a matter of several days, pretty much all that I thought about was how wonderful it would be to implement *my* ideas, to build an organization from the ground up. It didn't dawn on me for a second to present my ideas in detail or to get in writing what I would need and when. They wanted *me,* and I wanted *it.* What was there to discuss? If I had come down from the clouds and talked details, it might have been a different story. I might have seen that maybe I should not have taken the position. I doubt it. I wanted the job too much." Although his remarks suggest that he had been aware of his tendency to accede too readily to "reality," it was my impression that it was an awareness that he had managed previously to suppress to the level of a "still small voice." His awareness with me seemed more a function of my persistent but sympathetic questioning than it did of the usual content of his introspections. He was, like

---

[4] I have seen this phenomenon three times over the years, although I have been told that it is not all that rare. Grown men are not supposed to cry in public. Far more frequent is the euphoric reaction: exultation, ebullience, undiluted joy. It was not until I pursued the question about the crying that I understood that both crying and exultation can set in motion the same kind of process.

most of us, the kind of person who resolved dissonant thoughts in a way that made life tolerable, however unfortunate the consequences might be in the distant future.

Although it is an oversimplified dichotomy, a distinction can be made between two types of leaders: those who seek leadership primarily for reasons of power, privilege, and attention, and those for whom the new setting will reflect certain substantive ideas. It is the difference between a person (for example, John Dewey) who creates a new school in order to implement and evaluate a set of ideas that are related to an existing body of knowledge and someone who creates a school in order to make money; he may be providing a valuable or needed service, but that is a means to more personal ends. It is also the difference between someone who creates a new setting for old people because of an interest in the substantive problems of aging and someone who does it because it may lead, in his view, to even more important positions of leadership. It is the difference between someone who seeks to be the leader of a new setting (arising from an existing organization of settings) because of the purposes of the new setting and someone for whom the new setting is an opportunity to demonstrate his administrative skills. These contrasting motives exist in varying degrees in all leaders. There are no pure types. The point is that the extremes psychologically approach the creation of a setting in rather different ways. The leader whose interests are primarily substantive tends to assume that those who chose him have similar interests or, if they do not, that they are committed to making it possible for the distinctive features of the new setting to be implemented unhindered by prevailing customs in the existing organization of settings. Basically, this leader is uninterested in the existing organization of settings. For him reality is the present and the future and history is unimportant. Since he regards the new setting as distinctive and superior, he may regard the existing organization with a condencension that further justifies in his mind the unimportance of history and custom. His selfless devotion to substantive matters, a characteristic that may have been important in choosing him as a leader, frequently leads him to expect that the existing organization of settings is at best similarly devoted to the cause or, at worst, neutral or uninterested. It is extremely difficult for him to entertain the possibility that there are people who do not wish him or his new setting well. When, as is inevitably the case, this type of leader begins to experience what to him are obstacles placed in his way by the existing organization, he tends not to look upon it kindly and views accommodation or compromise as inherently immoral. For example, if he has developed a concrete plan about the composition and level of his core group and learns that in some way they conflict with prevailing custom, his prepotent tendency is to criticize custom and to seek ways of changing it for his purposes. He may even succeed, unaware that in resorting to the use of power and influence (most strong in this "honeymoon phase") he has changed the relation between the new and existing settings. The point, of course, is *not* to suggest that the leader should not fight for his ideas and plans and that he should readily compromise in the face of conflict but rather that in doing so this type of leader who tends quickly to transform each issue into a moral one does not comprehend the antecedents and consequences of the conflict. His ahistorical stance may help win battles in the present and prepare the basis for future wars. (I have seen instances where there was no future war because the initial battles were lost and the leader left the scene—or was asked to leave.) Such a leader may take public pride in his absorption with and devotion to substantive matters and view anyone and anything that distracts him from these matters as positive proof of the alarming degree of stupidity in this world.[5]

The other type of leader tends to be far more attuned to, and usually far more knowledgeable about, the existing organization of settings. It is, in fact, his stock and trade. He seeks to know how things work, what the prevailing customs are, and the formal and informal sources of power. He prides himself on his practicality, his capacity to distinguish between the possible and the impossible, and the importance of compromise. Far from being ahistorical, he is interested in how things *were* and how they led up to the present. Although he identifies himself with the purposes of the new setting, and no less than the other type of leader he wants it to be successful, its purposes are less central to his being than are considerations of power and status. This in no way implies that he is hypocritical because frequently he was chosen more because of his "administrative skills" and less because of his expertise with the substantive purposes of the setting. And by administrative skills is meant, among other things, that he is "realistically" sensitive to the problems of power, status, and

---

[5] As I shall try to make clear later, it does not follow that such a leader will not create a setting which by most standards will be successful, namely, he creates the conditions that allow his people to fulfill the purposes of the setting in ways which enhance their own development. This does happen, but in my experience these conditions exist for a limited period of time, namely, until that point at which changes in the phenomenology of the leader and the strength of forces in the existing organization interact to change qualitatively the atmosphere of the setting.

intersetting relationships. For this type of leader obstacles are pre-
potently experienced as political rather than moral issues, as threats to
his personal position rather than to purposes of the setting, as interpersonal issues rather than conceptual ones. The phenomenology of
this type of leader facilitates compromise and accommodation, frequently to the point where the innovative purpose of the setting has
begun to be undermined. Whereas the first kind of leader may be a
victim of his denial and ignorance of reality, the second type falls
victim to a too easy acquiescence to perceived reality. Although both
are committed to the setting in very different ways, the consequence
for the failure of the setting may be the same.

     The strong desire to become a leader, the exultation in becom-
ing one, and the satisfactions that begin to accrue in being one occupy
prominent places in the leader's thinking. They help produce a kind
of euphoric expansiveness affecting both emotional and intellectual
spheres, namely, he feels and acts in the present and begins to plan for
the future as if he were on the near side of utopia. In these very early
days his feeling and thinking take on some of the characteristics of
the child's leadership fantasy: he will do great and good things, he
will love and be loved, and he will give and get. This is particularly
true of first-time leaders, and it makes surprisingly little difference if
the projected new setting is modest in size and significance. But there
is one important difference from the earlier leadership fantasy: a sub-
dued fear about inadequacy and possible failure. By ordinary standards the leader may be a very self-confident person who has little
doubt that he can create a successful setting. This self-confidence may
be matched by the opinion of others that he is highly effective and
self-assured and destined for "success." Nevertheless, he harbors occasional thoughts that are not so optimistic, but they are and must be
kept private. These occasional thoughts are related, of course, to possibilities in the real world. That these thoughts may bear the stamp of
an individual's personality goes without saying. But in addition, and
from earliest days, an equally potent source of these thoughts is comprised of three related types of knowledge: that he is dependent on
many kinds of people and settings to get to the point where his setting
exists, that he can make errors, and that the world does not exist
primarily to help him fulfill his plans. In the earliest days these may
be the most fleeting of thoughts receiving no strong external support,
but sooner or later the new leader realizes that there is or will be a
permanent disjunction between fantasy and reality. This lesson in the
socialization of the leader is less significant for him and the setting than
the conditions in which it is learned. Under favorable conditions and

with luck, the lesson may be learned slowly and without feelings of defeat or bitterness toward others. He may feel disappointment (one does not give up a compelling fantasy without some scars) but not to the point where he feels he has lost self-respect or abandoned hope that the projected setting will approximate its stated purposes.

The leaders of new settings with whom I have talked describe a more gloomy picture. A number of them report that from the time they became the leader and began to form their core group they were inwardly traumatized by the disjunctions between the words and deeds of others, between promised and actual time schedules, between promised and delivered resources, between the initial atmosphere of enthusiasm and agreement and the appearance of minor and major obstacles by minor and major figures. The most bitter of these leaders were those whose setting arose from an existing organization of settings either steeped in tradition (for instance, a university) or of a size and complexity that defied easy comprehension (for instance, city, state, or federal government). One leader described it this way: "My education began the first week. I spent the better part of two days visiting offices and filling out forms to make sure *I* was on board. I could not get an appointment with the president until the end of the week. It took me a day to find out how to get a secretary only to learn that somebody else would do that for me. When I found out the salary schedule for secretaries my heart skipped a beat. People were friendly but disinterested. No one was putting out for me. I had lunch each day with a different person, on my initiative. In subtle but unmistakable ways I was told that there were a bunch of bastards running around and some of them might not like me—in fact two of them had wanted my job. I felt uneasy, questioned myself about how I had misperceived the atmosphere, and I was angry and scared. I came floating in on a silver cloud and when I hit the ground, I was hurt. It took me two months before I was able to hire my first staff member. If you could speak to my wife, she'd tell you I was hell to live with. I was." Later in our discussion after he described in detail the obstacle course he encountered, I asked him if he had thoughts of leaving at that time. "Leave? Of course. There were times when I wanted to say that unless they cut the red tape and started to really help me get things started, and told certain people to stay the hell out of my way, I would leave. But how could I? I had moved my family, and the kids were in a new school. Where would I go? How would it be regarded if I quit so soon? I *had* to stick it out. I am glad I did. It was quite an education." This was the same person who said: "One of the things I learned is that it is a lot better to take over a deteriorated situation and try to build it up to fit your ideas. You can only go up. When you start from scratch, you can only go downhill. You start off with dreams, and you quickly learn that your dream will be no more than that. A dream."

These kinds of expressions can distort too easily the picture one gets of leaders in this presetting stage. For one thing it is sometimes the case that the leader's view of this period is colored by later events which serve as a basis for reviewing the beginning. More important, however, in judging these reports is the fact that at the same time that the leader senses that all is not going smoothly, that there is trouble ahead, and that he may fail, his thinking is dominated by hope, planning, and the feeling of personal satisfaction that he is in the position he has long wanted. These positive feelings usually "contain" and dilute the effects of the dysphoric feelings. However, some leaders were emphatic that a sense of failure gripped them from the earliest days, and that dominant in their minds was hostility in two directions: toward themselves for being naive or stupid fools and toward others who, because of their stupidity or cupidity, interfered with the leader's actions.

If the reader has the impression that creating a setting is for the leader, even in its earliest stages, a kind of obstacle course which some do not complete and no one completes unscarred, he has no good basis for being surprised. The process of socialization, be it of a leader or a young child, is always a series of encounters, each of which has internal and external aspects in some conflict with each other. The degree of conflict and the resulting form of accommodation is in part a function of the gulf between the nature of the external social reality, on the one hand, and the strength, relevance, and content of internal conceptions, fantasy, and goals on the other hand. The leader may dream about complete success, but he comes to know that such perfection is not possible. He may want the world to bend to his needs but he comes to know the difference between learning and bending. He may imagine himself as the ever smooth, unruffled, creator and developer patiently and wisely defining and pointing to success, but he comes to experience internal turmoil, doubt, and the poignancy of being in error.

The pace and quality of the socialization process depends on many factors, and it is never a function only of internal or only of external factors. It is understandable but misleading if leaders tend to view the process as primarily caused by external factors. It is no less understandable and misleading if external forces view the process as caused by characteristics of the leader. On numerous occasions I have been at meetings in existing settings (part of a larger organization) in which a new setting was being created. It took me a number of years and a good deal of reflection to realize that when the new setting was brought up at these meetings because it presented a problem to the existing setting, the cause of the problem was frequently attributed to the new leader, namely, his ideas and style.[6] If he was different, if he was more cooperative, if he was less competitive, there would be no problem. It was difficult, indeed impossible, for them to see themselves as part of a socializing force, as one of a number of such forces. The cause was simplistically seen as external.

I have been talking about an early stage in the creation of a setting, from the time the leader has been chosen until he begins to form his core group. This time interval can vary greatly from a matter of weeks to over a year. It is a time popularly known as the "honeymoon period," and I have heard scores of leaders refer to it in this way and plan their moves to take advantage of it. Implied in the concept of the honeymoon period are all the major points I have made: In the beginning there is a level of hope, love, enthusiasm, excitement, and joy not likely to be experienced again; it is a prelude to a time when reality is demanding and must be dealt with; accommodating to this reality and trying to get reality in turn to be accommodating produce problems and conflict that change conceptions of self and others. But what many leaders learn in addition is what over the ages many couples have learned: The honeymoon period is not always an undiluted joy; it can contain the beginnings of later serious problems, and in extreme cases it can be followed quickly by termination of the relationship. The discrepancy between dream and reality has been too much for some couples and some leaders.

[6] I have never talked to a leader of a new setting who did not say that he had underestimated how long it would take for the setting to become operational. Some of the leaders said that they had vastly underestimated how long it would take and that this had adverse personal and organizational consequences. This underestimation was more understandable in those leaders who were relatively young, had had no previous substantial leadership experience except of an informal variety, or had little intellectual interest in or conceptual knowledge of organization. It was less understandable in those leaders with (sometimes) vast experience and conceptual knowledge. I attribute this primarily to two factors: they had never created a new setting, and their previous experience and accustomed ways of thinking and conceptualizing were inadequate to the new task: more than inadequate, they were a source of interference. The second factor resides in that initial burst of hope, excitement, and enthusiasm that screens out the social and organizational realities in which the new setting will arise. The opportunity to realize a long standing dream has mischievous effects in one's time perspective as well as how one perceives the world.

I must remind the reader that from the standpoint of the leader this early period is usually *remembered* as the best time. It is only when leaders are forced to think more systematically about this early period that they recall events and processes that had been only dimly noted but later turned out to be significant. Some leaders reported that they were blissfully ignorant of, or had grossly misinterpreted, some early events, the significance of which was learned only at a later time. What struck me in these discussions was the attitude of many leaders toward the past of the setting. By and large their remembered past is neither extensive nor usable. That is to say, they are so rooted in the present and pulled by the future that the significance and use of the past play a surprisingly small role in their phenomenology. This is not because leaders as a group may be a different breed (although in some respects they may be), but that even in the earliest period, when he has not yet formed his core group, the leader views each day far less as a function of yesterday and far more as a determinant of tomorrow. The possibilities of tomorrow are far more attractive than the constraints of yesterday. The leader of a new setting is like the artist who is gripped by a conception or internal picture which he decides he must translate into a palpable reality: There is a burst of activity that fills the present, and every change in that present is measured by an internal conception that defines the future. The past fades away in the rush to the future. When something goes wrong, the past may reemerge and be examined but first there must be something wrong, something that breaks the continuity between present and future, something that intrudes, and then perhaps the past is confronted. But it is at the point of confrontation that the similarity between the artist and leader tends to break down because while the former will tend to "remake" the past (he can literally start all over again) the latter does not have such an option and, more important, his faith in the future tends to persuade him that whatever is wrong in the present will be cured by the future. In short, in these earliest days the leader tends to underestimate the strength of negative events by projecting a healing quality to a benevolent future. This Gesellian view of development, in which what happens in the present is seen as normative and will be supplanted by newer and more mature processes, is one that is congenital to leaders in this early period. It makes the present seem far less threatening and the future far more pleasant. (As we shall see in a later chapter, the point at which the leader no longer can continue to believe that the future will be positively different than the present and the past is one of the most fateful points in the life of the leader and the setting.)

There will be readers who will feel that I am painting too gloomy a picture of the creation of a setting, that I make it seem too much as if the world conspires against the leader to turn his dreams into nightmares, and that it even robs him of the joys of the honeymoon period. As someone once said to me: "You make it sound as if creating a setting is one of the most complicated obstacle courses devised by man or God!" *It is.* Failure to understand this before the setting is created is the single most important factor contributing to the failure of settings. This failure is not restricted to leaders but is far more general, and it has several sources, not the least of which are the incomplete and misleading ways in which new settings are described (when they are described, and that is relatively rare). How many times does one read in the newspaper that a new setting is to be created, that a leader has been appointed, and, as a result, a problem will be solved or a social need will be met? These are not usually tepid announcements; they are loud fanfares heralding innovation and progress. The formal opening of the setting may get quite a public play, and its ongoing program may even get into national media. Why should a reader disbelieve what he is told, particularly if the new setting fits in with his beliefs and goals? How many times are these announcements and descriptions at best a valid statement of *hope?* How many times do our media searchingly contrast projected image with internal workings?

During the 1960s, when new settings were being created at a bewildering rate, I and my colleagues had numerous opportunities to observe the discrepancy between reality and projected image (Sarason and others, 1966; Sarason, 1971). What I observed is what Smith and Keith (1971) have described in some detail. They had the opportunity to spend a year in a new school in which a variety of innovative ideas were to be implemented. The school got quite a public play. As Smith (1971) reported:

The public image presented was not the reality that we observed from our day-to-day observations. The facade was written up in local newspapers and in national periodicals (on two occasions). Literally hundreds of people like us were in and out of the school on one- or two-day visits to find out what it was like and they got the facade—the party line. They did not get the realities as we did as we sat in the school. . . .

My summary comment, in a sense, is the only quantitative data in the monograph that we published, and it occurs in the first part, in a discussion of the faculty at the end of the first year, the turnover. Out of some twenty or twenty-two faculty members at the end of the first year, only 8 returned for the second year and only two for the third. At the end of the first year the superintendent took a leave of absence. The principal left in the middle of the semester during the second year. I don't know the base rates for the phenomenon of a principal's leaving his school in February or March, but there is little question that it is highly unusual.

It probably is highly unusual for a new principal to leave his school in February or March, but in my experience it is not that unusual for a principal *to want* to leave. What Smith and Keith report, I regard as the fairly frequent fate of new settings. Once this becomes recognized and the creation of new settings begins to receive the systematic study and clinical attention that the consulting industry (in and out of the university) gives to chronologically mature, malfunctioning settings, readers will not have to be convinced that creating a setting is and has to be an obstacle course true of the beginning as it is of any subsequent period. If readers will not have to be convinced, it will also mean that leaders will tend to come to the creation of settings with more wisdom and a more heightened consciousness about what they are undertaking. It will be a wisdom that acknowledges reality without sacrificing dreaming, that distinguishes and confronts the conflicts between the realities of social organization and the needs of individuals, that does not confuse what people are with what one wants them to be, that does not confuse what people are with what they always will or have to be, and that does not leave to a benevolent future the task of healing present unpleasantries. Finally, it will be a wisdom that will not tolerate the fantasy of perfection. But more of this later. Let us continue the creation of a setting from the standpoint of the leader by examining how he forms his core group.

Forming Core Group

When the new setting is an outgrowth of an existing organization of settings, there are many constraints on the leader's selection of a core group. Salaries, titles, length of experience, fringe benefits, and moving expenses are some of the things about which there may be standards and over which the leader has little control. Far from confronting these mundane matters in his fantasies, he has tended to project a future in which he can attract precisely the kinds of people he will need. I have seen instances in universities where a person has had the opportunity to create a new department or institute for which there was a good deal of financial backing, a situation which led the leader into believing that "he had it made" in the sense that he would be able to hire others in the way he had been. Not in a single instance did the leader attract all the people he wanted, and in most instances he got far less than he had hoped. Sometimes this was because existing standards and practices could not be changed or circumvented; most times it was because the quality of person the leader wanted was precisely the person who was likely already to have satisfactory working conditions. The enthusiasm with which the leader comes to the new setting, the high hopes he has for it, and the deeply personal significance the venture has for him contributes to his tendency to expect others to respond like himself to the ideas of the setting and to his overlooking those existing factors which will make attracting others far from a routine task. Like a person in love, the leader has trouble anticipating that others may view him as overevaluating his love object, namely, the projected setting.

I have never met a leader of a new setting who said he was out to hire second rate or even second choice staff. When he is chosen as leader, he convinces himself that he will seek and attract the best; at that point the possibility that he may have to be satisfied with less than the best cannot intrude into his thinking. Of course, when leaders talk publicly about their core group they talk as if each member was the most fortunate and sterling choice a leader ever made. Privately, they know and admit otherwise. The point is that choosing a core group inevitably is a disappointing experience for the leader. The disappointment may be tolerable; it may also be catastrophic to the leader, especially if it is apparent to him that the core group he is forming is not the group who is likely to help him achieve the setting's purposes. The more disappointment the leader experiences in forming his core group, the more likely that this has been preceded by disappointments stemming from eye-opening experiences with the existing organization of settings. This is not necessarily because one causes the other but rather that one feeds on the other. Regardless of their sources, the speed and strength with which the leadership fantasy is exposed as a fantasy are among the most important determinants of the phenomenology of the leader and the fate of the setting.

But now let us come to a deceptively simple question: On what bases can a leader attract the members of his core group. When a leader tries to sell the new setting, what is he asking the prospective core member to buy? I deliberately use the words *buy* and *sell* because they convey well the phenomenology of the two people, namely, each has something he wants and something he can give. In practice it turns out to be a rather unequal bargaining situation because, more often than not, it is the leader who does most of the selling. When the prospective core member is someone the leader wants (regardless of reason), he will describe the setting's prospects in glowing terms, emphasize the opportunities for growth, and indicate how much the core member has to contribute. Even when the prospective core member desperately wants to join the setting, he must not reveal this. He must be wooed and whatever wooing he does must be subtle and indirect. Just as the young woman is supposed to help her young man pop the question of marriage, the prospective core member has a similar task. The leader, like the young man, must make the best case he can and, as a consequence, whatever negative features or ambiguities may exist in relation to the setting are bypassed or only alluded to. It is not infrequent that the leader is quite aware that he is suppressing information and that he is not painting reality the way it is, and he may justify this on two counts: that the present difficulties will somehow be surmounted; and that if this prospective core member can be attracted to the setting, the difficulties will be diluted. In attracting his core group the leader is usually quite aware that he feels he cannot put all his cards on the table; indeed, he feels, he must not. What the leader is not aware of is that he has started a process that will produce two of his most thorny problems: the sense of aloneness and interpersonal distance, and the ubiquitous "faulty communication." This should not be taken to mean that these are avoidable problems because they are not. What I am suggesting is that the problems begin early and they need not be as destructive as they usually are. It is not that the leader causes these problems, but rather that they are frequent consequences of the dynamics usually at work in the formation of the core group. There can be no question that the leader plays the most crucial role. He is the most visible and influential model of how one should think and talk, what one should talk about, how one deals with reality, and how one anticipates and deals with problems. And the kind of model he is already is reflected and tested in the formation of his core group, a fact which many leaders ignore and which many core group members learn about later.

If the basis on which the leader attracts his core group emphasizes the opportunities the new setting offers *them* in fulfilling *their* ambitions, how does that square with the ambitions of the leader who did not strive to be a leader in order primarily to help others realize their goals? The platitudinous answer is that there should be no conflict between the ambitions of both, which is to say they need each other, and although they may have different ambitions, it should not mean that they have conflicting ones. Although the leader and the core group member may think this way, it usually turns out to be otherwise. In his desire to attract the core member, and in the core member's desire to be attracted in ways fulfilling of his ambitions, they arrive at an "understanding" not based on any explicit discussion

of personal and professional ambitions. More accurately, their discussion does not explicitly and directly deal with possible conflicts of
ambitions. The fact is that the new setting is for the leader a deeply
personal affair precisely because he sees it as the opportunity to fulfill
his dreams, as a way of satisfying a variety of needs and ambitions, as
a way of realizing concretely what had been pictured only in his
imagination. His fantasy of the new setting was populated by only
one "real" person, the leader; all other actors were his creation and
their actions were in accord with his needs and ambitions. The leader's
attitude is not a selfless one. He may temporarily see or present himself as selfless, and others may see him that way, but as the setting
begins to evolve, the leader's thinking and actions primarily revolve
around his ideas and goals. To say that the leader is not selfless is
not to say that he is selfish. The point is that he sought to become the
leader and was chosen as such because he stood for something which
would appropriately shape the new setting. He is expected to choose
people who will help him, and it is expected that if they "come
aboard," it is because there is a "captain" who decides directions. I
have heard leaders of new settings proudly use naval language in the
context of forming their core group, unaware of the ambiguous basis
upon which the relationships have been started.

The theater provides some of the best examples of the problems
in forming a core group. It is not unusual that even before the first
performance, core members have left, leaders have been deposed, and
the whole production consigned to a warehouse. Tradition and the
mythology of the theater have it that artists are a breed apart: sensitive, high strung, narcissistically ambitious, and with a marked tendency to confuse fantasy with reality. If the general public accepts this
tradition, it is because they believe what theater people tell them and
because when similar things happen in other types of new settings, they
do not receive public attention. The similarities far outweigh the differences.

Like most new settings the creation of a new production for
the theater begins in a glow of love, hope, and enthusiasm. The
producer has purchased a playwright's work, he usually then hires a
director, and then comes the casting. Although all this is accompanied
by legal contracts specifying rights, obligations, and financial arrangements (in themselves indicators of what has happened again and
again in the creation of such settings), togetherness and excitement
characterize the beginning. In purchasing the work the producer has
assured the playwright that the spirit and letter of his literary creation
will be observed. In attracting the director he has assured him that
there will be no interference with artistic matters. And so it goes. If

stars are sought for leading roles, no doubt is left in their minds that they are crucial for ultimate success. Each person is satisfied that his goals will be achieved. Everyone assumes that there is agreement on goals. That each person may have read the play differently, that each may have a different conception of what changes and additions he would be permitted to make, and that each may have a different conception of what or who the leader is are possibilities lost in a haze of imagined self-fulfillment. In wooing his director, the producer (leader)' usually does not take up the problem of what one does with a recalcitrant star, a stubborn playwright to whom changing a scene is a form of prostitution, or the need for more money in the event new scenery is needed. The producer may have definite ideas about these and other matters but they do not meaningfully surface at this time. The producer will have assured his stars that precisely because of their particular abilities and styles, no one will require them to do anything out of character. Besides, he may also have told them that in light of the director he has attracted, the star need not worry about unreasonable demands. In short, the producer proceeds as if he is a selfless person dedicated only to the fulfillment of the dreams of others. He makes no claim to artistic expertise or to seeking of glory. Of course he will admit he wants to make a profit, but that should not conflict with artistic success so why talk about it?

There are times when the stature of the director and his arrangements with the producer are such that he is essentially the leader. Or, as in the case of Shaw's English production of Pygmalion (Huggett, 1969), the playwright, producer, and director are one person. Huggett's sidesplitting account illustrates a number of points. For example, and not surprisingly, there was never any doubt in Shaw's mind about how the play should be staged and acted. In fact, the world premiere of *Pygmalion* was in a foreign country, and its English production was delayed several years because Shaw did not think it could be appropriately staged, acted, and appreciated in England. To say that Shaw knew what he wanted is to understate the truth. How he wooed Mrs. Patrick Campbell for the role of Eliza Doolittle! Mrs. Campbell very much wanted the role but refused to come to terms unless she could chooose *her* Higgins. She wanted no part of Robert Loraine who was Shaw's choice. The imp in Shaw knew how to woo Mrs. Campbell:

I don't want anything put before me. I am an artist and don't understand finance. I want my Liza and I want my Higgins. If you are unkind about them I shall sit down and cry until I get them. I won't choose between them. I must have my Liza and no other Liza. There is no other Liza and there can be no other Liza. I wrote the play to have my Liza. And I must have a proper Higgins for my Liza. I won't listen to reason: I will sit there and howl. I can howl for twenty years, getting louder and louder all the time. . . . I won't be offered the Best and then refused poor Bobby, who is the best. I will have a better if you can find him, because nobody is good enough for my Liza. . . . I don't want to force anybody into anything. I only want to see my play with my Liza properly supported in it; and until I get that I want to do nothing but yell. . . .

I have gone through my card index and could name you twenty far better Higginses than any you have thought of; but they are none of them good enough; I'd rather die than see you dragged down to second class by them: I'd as soon ask you to wear a contract dress at £3.4s.2d. If you won't have Loraine then we must wait until somebody else whom you will have comes to the front and proves his mettle. And I shall cry, cry, cry all the time, and there will be a great wave of public feeling against you for your cruelty. And I will write such a play for Lena Ashwell, my dear Lena who really loves me. So there! (P. 34–35)

Choosing and wooing Sir Tree for the role of Professor Higgins were done more subtly and with consumate skill by Shaw. When the core group was finally formed, happiness reigned.

In one respect *Pygmalion* is atypical for the behavior of the leader: Shaw, neither publicly nor privately, viewed himself as selfless, as no more than a vehicle for enhancing the glory and accomplishments of two stars. What Shaw did not bargain for was that that was precisely the way Mrs. Campbell and Sir Tree viewed Shaw. He had made them feel absolutely crucial; they were doing him a favor. In Chapter 4 I very briefly described the war that took place up until opening night. Huggett states that if Shaw had known what he was getting into by having two stars who viewed a leader like Shaw as someone who would benefit from their radiance, he would not have gone ahead. This conclusion seems more true for the two stars than for Shaw who, realist that he was, knew what he was up against and would have to do. Indeed, Huggett seems unaware that he describes Shaw as relishing the whole affair. Shaw knew more about what was going to happen than either of his stars. He judged them far better than they did him. Shaw felt he could pull it off, namely, that he could stage a performance that would meet his standards as well as meet the needs of his stars. He was temporarily successful. When Shaw left for vacation after the opening, Mrs. Campbell and Sir Tree slowly but steadily changed the production according to their styles. What he had won by virtue of his authority and authoritarianism was lost in his absence, exposing the vulnerability of the setting.

As a leader, Shaw had advantages that very few leaders of new settings have. For one thing, Shaw was a self-appointed leader with the material resources to create the setting. He was beholden only to himself. Furthermore, no one, least of all Shaw, could seriously question his knowledge of the theater or his accomplishments in it. In becoming a leader Shaw did not have to prove himself to himself and, being Shaw, he did not have a strong need to prove himself to others. When he became the leader, he was already a world known literary figure and personality. Shaw may have had questions about the significance of history for his destiny; he had no question about the significance of Shaw for history. In a real sense Shaw had little or nothing to lose. If he failed, it would be a wound but not a deep one. These advantages are in startling contrast to the situation in which most leaders of new settings find themselves. In most instances the leader has a great deal to lose, and failure, partial or complete, is a deep and everlasting wound. For most leaders the opportunity to create a new setting is the vehicle for acclaim and status in their particular worlds; it is not, as in the case of Shaw, another link in a chain of acclaimed accomplishments. Unlike Shaw who could and did wait until the right conditions existed, most leaders of new settings feel tremendous internal and external pressure to get started. Shaw formed his core group on the basis of wooing and cajolery and in this impish way he left no doubt who was leader and why. If the two stars did not fully understand this, it was as much due to their monumental egos as to Shaw's initial meeting of his conception of his role, and, in my opinion, his insight about what would (and would have to) happen. Unlike a leader who attracts his core group far more on the basis of what he will provide them than on what they will provide him, usually an unwilling form of self-deception, Shaw was discerningly more candid. Finally, precisely because the beginning of a new setting is suffused with feelings of love, excitement, and zeal, and because the leader operates under a variety of constraints, and because he usually does not have an excess of self-confidence, in addition to the fact that he views his future as depending on the success of the setting, emerging differences of opinion and practice tend to be avoided rather than confronted. Shaw was a confronter par excellence and he understood when others confronted him. He fought for his ideas and he seemed to respect those who fought for theirs. As a leader he was a model of directness. Love was not enough, and too much was at stake to buy continued peace at the expense of dangerous compromise! To bury conflict when it meant burying the promise of the setting was not a possibility for Shaw. Unlike most leaders Shaw not only confronted issues quickly, he tolerated considerable confrontation from others.

Some would argue that all I am saying is that most leaders of new settings are not George Bernard Shaw. This is a specious argument because it rests primarily on the assumption that whatever happened was due to Shaw's personality, as if his ideas, planning, foresight, and strategy were secondary factors. For example, his refusal to accede to Mrs. Campbell's demand that she choose her leading man not only reflected his understanding of Mrs. Campbell (how she would choose and why) but the disastrous consequences that could follow. Shaw evaluated each step on the basis of principles and goals, and he did not disregard the prehistory of his core group. Shaw was a moralist and a calculator who, behind the facade of impish clown and iconoclast, approached his task in dead serious fashion. To explain what happened as a function of his personality is to miss the point that he had a highly sophisticated conception of the complexities and dangers in the task ahead. One does not have to be a Shaw to grasp the conceptions. One does not have to be a Shaw to be clear about whether the conditions are appropriate for creating the setting, and, if they are not, to pass up the opportunity. One does not have to be a Shaw to distinguish between the demands of the needs and goals of a setting, on the one hand, and one's desire to be loved, on the other hand. And one does not have to be a Shaw to view conflict not as an evil but as an opportunity for learning and change; not as a sign of failure and therefore to be avoided and suppressed but as an inevitable occurrence that must be confronted.

The personality argument prevents recognition of the fact that Shaw was a leader in the context of certain condtions and that under other conditions he might have been a miserable failure. Shaw's insistence on certain conditions reflected, I think, his knowledge of himself, and it is not hard to imagine what would have happened if he had acceded to the demands of Mrs. Campbell and Sir Tree. Or if there was a producer to whom Shaw was responsible! Shaw's tenure would have been short-lived, and there probably would have been no production. Shaw knew himself and the conditions he needed, unlike many leaders who, faced with an alluring opportunity to create a setting, succumb to the temptation of greater glory without confronting who and what they are. Because there are mountains to be climbed, does not mean that everyone should or could climb them. I do not know how many people turn down the opportunity to create a setting, but in light of what happens to many new settings one can only conclude that the number of turn downs should be higher than it is.

How successful was Shaw as a leader? From the standpoint of public reaction the production was successful and Shaw also seemed to be satisfied. But what about the fact that when Shaw left for vacation, he started to receive messages that his core group was regressing to their accustomed style of acting and improvisation? That his stars had little love for each other and even less for Shaw? Was the temporary success achieved in ways that, as in the case of many new settings, lead to deterioration? Did Shaw err in not anticipating what would happen in his absence? Did Shaw make the mistake of getting his way to an extent which unduly frustrated his stars' accustomed ways of performing, which is to say, did he satisfy his needs and ideas at their expense? At the very least these questions suggest that Shaw as leader was not without fault, and they require us to look further into the bases of the relationship between the leader and his core group.

Obligations of Leadership

What obligation, if any, should a leader have to help his core members develop those interests, skills, and understandings that are distinctively theirs, and, related to that, to what extent, if any, should he be prepared to accommodate to their distinctive styles? The question can be put in a somewhat different way: To what extent should a core member prevent the situation in which he does not experience the sense of an autonomous existence, namely, he feels that the leader constrains and inhibits his need for and sense of productive development? The failure to pose this issue clearly is one of the most potent sources of conflict in the relationship between the leader and core members. In attracting a core member, no leader will describe a relationship in which the core member exists for the sole purposes of the leader, and no core member would be attracted if he feels that the leader will determine the shape and quality of his existence. Both the leader and the core member would readily agree that it is wrong for one person to use another as if he were a thing. They would further agree that no two people are alike and that differences are inevitable and should be respected. With this much agreement, they would say, the crucial factor is the degree of agreement about goals. If two people can agree on verbally stated values and goals, the major ingredients for a successful relationship are present. Why should there be problems? Why, like in other forms of human marriage, should there be a falling out? One answer is that agreement on values and goals does not inform one about how to implement values and reach goals. Because two people agree on a statement detailing the values of individual freedom in human dignity does not mean they will agree when these values are concretely tested. Numerous times I have had core members say about the leader: He says one thing and does another. He talks about democratic procedure but acts unilaterally. And the damned thing is that when he talks he is sincere but he doesn't see the contradictions between what he says and does. Equally numerous are the times leaders have said similar things about core members. The point is not that the chances are staggeringly high that people who agree on values and goals will find themselves in disagreement in practice, but rather that the leader and the core member begin their relationship as if the chances are low or nil. The inevitable is ignored or given the silent treatment, and until the conflict surfaces with disruptive effects, the chief vehicle for dealing with it is similar to the way it was dealt with initially: silently, indirectly, or by denial.

The second answer is one I have already dealt with and it stems from that complex of factors leading to the choice of the leader for the new setting. Put most briefly: From the standpoint of the leader the opportunity to be a leader is to realize a dream, the setting is *his* in the most personal and pervasive way, and his feelings of worth are perceived by him as depending on the success of the setting. These are a combination of factors which make it extraordinarily difficult for the leader to give any degree of equality, let alone precedence, to the distinctive needs and goals of a core member. But, someone could argue, do not the needs and goals of the leader take precedence over those of a core member? Does not his unique responsibility require him to give precedence to what he thinks has to be done, even though this adversely affects a core member? There are two replies. I could answer affirmatively to both questions if the possibilities they describe had been anticipated and discussed, and there was agreement in principle about how they would be handled. The fact of the matter is that when the leader is seeking to attract a core member, these possibilities are almost never discussed. If they were, the two people might see that their values were not as identical as they thought.[7] Regardless of type of setting, it is not at all difficult for a leader and prospective core member to imagine and discuss possibilities in which they might be in conflict.

The second reply is that when by virtue of giving precedence

---

[7] In Chapter Four, I give an example of how a leader and prospective core member can predict and should discuss possible and predictable sources of disagreement involving their rights and status.

to his needs and goals the leader denies the core member the agreed upon right to some degree of autonomous activity, frustrates the sense of productive development, he is being inconsistent with his own values. Here again, some would argue, does not the general welfare of the setting as the leader perceives it take precedence even at the expense of an individual? Aren't there times when for the general welfare the leader may have to be inconsistent with his values? These arguments can be accepted only if it is recognized that a leader is seen as justified in treating someone as a thing, namely, as a possession whose shape and direction are determined by outside forces. Furthermore, these arguments are about *an* individual, whereas my observations indicate that in many settings, indeed most settings, one of the most frequent complaints of core members is that they have little or no opportunity to experience the sense of autonomy, learning, and growth. The tendency for the leader to give precedence to his needs and goals, to see them as identical with the success of the setting, adversely instead of positively affects the general welfare of the setting. In reality, the issue rarely concerns the leader and one individual but many individuals in the setting. To often the leader's use of the principle of the general welfare is based on a most distorted conception of how "his" people view the principle.

And so we are back to the question: Does a setting exist primarily for others (in terms of a service or product) or for the growth and learning of those who populate it? To most people it is obvious that the justification of a setting is in whatever form of service it renders to others, and it is equally obvious to them that a leader has to be governed by this criterion. However else leaders may differ from most people, they agree on the obvious, unaware that the nature of the justification works against the general welfare. I have seen leaders who said that coequal with any other value and goal was the quality of life within the new setting, and I had no reason to question their intentions or sincerity, but as soon as the first real test arose, the fragility of the intent became clear. Leaders who pose these questions of value are rare, and rarer yet are those who when the crunch comes, when the moment of truth arrives, can be consistent with what they have said they believed.

By the time the leader has chosen his core group he is aware that he has learned and perhaps has changed a great deal. Whereas at the beginning he could dream, savor possibilities, indulge the joys of a new-found status and power, and see the future as cloudless, he now knows that he has become (or must become) a "realist," that he has become *dependent* on those whom he has attracted, that the surrounding world tends to be indifferent, or demanding, or hostile to his setting, that the problems of today and tomorrow crowd out the future, that there are no isolated problems but rather that everything is potentially related to everything else, and that there is in him a tension between what is and what may be and between his needs and ideas and those of others. Whereas at the beginning he had no reason to doubt that he was master of his fate and captain of his soul, he now knows that although he feels he is still captain of his soul, he is not the certain master of his fate. The strength of the poignant feelings which accompany this learning will vary, of course, with a variety of prehistorical, before-the-beginning, and personal factors. Some leaders do not survive and leave even before a core group is formed. Most leaders survive, none unscathed. But, as we shall see in the next chapter, as the setting differentiates, the tensions within the leader, however minimal they have been, build up in ways and around issues that force him to ask: What am I? What do I want to be? How do I want to live?

CHAPTER 10

Leader's Sense of Privacy and Superiority

A leader newly chosen for a chronologically mature setting knows that there is an existing structure, stated goals, and people (all of whom may be unknown to him). He may have plans to make a variety of changes, but even if the shape of his plans is vague, he knows that he must familiarize himself with what exists and how it works. There is much he has to learn, and the directions in which he proceeds are in large part a function of what exists. However much he may not like what exists, it nevertheless has the function of giving him direction. He is, so to speak, told what to think about.

The leader of a new setting is in a different psychological situation. He must forge a structure, state goals, and choose a staff. Far from his thinking being directed primarily by an existing structure, its direction is largely due to internal factors. The major spur to thinking and action is from within. Granted that there are always internal and external factors, he does not have the comfort of any existing external structure to absorb his thinking and energy. Everything which makes the creation of a setting seem magnetic and attractive, to build something according to one's desires and images, can become a source of anxiety precisely because the ambiguity of the external situation requires an unusual degree of internal clarity and direction, and these are not frequently found characteristics. Even where these characteristics are present, the inevitable ambiguity of what is and will be, the clear sense of becoming without an equally clear sense of *what* one is becoming, can produce reactions ranging from a quiet unease to unmistakable anxiety. These are disquieting reactions because they were not expected and they conflict with the leader's conception of how a leader should feel. They remain private, but if they are strong reactions, they are always reflected indirectly in some form of action.

An additional factor that contributes to the leader's unease, its presence and strength, is the knowledge that the consequences of his actions are frequently surprising and more complex than he thought. This knowledge, of course, is not unique with leaders, but what gives it significance is the feeling that what is at stake is no less than the dreams and adequacy of the leader, although to an impartial observer, the different actions of the leader may appear to be unrelated because they bear on the setting which he experiences as a reflection of himself. He feels and is responsible for the setting, and whatever happens to it, good or bad, happens to him. Psychologically it is his "baby" and, like every good parent, he cannot be indifferent to his offspring. The similarities between the first-time parent and the leader of a new setting are many and genuine, but I wish here only to emphasize the anxiety both experience about the well-being of the offspring. The difference is that the parent frequently does not hide the strength of his anxiety whereas the leader does.

The creation of a setting is a process, the characteristics of which always engender some uneasiness and anxiety in the leader. Their strength can be exacerbated by the variety of factors described in previous chapters, and, paradoxically, one of these factors is the tendency of the leader to keep these feelings private, to view them as dissonant with his conception of what a leader is. Such a conception is identical to that of most people, who confuse outward appearance with internal states. It is a form of mutual deception which characterizes the relationship between the leader and his core group.

The leadership fantasy which I discussed in the previous chapter helps us to understand the leader's prepotent tendency to keep significant feelings private. In the fantasy's more primitive or undifferentiated form the leader is omnipotent, all-conquering, and selfless. His motives are simple and clear, and there is an identity of feelings and goals between the leader and his people. In its more differentiated form the leader becomes aware that his motives have a public and private component and that the latter is tinged with guilt because its contents are in such contrast not only to the more primitive fantasy but to the leader's perception of how others want him to be, namely, selfless, rational, and quite in control of his destiny. In striving to become a leader he learns that he must be publicly modest about the strength of his strivings and competitiveness but not necessarily about his talents and accomplishments. He learns that one does not publicly proclaim one's self-doubts even though one is quite aware that he has them. The leadership fantasy and the social process in our society whereby one becomes a leader insure that the leader will be and will remain a private individual, particularly in regard to thoughts and feelings reflecting anxiety or self-doubt.

I have never talked to a leader who denied such private feelings or who enjoyed living with them. The longer a person had been a leader the more he seemed to resent the necessity to act as if he was adequate to whatever came his way. The knowledge that he is acting is tinged with guilt, but its strength is diluted or controlled by the attitude: That's the way it is and has to be, and that is the price you pay for being a leader. To give other people strength requires that you appear strong, even though inside you do not feel that way. This attitude, as we shall see later, is complex and important, but there is one aspect of it that is crucially relevant for the attempt to understand the strength of the tendency to keep self-doubt private. From the earliest leadership fantasies and through the process leading to the time when he indeed becomes a leader, the leader regards himself as a superior being, superior, that is, to whatever group he leads. The basis for this feeling of superiority may be seen by the leader as residing in superior wisdom, or strength, or values, or vision, or some other attribute. But in whatever it resides, it is the basis on which the leader sees himself as a superior person. This is particularly true in the case of leaders of new settings where shape and direction are reflections of the leader. When the leader talks of *my* setting, he is saying, and he knows that he is saying, something that no one else in it can say. This feeling, compounded of uniqueness and superiority, may extend far beyond his setting to include all other similar settings. He may not conquer the world but he will *show* it. Leaders ordinarily do not proclaim their feelings of superiority if only because it is not considered socially acceptable to do so. In fact, there are leaders who vehemently deny that they possess such feelings. They would agree that they may be the most important person in the setting, but they do not pursue the significances of viewing themselves in such a unique way.

The feeling of superiority and the desire to be so viewed make it extraordinarily difficult for a leader to make public whatever doubts and anxieties he may experience about himself in relation to the setting. An additional factor is that the sense of superiority unwittingly leads to viewing others in the setting as if they must be protected against a stern reality which they could not comprehend, would find upsetting, and about which they would not know how to act precisely because they are not leaders. This factor is further reinforced when there is a discernible age difference between the leader and his group, in which case the tendency to regard others as immature, dependent, and in need of protection is very much in the forefront of the leader's mind.

There are instructive similarities between the leader and the classroom teacher who each year creates a setting with children. In numerous ways the pupils regard the teacher, and the teacher regards himself, as a superior being. A number of years ago we did a study in which observers were placed in classrooms every day for the first month of school (Sarason, 1971). One of the purposes of the study was to study "the constitution" of the classroom: the ways in which the rules governing the classroom were developed. The task of the observers was to record any statement by teacher and child that was relevant to constitutional issues.

The results were quite clear: (1) The constitution was invariably determined by the teacher. No teacher ever discussed why a constitution was necessary. (2) The teacher never solicited the opinions and feelings of any pupil about a constitutional question. (3) In three of the classrooms the rules of the game were verbalized by the end of the first week of school. In two others the rules were clear by the end of the month. In one it was never clear what the constitution was. (4) Except for the one chaotic classroom neither children nor teachers evidenced any discomfort with the content of constitutions—it was as if everyone agreed that this is the way things are and should be. (5) In all instances constitutional issues involved what children could or could not, should or should not, do. The issue of what a teacher could or could not, should or should not do, never arose.

On a number of occasions I have presented these findings to groups of teachers with the question: How do we explain them? In every group the question produced silence. In one group a teacher responded in a way that I think verbalized what most teachers were thinking: What is there to explain? I would then follow my initial question with another question: What do we have to assume to be true about children and teachers in order to justify these findings? These discussions were by no means easy or pleasant, and understandably so, if only because the teachers had never been called upon to make explicit the conceptions and values upon which these practices were based. But what were some of the assumptions that teachers could, after prolonged discussion, recognize and state? (1) Teacher knows best. (2) Children cannot participate constructively in the development of a classroom constitution. (3) Children want and expect the teacher to determine the rules of the game. (4) Children are not interested in constitutional issues. (5) Children should be governed by what a teacher thinks is right or wrong, but a teacher should not be governed by what children think is right or wrong. (6) The ethics of adults are obviously different from and superior to the ethics of children. (7) Children should not be given responsibility for something they cannot handle or for which they are not accountable. (8) If constitutional issues were handled differently, chaos might result.

If one does not make these assumptions, which is to say that one thinks differently about what children are and can do, one is very likely to think differently about what the role of the teacher might be. In this connection it is instructive to note that as I pursued the issues with the groups of teachers, and the assumptions could be clearly verbalized, many of the teachers found themselves disagreeing with assumptions they themselves recognized as underlying their classroom behavior. Equally as instructive was the awareness on the part of a few that if one changed one's assumptions, one would have to change the character of one's role, and this was strange and upsetting, as indeed it should be, because they realized that life in the classroom for them and the children would become different [pp. 175–177].

That which characterizes the thinking of teachers about children is found in leaders in regard to their "pupils." There was one other finding in that study which deserves special emphasis: No observer recorded that a teacher said, "I don't know" or in any way verbalized any form of self-doubt in relation to anything he did. This is similar to what I have observed in leaders and has similar origins, namely, a conception of leadership based on some perceived superiority that would evaporate if internal doubts, anxieties, or any meaningful kind of inadequacy were verbalized to people seen as unable to cope with such expressions.

What I have been saying about the leader has to be viewed on a time continuum. In the early life of a setting when everyone's enthusiasm and sense of mission are at their highest, and there is an exhilarating feeling of togetherness, it is easy for the leader to manage internal unease and the consequences of a self-imposed separateness. It is easy to overlook that this is a time when the leader and his core group spend a great deal of time together, more time than they will in the future when each core member will have formed his subsetting and be occupied with its tasks and problems. It is also a time when there is no question in anyone's mind that the leader knows the most about what the setting should and will be. The leader not only can contain the expression of internal doubts, but his need to express them is minimal or nonexistent. Given his conception of leadership and sense of superiority, it is impossible for him to recognize that he has structured his relationships in decidedly unequal ways: he expects to be trusted without limit but he cannot give such trust to others; he regards himself as a source of control against the inadequacies of others, but he cannot regard others as playing that role for him; the privacy of feelings, ideas, and doubts about the setting, which he feels he must maintain, he views in others as detrimental to the setting. This self-imposed privacy is one of the most potent sources of the ubiquitous communication problem and it is present in the early stages when the leader and his core group cannot even envision such a problem.

The setting grows larger and becomes more differentiated. The amount of face-to-face contact between the leader and his core group noticeably lessens. The leader's knowledge of what is going on is increasingly obtained second or third hand. The number of problems increases within the setting and between this and other settings. The leader must make decisions and resolve issues and conflicts, and usually not on direct experience. There is usually one formal meeting each week between the leader and his core group to serve two purposes: to bring important issues to the attention of the leader, and to provide an opportunity for the leader to state and clarify policy and direction and to bring up problems. There are many more meetings between the leader and each of his core group, and these individual meetings usually center on problems which either the leader or core member cannot bring themselves to raise and discuss in a group or which they regard on some basis as not belonging to the larger group. The problems vary considerably: criticism of the core member, competitiveness among core members, discussion of policy, or some noninterpersonal question bearing on the core member's sphere of responsibility. These individual meetings are far more informal, personal, and productive of decisions than the group meeting. The substance of these individual meetings may (and usually does) have little overlap with that of the group meeting.

The consequences of these developments for the leader's privacy are three-fold. First, he becomes increasingly aware that his group meetings are interpersonally unsatisfying and unproductive, rituals by which conflict-arousing problems cannot surface except in indirect ways, that is, he cannot put on the table what he knows generates conflicts in the ways it generates conflict. Second, the knowledge that his core group is not homogeneous in personality, effectiveness, and in their feelings for each other not only restricts what he can talk about with each but also engenders feelings of anger and inadequacy that the situation is not otherwise. Third, the leader is quite aware that he feels differently toward each core member but that he must not show that he likes some more than others, that he respects some more than others, and that he trusts some more than others.[1] Each of these consequences rarely takes place in insulation from the others, and the result is that the leader is constantly being reminded of the contrast beween his leadership fantasy and his realities, between his utopian dreams and what actually exists. If he tends to blame himself or others (or both), it is still a "narcissistic wound" he keeps to himself. Publicly he may proclaim his satisfaction about the existing state of affairs or adopt a seemingly realistic and candid stance about how long it takes a fledging setting to shake down to productive stability, but inwardly he knows that he and the setting are falling short of his goals. The severity of these private feelings will vary with a number of factors, for example, the degree of strife within the setting; pressure and criticism from external sources; and unforeseen events like budget cuts, illnesses, and even death of a core member.[2] An additional factor,

---

[1] It is almost always the case that the leader has one core member whom he trusts above all others and to whom he will confide *aspects* of his private thoughts and concerns. The leader considers this a special relationship and he is aware that it serves the function of lessening, albeit temporarily, his sense of aloneness. It is testimony to the strength of the leader's belief in the necessity to appear to feel and act similarly to every core member that he is usually unaware that this special relationship is obvious to all and is a source of difficulty within the core group. The leader is like the classroom teacher (or parent) who publicly proclaims equal affection for and interest in all pupils. The pupils, of course, know otherwise, and this knowledge creates in some a feeling of rejection at the same time they try to build their own special relationship with the teacher.

[2] In creating a new setting and forming his core group the leader implicitly assumes that what he is doing is taking place in an orderly and predictable world, namely, that he and his core members will remain healthy and alive. His future planning is based on this assumption and when events prove otherwise (such as a serious illness or death of a core member) he and others can become disorganized. Illness and death are not very frequent in new settings. A current example of what can happen when new settings are based on the assumption that planning for catastrophe is only for those with morbid inclinations can be seen in numerous new settings that have gone out of existence or whose purposes have been defeated by a national economic recession. My sensi-

of course, is the relationship between the validity of the leader's diagnosis and the appropriateness of the treatment of the situation (about
which I will say more later). Suffice it to say that any solution that
depends on the leader's use of power to legislate change bespeaks of
a diagnosis that is as invalid as it is frequent.

Some leaders like to talk about their loneliness as if it inheres
in the role to which they are willing, self-sacrificing slaves. Other
leaders verbalize the loneliness as a necessary consequence of their
conception of effective leaderhip: The leader cannot be open about
many of his attitudes and feelings, besides which, they go on to say,
their staff would not want him to be. On the contrary, the argument
goes, their staff wants protection and direction from the leader, and
not his dilemmas and problems, personal or otherwise. The leader is
supposed to lead and not to upset, to keep morale high and not to
discourage, to be strong and contained rather than weak and revealing.
The more I observed and talked to leaders the more it became clear
that they viewed themselves as classroom teachers do in relation to
their pupils. And it is not fortuitous that one of the most frequent and
poignant problems of the classroom teacher is the feeling of loneliness,
despite the fact that he is in one of the most densely populated settings
on this earth (Sarason and others, 1966; Sarason, 1971, p. 105).[8]

One source of the leader's loneliness is universal; each human
being knows there is a part of him that he cannot or will not publicly
articulate and that even when he tries to do so words are inadequate
vehicles for reflecting the concreteness and nuances of experiences.
The other major source does not inhere in the role of leaders, but in
his conception of what a leader is or should be, and this conception
always involves considerations of mutuality: What he expects of and
gives to others and what others should expect and give to him. The
substance of this mutuality (and its underlying values) are rarely very
clear in the leader's mind and, consequently, he cannot make it clear
for others except as their experience with him helps them come to

---

tivity to this point is largely due to the fact that my formative years were in
the catastrophic depression of the thirties, as a result of which I have always
operated on the assumption that sources of money (particularly governmental)
could disappear quickly. Inwardly, I would envy those who started new settings
as if to question the stability of sources of money was to lack courage or to be a
victim of anxious pessimism.

[8] In our 1966 book there is a chapter "Teaching Is A Lonely Profession."
To our surprise this chapter elicited from teachers more spontaneous comments
than to any other chapter, and common to all the comments was, "How did
you people know so well how teachers feel?" It was relatively simple. We each
spent a great deal of time in classrooms and with teachers, and once we got to
know and trust each other, the private feelings were publicly verbalized.

some understanding of his conception of mutuality. The point is that the leader's conception of his role prevents him from making his view of mutuality explicit in structuring his relations with his core group and, equally important, there is no way whereby it can remain a focus of their continuing relationships. There are no agreed upon "constitutional" arrangements which require the leader and his group to deal with the issue and problems of mutuality. How can such arrangements be developed, how can the very idea of a constitution arise if the leader's conception of mutuality rests on his perceived necessity for a unique degree of privacy as well as on a perceived superiority? What this conception does is to prevent the leader from recognizing something which he may well have experienced in other settings, and that is that any difficulty which arises in the early life of a setting always has impact on the relationship between the leader and his core group. Regardless of the source or nature of the difficulty, its effects are perceived and felt by all, personally and professionally. If there are no agreed upon means by which this surfaces and can be dealt with, everyone becomes more private, and individual goals begin to take precedence over those of the setting. This is a familiar consequence, and its major root is the leader's conception of leadership, namely, a model of thinking and acting that produces for him and others a sense of privacy that quickly becomes a feeling of alienation. The fact that leaders speak so eloquently about *their* loneliness reflects, among other things, their inability to conceive of the loneliness of those around them or to conceive of his and their loneliness as an outgrowth of implicit rules about how they should live with each other.

I have seen new settings die at a very early age, and I have seen even more settings fail rather early in their stated purposes, even though as an entity they survived. In every instance a contributing factor was some form of strife between the leader and some core members that had never been able to surface in a way that could have led to resolution or compromise. This statement should not be taken to mean that the cause of failure was purely interpersonal, but rather that the inevitable problems encountered by the new settings affected and transformed relationships, the effects of which could not be dealt with except in self-defeating, indirect kinds of ways. The rate of change in a new setting (like that in a newborn infant) is greater than it ever will be again, and this is mirrored in the transformations of relationships within the setting. This holds for the leader in relation to the core group as well as for each core member in relation to every other one. If the consequences of this rate of change and transformation of relationships are not clearly recognized and dealt with, and they usually are not, substantive and interpersonal differences become fused and confused, rumor and gossip become major vehicles of communication, and the loneliness of everyone is heightened.

Let us look at what happens when a leader conceived of leadership in a very different way. In Chapter Six, I presented in some detail the creation of a Residential Youth Center (Goldenberg, 1971). The reader will recall that this center was for hard-core, inner-city youth, that Goldenberg was its leader and the sole professionally trained person, and that the rest of staff (the core group) were so-called indigenous people. The core of Goldenberg's thinking is best given in his own words:

> If there was anything we had learned (and learned well) from our involvement in different organizations, it was that one could be certain of only one thing: There would always be problems. The problems would vary in content and intensity, but they would always be there, always pose some present or potential danger to the organization, and always threaten the goals of the setting and the welfare of its people. To say that one could always count on the existence of problems seems to be little more than a glimpse of the obvious. Our past experiences, however, had left us with a residue of unhappy examples of just how rarely this apparent truism is taken seriously enough to be translated into, or lead to the development of, the kinds of organizational vehicles that might enable a setting to deal with its problems in nonself-defeating ways. To be aware —however dimly, perhaps even unconsciously—of the inevitability of problems is one thing; to anticipate their occurrence and to plan or devise internal mechanisms for handling them is quite another. . . .
>
> The anticipation of problems and the realization that we would have to develop a vehicle for dealing with them were only a few of the reasons for turning to sensitivity training, for wanting to "institutionalize" it, and for making it a formal and permanent part of the organization's structure. We were acutely aware of the fact that problems would never be "solved," but we hoped to be able to use these sessions to deal with our problems in a preventive, albeit tertiary preventive, manner. Institutionalized sensitivity training was to be used as a mechanism, indigenous to the setting, through which we could deal with our problems openly and regularly, and hope that by so doing they would be kept from interferring unduly with the goals of the program or the individual and collective growth of the staff [pp. 160–161].

Goldenberg goes on to criticize the usual way in which sensitivity training is used in organizations and why it was inapplicable to the purposes of the Residential Youth Center—a critique as incisive as it is brief. He then describes several types of meetings which became a weekly routine. We are indebted to Goldenberg and his publisher for the fact that verbatim transcripts (by an experienced court reporter) of these types of meetings are in the book. Obtaining these transcripts was an expensive affair, but they were considered an essential means whereby each individual could review what had gone in the meetings. Their presence in the book reveals to the reader an amazing degree of conceptual and interpersonal depth, in marked contrast to the usual superficial and stultifying staff meetings in most settings.

What permitted Goldenberg to give of himself in the same way and degree he expected of his core group? That is to say, what made it possible for him to suggest and agree to constitutional principles that were mutually binding? He makes clear that he did not approach these meetings without anxiety because of the likelihood that he would have to talk about himself, or others would, in terms that would expose his shortcomings. In the most simple terms: He was agreeing to something that could only reduce the extent of his privacy. This, of course, was what he was asking his core group to do. There was more pressure on him than on others because he was the leader and if he was perceived as not abiding by the rules, it was going to make it difficult for others to do so.

Goldenberg emphasized that from the time he knew he was to be the leader of a new setting his thinking was dominated by the knowledge that there would always be problems and that means had to be developed and institutionalized that would not make it easy for anyone to forget that fact. As he makes clear, the driving force behind this knowledge was his experience in and observations of other settings where, at best, lip service was paid to this knowledge and, at worst, the principle was denied. (They would never deny the inevitability of death and taxes!) As important as this first principle was the knowledge that the most serious problems involved personality *and* conceptual differences among those in the settings. Goldenberg did not make the error of seeing differences and conflicts in purely personality terms. Unconfronted conflicts in the realm of ideas and values can destroy a setting no less effectively than so-called personality clashes. In my experience they are more destructive, and wherever I have been given explanations in terms of personality, it seemed obvious to me that it obscured conceptual differences. It is far easier *to see* personality differences than *to hear* the conceptual ones. Goldenberg knew this, and this, I believe, explains his discomfort with the phrase sensitivity session or training in which personality factors dominate or obscure conceptual ones.

What Goldenberg was able to do was also a consequence of a

set of considerations I discussed earlier (Chapter Six): Coequal with any other goal of the setting, indeed necessary to maximize achieving any other goal, was creating an atmosphere and conditions that would allow staff to change and develop. That is to say, if the young residents of the center were to alter their ways of thinking and acting, those who were to help them do so would themselves have to experience the sense of change. If youth was to learn to live productively with each other and the staff, it was crucial that the staff learn how to live with each other. These were not tasks to be learned by a certain time; they were ever present or recurring tasks requiring constant vigilance and new solutions. The amount of time that Goldenberg and his staff devoted to their development is explicable only on the basis of the principle that their learning and changing were as important as those of whom they served. The techniques employed are less important than the considerations that gave rise to them because these considerations were as explicitly applicable to the leader as to others. Techniques may and should vary; there is not only one way in which basic principles can be reflected in practice.

Many leaders would probably subscribe to the principle that the learning and development of the leader and his staff are coequal with any other of the setting's goals. This is rarely reflected in practice, however, because it conflicts with the leader's sense of superiority and his perceived need for privacy. In practice he is far more willing to apply the principle *to* his staff than to himself *with* his staff. After all, for the staff *and* the leader to be bound by this principle makes it it very likely that the leader's privacy and sense of superiority will be challenged and changed. What allowed Goldenberg to take the risks? Was it that, far from having a sense of superiority, he was quite the opposite and instituted the procedures as a kind of compensation? Or was he an idealistic missionary-type, all too familiar today, whose approach to reality is distorted by a confusion between what is and what should be? As I can personally attest by virtue of having worked with him and observed the development of youth center, Goldenberg was a singularly self-confident young man, quite clear about his assets and liabilities, absorbed (if not obsessed) with the mammoth obstacles preventing consistency between values and action, and, crucial for our present discussion, confident that he could handle himself in and derive benefits from any situation in which he willingly placed himself. Furthermore, he was doing this with people he had chosen, trusted, and each of whom he felt had a legitimate basis to feel superior to him, just as he had a basis to feel that way toward each of them. There was never any doubt in his or anyone else's mind about who was the leader, and this was as true when he left the setting as when he began it. The fact that from the very beginning it was explicit that Goldenberg would be the leader for six months, and the identity of his successor was also known, was an additional stimulus to instituting procedures which would give everyone a chance to think through and adapt to the consequences of such a plan.

Many of Goldenberg's characteristics are shared by other leaders. Self-confident, a sense of superiority, courageous, hard-working, inspiring—many leaders have demonstrated that they possess these characteristics. Where Goldenberg differed from most leaders was not in personality characteristics but in his conception of what a setting was for and what this meant for how a leader and his group had to be with each other, what this required for forging appropriate porcedures, and how all of this had to reflect one of the most obvious facts about social reality: there are and will always be problems.

Regardless of his conception of leadership, the leader inevitably remains a private being like everyone else. (As Goldenberg makes clear in his diary, there was much of him that remained private.) The degree and content of a leader's privacy become a problem to the extent that he has not built into the new setting procedures which serve as external controls against all the errors to which private thought and feeling are subject. If these controls do not exist for him, he drastically limits the extent to which he can serve as a control for others. When in a new setting its problems begin to be explained as due to a lack of communication, it is a clear sign that at the very beginning the issue of mutuality was probably never squarely faced.

Challenge, Novelty, and Boredom

The opportunity to create a new setting engenders a complex of feelings not well described by overworked language. As soon as one resorts to language the process of dissection of experience begins, and although this is both inevitable and valuable, it fractionates that which is whole and the ensuing array of part-characteristics renders difficult the task of understanding their strength, duration, and vicissitudes. The problem can be immeasurably complicated if those whose feelings and ideas are being dissected are, wittingly or unwittingly, poor reporters, or if those doing the dissection have never been in the role of those they are trying to understand. I have already indicated that I believe that what leaders tell us is an inadequate sample of what they experience, and this is particularly true of leaders of new settings. Every now and then (mostly then) someone comes along who manages to transcend these difficulties, at least to the point of illuminating hitherto dark or inadequately attended to aspects. Usually, it is not that something new is discovered but that a different emphasis is provided that forces one to rethink old formulations. An example of this is provided by Anderson (1970) in his book *The Ulysses Factor*. At first glance this book would not seem to be particularly relevant to our purposes because it is concerned with individuals, past and present, who performed a prodigious feat of exploration involving physical strength and danger, the conquest of natural obstacles, and confrontation of the unknown. (The subtitle of the book is *The Exploring Instinct in Man*.)*

> Man has lived in communities from the beginning of the human story, and as communities have grown they have required more food, wood that would float better or split more readily than the trees in their immediate environment, new needs in almost infinite variety. Most can be met in fairly obvious ways: food by the improvement of techniques for hunting and growing things or by the sadly simpler method of attacking neighbors and taking their land and sources of food supply; better timber, new materials of all sorts can be found by experiment, by looking for new kinds of trees, by digging into the earth. Every now and again, however, something so novel that its existence could not even be guessed has been brought into communities to give them a wholly new rung on the ladder of development. Someone has looked at a range of mountains regarded as an absolute barrier to the territory of his tribe and decided to climb them, to find out what is on the far side. Someone has looked at a sea known to everyone as marking the end of the world and set out with a raft or log of wood to discover if it really is the end of the world.
>
> All very well, but is this any more than a love of adventure? Most healthy human beings have a piece of adventure in them that sends little boys up trees, makes people want to change their job, or even to move house. But this explains the how rather than the why in the achievement of scaling unclimbable mountains or crossing—from choice—an ocean in a rowing boat. You use your arms and legs as you have been taught from infancy, and without an innate sense of adventure the teaching would not have got far. The normal man or woman enjoys a good country walk, a scramble over rocks, or a sail, but does not particularly want to climb an ice face or to tackle an ocean in an open boat. Some force other than mere adventure must be looked for to discover what prompts a man not only to feel that it would be nice to know what is on the far side of the hills but to contract a fewer of desire to know and then an absolute determination to find out.
>
> Men do extraordinary things in the hope of gain: a love of adventure coupled with a desire to make money may be explanation enough for all these feats of human endeavour. To write this is at once to dismiss it, for it is patently untrue. Men have beggared themselves and done so

coldly and deliberately to build boats to cross an ocean for no apparent purpose or to finance an expedition in search of no tangible treasure. Sometimes they have come across treasure and have been glad enough, no doubt, to find it, but treasure-seeking in the ordinary sense cannot be the driving force I mean. Nor can that almost equally powerful motive, the lure of fame. Men like to be famous, and publicity of one sort or another has often been sought in connection with some enterprising feat. But sometimes the proposed feat is in itself an effort to attract notice to some project or manufacture, in which case it comes under quite another heading. Sometimes, particularly in recent years, publicity has been a method of trying to finance an expedition, but that does not make it necessarily the object of it. Sometimes a man dominated by the need to climb his mountain or to cross his unknown sea may have a considerable distaste for publicity at all. Of course, in some circumstances to shun publicity or to play hard-to-get is a method of courting notoriety, but certainly not always. Tilman, for example, any one of whose exploits could have made the name of a lesser man into a household word, has been content to be known to those who care to read his books. Adrian Hayter, whose remarkable first voyage in *Sheila* has never had the recognition it merited, is another who has sought no popular reputation for himself.

Neither gold nor fame will do. They may be won by a successful endeavour, but they do not explain this particular kind of endeavour. The anthropological approach remains: There is some factor in man some form of special adaptation which prompts a few individuals to exploits which, however purposeless they may seem, are of value to the survival of the race. I call this the Ulysses factor. But, if so, why is it manifest now; how, when the terrestrial globe is mapped and explored, its resources known, can there be any survival value in crossing an ocean by the primitive means of sail or oars? [pp. 15–17]

Anderson analyzes in detail the feats of a number of people (Heyerdahl, Herzog, Chichester, Tilman) but always from the standpoint of how they illuminate the psychological characteristics comprising the Ulysses factor. Using his own experience as well as the extensive reports and diaries of many individuals, Anderson describes the Ulysses factor as comprised of the following ingredients: courage, selfishness, practical competence, physical strength, powerful imagination, ability to lead, self-discipline, endurance, self-sufficiency, cunning, unscrupulousness, and strong sexual attraction. Anderson points out that each of these ingredients is complex and requires qualification.[4] The relevance of certain aspects of his discussions both for the

---

[4] Anderson's list (and his discussion of it) is refreshingly different from what is given to us by most leaders or, for that matter, by the research literature on leaders. There is overlapping, of course, but his inclusion of "negative" qualities (selfishness, cunning, unscrupulousness) and the quality of "strong sexual attraction" introduce notes of reality reminiscent of Machiavelli. Putting

problem of leadership and the creation of settings is made clear in
the following:

> Can a purely intellectual search for knowledge be put down to
> the Ulysses factor? It demands similar type-qualities: Newton, Einstein,
> Fleming, all who have crossed the frontiers of existing knowledge by sheer
> intellectual capacity have manifested a compelling driving force requiring
> self-dedication, self-discipline, endurance, a restless need to know, many
> of the qualities inherent in Ulysses. But to be similar is not to be the
> same. The factor in man that makes for intellectual exploration is related
> to the Ulysses factor, but it is different in that it does not require personal,
> physical action. The Ulysses type cannot find fulfillment without per-
> sonally being there: Your own foot must reach the mountain top, your
> own eyes see the waves, your own hand be on the tiller. This is a funda-
> mental difference.
>   Can individuals strongly influenced by the Ulysses factor work as
> a team? This is a difficult question. Leadership is inherent among the
> type-qualities, and the Ulysses man can certainly lead a team: manifesta-
> tions of the factor which have produced some of the greatest of human
> achievements have required the leadership of others, crews, companions
> on a mountainside, expeditionary forces. But this is to use a team for
> one's own purposes; it is not the same as being in a team. Yet when a
> handful of men set out to climb an all-but inaccessible Himalayan peak,
> or deliberately drift together in a raft across an ocean, it is likely that, as
> individuals, all will be influenced by the Ulysses factor. And such teams
> have lived and worked together splendidly: One man is accepted as the
> leader, but the achievement is the work of the whole team. I think that
> the conclusion here is that the Ulysses factor enables men to work in
> small teams, but that is not the motive for large collective performance.
> A general may be motivated by the Ulysses factor, but not his army. The
> ability of man to undertake big collective actions is due to other factors.
> A community may use the results of Ulysses-type exploration by sending
> out groups, or other individuals. Each must have enough self-discipline to
> subordinate himself to the purposes of the leader and the needs of his
> companions—self-discipline is one of the type-qualities. But the individual
> must be able to feel that he is an individual, that his hand on the tiller or
> his work on a rope has a direct part in whatever is being done. Unless he
> can call on other qualities to suppress his Ulysses inclinations, the Ulysses-
> type is unlikely to show the dog-loyalty of accepting orders without asking
> why. He is capable of intense loyalty to others, but he must understand
> what is going on, and feel part of it [pp. 34–35].

This is as good a brief statement as one will find about what the
relationship between a leader and his core group should be, and

---

Anderson in the tradition of Machiavelli may seem strange or outrageous to
those who associate evil with Machiavelli. For these readers I recommend Levi's
chapter on Machiavelli, Von Clausewitz, and Herman Kahn in his book *Humanism and Politics.*

Anderson provides splendid examples illustrating how "atypically" the leaders he writes about viewed and handled their privacy and sense of superiority. But what is most germane for my present purposes is Anderson's emphasis on something that I think is very important in the phenomenology of the leader creating a new setting: "Can *I*, with *my* ideas and personal talents, create a setting that will demonstrate to *me* that *I* have successfully done what *I* felt *I* *had* to do because if *I* did not do it, there would always be a part of *me* about which *I* would have questions. If *I* don't do it others will, and *I* will never *know* something *I* want to know about *myself*." For many leaders the creation of a setting is something they want and have to do.[5] It is a blend (among other things, of course) of a sense of challenge to and curiosity about one's self in the realm of action.

This personal challenge and curiosity are important parts of a complex of factors that motivate and propel the leader and his group and give to the beginning stages their aura of mission and excitement. In these stages each day is eagerly awaited because the things that need to be done and the problems that will come up have some quality of novelty and bear directly on how one feels one is meeting the personal challenge. What I am describing is a rather frequent phenomenon. It is what a teacher experiences in the early months of his first teaching job, what a psychotherapist feels with his first series of clients, and what a surgeon feels when he first asumes responsibility for operations. There is anxiety because there is novelty, danger, and personal challenge mixed in a way and to a degree that is absorbing and exciting. At first the question, Can *I* meet the challenge? has little specificity, but once the individual becomes the leader and the process of creating the setting begins, novelty abounds, and the global sense of challenge becomes differentiated in terms of concrete situations, individuals, and relationships. But each aspect of this differentiation is always related to and helps answer the question: Am *I* meeting the challenge? It is a question asked and answered each day because in these early stages the relatively unformed character of the setting makes it seem so vulnerable to pressures and problems. Despite the anxieties and problems, one looks forward to, indeed rushes toward, tomorrow.

There are different ways in which different leaders find themselves answering the personal challenge and, as one would expect, positive and negative answers have somewhat different consequences.

---

[5] The leader knows that he starts with nothing and that at some distant end point there will be something and that in between he will have been engaged in a variety of new relationships and actions.

The most frequent answers are in varying degrees negative and stem from the realization that there is and will be a marked discrepancy between what is and what the leader expected. It is not central to my purposes to go into the complexities of personality dynamics which in part determine how the negative answer is formulated and how it in turn affects personality dynamics. The important point is that the more negative the answer the more the leader tends to disaffiliate himself psychologically from the setting and to cease viewing or experiencing it as part of himself. He may be interested in what is going on in the setting and expend a lot of energy in dealing with its problems, but he does it more because it is a job and less because it bears on how he answers the question of how he met the personal challenge he accepted in creating the setting. He has more or less answered that question. The personal challenge is gone or markedly weakened, as well as any eager anticipation of novelty. Far from rushing toward tomorrow, the leader tends to shrink from it because it will be filled with reminders that what he wanted to create does not and will not exist.

The negative answer is a bitter pill to swallow. It is as difficult to accept as a parent's knowledge that he is in some way responsible for his child's failures and deviancy. It is not an answer that, so to speak, lets one alone, and one goes on to new questions. It is an upsetting complex of ideas and feelings that gives rise to new actions, not necessarily because they will change the negative answer but because, hopefully, they will have the effect of cutting one's losses. It is hard to generalize about the consequences of these new actions because they depend on the extent of the negative answer, its relationship to the age of the new setting, the number and kind of job opportunities to leave the setting, and the kinds of existing satisfactions stemming from the leader's status and power. The one generalization strongly supported by my observations is that the leader initiates a series of administrative reorganizations that have two characteristics: they increasingly insulate him from direct contact with or knowledge of the setting's problems, and they seal over rather than deal with the substantive and interpersonal issues existing in the setting. Aside from the fact that these maneuvers rarely have productive consequences for the leader and the setting, the leader increasingly feels more lonely, inadequate, and bored. The sense of personal challenge disappears, and a new task appears: How to put meaning and novelty into one's days?

The grim personal consequences of a negative answer can only be understood in light of the intensity of the sense of personal challenge with which the leader began, an intensity that insures that fall-ing short of the mark will have serious repercussions. The leader is like first-time parents who are willingly prepared to give their all to the extension of themselves; conscious that they have embarked on a task that will fascinate, absorb, and test them; convinced that what they will create will be distinctive, if not unique; and with little doubt that at the end they will feel the joys of success. One does not have to fall too far from such heights poignantly to feel failure.

Leaders in general are a self-selected group, if only because they actively seek leadership. Leaders who create a new setting may well be a somewhat differently self-selected group because they strive not only to lead but to create something "out there," the origins of which are deep within themselves. Although they may have been the leader of an existing setting bearing the stamp of other people, ideas, and times, they do not regard this as fulfilling or as personally chal-lenging or as "good" as what they could create. In seeking the oppor-tunity to create their setting, they are not only challenging the world but themselves as well, and in a public way. How the leader ulti-mately answers the *personal* challenge is frequently not the same as how others see him as answering the question. I have known of many instances where the leader's answer was far less positive than that of others; indeed, the disjunction can increase the leader's loneliness because he cannot talk about or justify his answer to others. He is perceived as successful although he does not feel that he met the personal challenge in the way he had hoped. One such leader put it to me this way: "No, I cannot honestly say that it worked out the way I wanted. The picture I had of myself when I started and the picture I had of how things would be are quite different than the way things are and I can't say it gives me pleasure. If you could talk to others, my guess is that you would get a very different answer. They see me as successful because they see me as having done pre-cisely what I set out to do. Every now and then when I am down in the dumps I find myself *hoping* they are right and I am wrong. Most of the time I know I am right because *I* know that what *I* hoped to do has only very partially been accomplished."[6]

[6] This was an unusually candid individual. When I talked to leaders of new settings, one of the questions I asked was: How well do *you* think *you* did what *you* set out to do? Understandably, this was not an easy question to answer (or to ask). All leaders became somberly reflective and silent, testimony, I believe, to its importance for them. The most frequent answer was a variant of "things never work out the way you want." Some leaders essentially never answered the question; some expressed bitter disappointment; others valiantly tried to give a balanced positive answer, usually accompanied by nervous humor;

When the personal challenge receives an answer, the level of novelty in the setting decreases for the leader. The answer does not occur at a particular time but during a time period in which the leader slowly becomes aware that *he* has answered the personal challenge, positively or negatively, and that the setting no longer has its earlier power to stimulate and excite. Strangely enough this is most clear when the leader has answered the personal challenge in a very positive way. As one such leader related to me: "I was dimly aware that something had changed. Things were going well, and I felt satisfied, but it wasn't the way it was. And one day it came to me: It could never be the same as it was because I had already done what I set out to do. I was no longer helping to create something but rather to maintain it." A leader of a business-professional organization put it this way: "We are now a going concern, and life is a lot more predictable. When it first started, I kept thinking of the time when things would be quiet and we would be a smooth-running organization. Of course it is never smooth and quiet, but what has disturbed me is that it is no longer as enjoyable or interesting as it used to be. I just don't have that get-up-and-go feeling because I am where I wanted to go!" Both leaders were puzzled and bothered by this strange, restless feeling that something was missing in their lives. I had the impression that they felt guilty about these feelings, as if in some way they were disloyal to what they created. When they started their settings, they were quite aware of the personal challenge, but they had no way of anticipating the consequences of a positive answer because they tended to see themselves in the setting for an indefinite future. They could not imagine a time, particularly if they were successful, when they would not feel a sense of heightened personal challenge and an eager anticipation of tomorrow. If you are successful, why should you feel bored and restless? The answer, of course, is that when an important problem is solved, it loses its mystery and attractiveness. There is no fun in solving the same problem again and again. It is not easy for a leader to say this out loud, namely, it is not socially acceptable for a leader to say: I have done it well. I can continue to do it well, but my heart is no longer in it. Goodbye.

---

very few (about whom I shall be talking later) gave an unqualified or decisive positive response. These were leaders of diverse types of new settings (new schools, businesses, communes, university departments and programs, community action programs, and so on) which had been in existence no more than two years. My overall impression of the group was that they were not satisfied with what they had accomplished or with the future they saw. This is not to say that they were unsatisfied but that the degree of satisfaction was not sufficient for them to say that they had met the personal challenge.

Furthermore, it is not too easy for leaders to move on to new challenges. If they are successful leaders, they may be offered opportunities to recreate elsewhere what they have already done, but this is ordinarily not a sufficient lure. It is like asking Hilary to climb Mt. Everest a second time. Where is the challenge and novelty? He has been *there*, why go back? What the successful leader of a new setting requires is a new personal challenge and, given social-economic realities, these are not easy to come by.

But what can happen when a leader has answered the personal challenge positively, and there are no new challenges on the horizon? The consequences are similar to those that follow a negative answer: The setting becomes more an object for, rather than an extension of, the leader, a kind of psychological disaffiliation; curiosity about what is going on is reduced; and vigilance for and diligence about problems lessens. When these dynamics come into play, and if they continue for any appreciable period of time, all the problems that can cause a new setting to fail begin to appear, albeit at a later time in the life of a setting and at a more leisurely pace.

The leader may be quite aware that in contrast to the beginning periods when he felt expansively creative, he now feels a prisoner of the setting, confined by loyalties, guilt, and (let us not forget) some continuing and real satisfactions. It does not occur to him that these private feelings may be reflected in different ways in his working day, for example, canceling or missing meetings, increased travel away from the setting, increasing irritability when dealing with the inevitable stream of problems, and sermonizing to his personnel. The consequences are usually subtle and slow in appearing, and for a long stretch of time the leader does not see the setting as changing. It is coasting downhill. Others in the setting sense something is wrong long before the leader does. They usually do not place what is wrong in an historical context but see the difficulties in terms of the here and now. They may sense that the leader has changed, but their explanations rarely point to where the trouble usually is: the consequences of the leaders diminished feeling of personal challenge.

There is an additional factor that contributes to the psychological consequences of a positive or negative answer, and that is that the answer remains private. It is a kind of nurtured secret that, in light of the fact that it refers to the leader in relation to the leader's setting as an abstraction as well as to people with whom he daily works, exacerbates the leader's sense of aloneness. One would suppose that the private negative answer, more than the positive one, would exacerbate the sense of aloneness. This may turn out to be the case, but my observations incline me to believe that the differences would not be as great as most people would suppose.

Power Corrupts

We are all familiar with the admonition that power corrupts and absolute power corrupts absolutely. The political history of nations provides too many clear-cut examples of this basic truth. There are many in our society at the present time, particularly younger people, who have reacted to the social-political calamities of this and past decades by denying the necessity of leadership and the implicit and explicit power that ordinarily goes with that position. By denying the necessity of a leader, it is assumed that a major source of individual and social corruption has been eliminated. Many of the communes that have been started in recent years have had as one of their goals to demonstrate that it is possible for people productively and happily to live and work together without a formal leader. That the demonstrations have been far from successful is perhaps less note-worthy than the fact that so many people view the role of leadership as inevitably destructive of the leader and the setting. Such a view, however, rarely provides us with an explanation of why this is so, especially in the case of new settings which in their earliest stages seem to be characterized by harmony, cooperation, and shared values and goals. Is it possible that like so many of the later problems of new settings, the corrupting influences of power already exist at the beginning when all seems sweetness and light? That the corrupting influences so obvious at a later stage have origins in ideas and structures which seem natural and innocent?

One of the most obvious features of a new setting in its earliest stages is that the leader sees himself, and others see him, as the most important person in the setting. After all, the setting is his idea or vision; he has taken or has been given responsibility for what happens; he has attracted people to join him because of what he is and hopes to do; and it is assumed that only he has the knowledge, skill, and power to organize resources and to move things forward. He is the most influential person in the sense that his opinions are given the greatest weight, not so much because he sees himself or others see him as powerful than because he is seen as more knowledgeable and as having the greatest stake in what happens. At this point in time it is as if everyone agrees that the setting belongs to the leader in much the same way as a child belongs to his parent. What right does a guest have, even an invited one or a close relative, to tell a parent how to rear his child? He may advise the parent, but obviously the parent has the right to do what he wants. It is similarly obvious to the leader and those around that his should be the decisive voice. There are three other major factors contributing to this seemingly natural state of affairs: the leadership fantasy in which the leader is in this obvious role; the attention and deference the leader receives by virtue of his primacy; and, most fateful, his enjoyment of his centrality. To receive little or no enjoyment from attention, deference, praise, and primacy is not characteristic of leaders of new settings. To dream about and then experience such enjoyment is not calculated to stimulate reflection about possible dangers in such an experience, and there is no external agent to raise such possibilities.

There are two intimately related dangers. The first is that what the leader enjoys he comes to expect and need. After all, both from within and from without he has been shaped up to expect certain rewards. And, let us not forget, this is taking place at a time when what the leader enjoys from others is given to him less because of his powers and more because of a perceived communality of values and goals. The second danger is in the inability of the leader to anticipate that what he enjoys is not likely to continue to be given him as readily or frequently as in the beginning. This is not only because critical problems develop, conceptual differences arise and get enmeshed in personality clashes, and the sense of communality in values and goals diminishes. What also happens is that those around the leader grow up and begin to develop a body of knowledge and skills that does not permit them to accede to the leader's opinions and decisions as readily as was once the case. It is what happens predictably in parent-child relationships in which the child begins to sense that he thinks and feels differently from his parents and that he wants to be different. This comes as quite a shock to some parents, who have seen their child as one with them, dutifully and willingly incorporating their vision of how things should be. Some parents understand and anticipate that these differences will occur; some never get over the shock and produce the *Sturm und Drang* about which countless books have been written. But leaders are a far more self-selected group than parents, especially in regard to their need for centrality and primacy in their relationships with those around. They have strived for it, they enjoy its consequenecs, they come to expect them, and when they begin to diminish, it is extraordinarily difficult for them to understand it in terms of the needs of others. Leaders often perceive a display of independence in others as disloyalty, arrogance, and divisive of the communal spirit. The leader experiences such conflict in terms of his needs, expectations, and accustomed enjoyments. It is literally inconceivable to him that the other person is fighting for his sense of separateness and independence. The significance of these conflicts is that they make explicit what was at the beginning implicit: that the leader owed less to his core group than each of them owed to him. That is to say, the loyalty owed the leader was far more clearly defined and accepted than that which the leader owed to others; the leader's opinions and ideas were expected to be given more weight than he would give to those of others; and it was the task of others to learn from the leader as it was the task of the leader to instruct and direct. Some would ask: What was wrong with that kind of relationship? Is it not right that by virtue of his role in creating the setting the leader should expect others to fit in with his ideas and plans? Should he not feel that he can count on their support to do what he feels needs to be done? Should not his vision be given priority? *Whose* ideas gave rise to the setting? All of these questions imply that a major function of the setting is to aid the leader to do what he wants to do, and the needs of others must recede to the background. These questions can be answered affirmatively in regard to the early stages of the setting, provided that the leader and others understand that the basis of their relationship will and should change as the setting develops and the disparity in knowledge and skills between the leader and others decreases and may even disappear. To expect such an understanding or even to entertain it as a possibility in the early stages is to run counter to what seems "natural" to the leader and others. And yet it is predictable that at some future time what will get called into question is the basis of the relationship between the leader and others, particularly his core group. And the call is for the purpose of changing that relationship and requires the leader at least to begin to view others as they once did to him, namely, he has an obligation to help them develop in *their* way. The leader is psychologically unprepared for such a change, and, indeed, he misinterprets and resists it. He tends to view it as a challenge to his primacy that would require him to revise his role, namely, to abdicate leadership to someone else. Far more often than not what is being asked of the leader is not a challenge to his primacy but a request for manhood. To the extent that the leader views it as a challenge, he begins to think about and use power as the basis for maintaining his primacy, and in so doing *he* has changed the basis of the relationship.

When the leader begins to use power (in the narrower meaning of that word), it is not difficult to observe how the use can defeat the purposes of the leader and others. Its use drastically alters the social climate and tends to create the conditions where power has to be used again and again. We then say that the leader's use of power unwittingly has corrupted him and prevents him from seeing how he has brought about and maintains a situation which he and others wanted to avoid. I have been suggesting that in the case of new settings the corruption began much earlier. It had its origins in a relationship markedly unequal in its mutuality, a quality of relationship willingly entered into and considered by all to be natural and enduring. The corruption begins in an innocence and ignorance in which the future is seen as no more than an extension of the satisfying present.[7] That both members of the relationship will change—the leader increasingly enjoying the rewards of his primacy and those around him becoming more knowledgeable and skillful as well as developing stronger needs for autonomy—is not even verbalizable as a possibility. It is only in rare instances that when this possibility begins to be a reality there is the insight that the old relationship has been outgrown.

[7] That innocence is a frequent antecedent of personal corruption has been described best by novelists and playwrights (who usually seem to be ahead of the academic researcher). The most recent and among the most beautiful portrayals I have read is Ignazio Silone's (1970) *The Story Of A Humble Christian*. This is a play about a saintly Franciscan monk who, in 1294, was elected Pope (Celestine V) as a compromise between two warring Roman families who controlled the college of cardinals. Like St. Francis, he was seen, as indeed he was, as a kind of "other worldly" person, concerned only with devotion to God and justice to man. Against his better judgment he is prevailed upon to become Pope. He fears that he will be corrupted by the corrupt people and practices in the church, but he finally persuades himself that this will not be the case and he will rebuild the church in the true spirit of God. And so he plunges ahead unaware of why he was chosen, the strength of the organizational and personal forces arrayed against him, the moral issues with which he will be faced, and the dubious power of love as the exclusive weapon in the fight against sin. The piercing question Silone is raising is whether it is possible for anyone in power to be and remain consistently moral, in other words, can one fight organizational sin without succumbing to some extent to these very same sins. The high point of this moving drama is when Celestine realizes how innocent he had been and how he will be corrupted. After a six month reign he abdicates, the only Pope ever to have done so. His heroic defiance costs him his life. Those who know Silone's life and literary works will not be surprised at how he answers the question because the most important forces in his life were his relationship to and disillusionment with the Russian Revolution, the largest instance in his generation of the creation of a new society by overthrowing an old, corrupt one (for instance, *Emergency Exit*, 1968). We will be dealing with the question Silone raises in a later chapter.

CHAPTER 11

Leadership and Problems of Control

Whenever I have presented the ideas contained in the last two chapters, several questions have been raised with some regularity. Although my audiences have usually been quite heterogeneous in respect to age, experience, and status, they did not question my description of the behavior, thinking, and dilemmas of leaders, including the developmental aspects of the leadership fantasy. This, of course, may in some measure be due to the politeness accorded an invited speaker (a tradition of courtesy that does not have serious consequences, but, ironically, can be quite serious when it characterizes, as if often does, the relationship between a leader and those around him!). I discount the role of politeness as a major factor because on each occasion several people would tell me afterwards that I had verbalized what they had experienced. Some of these people were or had been leaders; several later wrote me about their experience in creating a setting, and in each of these instances the setting had been terminated early in the game. These anecdotes provided me with insights and materials, and I am grateful that the

241

writers graciously allowed me to use them. In this chapter I shall deal with the most frequent questions my presentations raised.

Contradictory Characteristics of Leaders

I have described leaders of new settings as possessing conflicting, if not contradictory, characteristics. They are dreamers and doers, knowledgeable and ignorant, selfless and selfish, absorbed by challenge and bored by its absence, strivers for "family solidarity" and protectors of their own privacy, convinced of their superiority and plagued by self-doubts, pursuers of the future and ignorers of the past, believers in the inevitability of change and resisters of the anticipation of its consequences. Are leaders all that different from other people? The answer, of course, is that they are not all that different in terms of the content and structure of personality, but they are different in that they have the opportunity to realize their ambitions. It is an opportunity which represents for the leader both an end and a beginning, and what takes this beyond the realm of an individual psychology is that for those around him, as well as for the larger society, we are witnessing a sustained social event and process. Creating a setting says something about individuals, but it also says something about the surrounding society. As long as we permit ourselves to be endlessly fascinated by the personality of leaders of new settings, we cannot gain perspective on the social complexity of the process of institutional creation and the way in which it influences and is influenced by the surrounding society. The most obvious way in which leaders of new settings differ from others is in their numbers, not in their personalities. That obvious fact should be viewed as reflecting two things: the pace and ways in which a society is changing and the explicit and implicit values and categories of thought that accompany and guide those changes.

I have learned that the question of the degree of similarity between leaders and others literally hides another question that is first in point of time: Are not these contradictory and conflicting characteristics basically unsolvable, namely, is it not true that these polarities never disappear? And once this question surfaces, the gnawing underlying feeling comes out: If, as is likely, these polarities are enduring ones, are not new settings doomed to slide downhill and to fall short of their mark? This is an unpleasant feeling which we resist mightily, in much the same way that we resist the affective consequences of the recognition of the fact of our own mortality. Why must a good thing end? It would be strange indeed if we did not struggle against and deny the idea that states of happiness and fulfillment cannot be permanent. Those who resist such a possibility have kinship to all those who begin new settings, except for the fact those who create new settings do not even consider the possibility that the future will not be continuation of the happy present. And therein lies the basis for hope because the important and practical question does not concern permanency but rather the degree to which awareness of what can and will happen helps prolong the period of challenge and satisfaction. I suppose I am saying that when you live your life as if you believe you will never die, you may be courting personal disaster. It does not follow that living your life knowing that you will someday die is a prescription for happiness. But the awareness of one's own mortality can and should be the stubborn fact forcing one constantly to justify the significance of how one lives.

Whether or not new settings inevitably decline and fall short of their mark can justifiably be viewed as a red-herring issue because how one answers the question in no way helps us understand why some new settings fail quickly and go out of existence, and others lose their steam rather early and remain a shell that has lost its living substance. As I have tried to show in this book, the creation of a setting is a fantastically complicated social process containing one booby trap after another. Among the most prominent is the interaction between the role of the leader and the human polarities that exist within him. Underlying this interaction is myth that denies that neither he nor the setting will basically change—except possibly for the better. Let us not forget, however, that the myth is also shared by those around the leader, each reinforcing the strength of the myth in everyone else. The myth is not created by the leader, and he is not the sole source of its shattering. Potentially, however, he is the only person who by his knowledge and actions can begin a tradition which requires in others and himself an awareness of and sensitivity to the presence of myth and other ordinarily hidden sources of destructive conflict. This, as we shall now see, is not a mere matter of open talk or expression of feeling as if these are virtues in themselves, justified by the purity or sincerity of motivation, and not requiring the control and direction of organized conceptualizations. Telling the truth is not the same as being helpful (although it sometimes is), and being helpful is not a simple function of one's desire to help (although it sometimes is).

Openness

Some, mostly nonleaders and usually younger people, have interpreted approvingly my remarks as if they rested on the value that openness is a virtue, namely, that the leader and those around him *should* make public what they think and feel. Others, mostly leaders and usually older people, have reflected in their questions misgivings that I was suggesting a degree of openness that was unrealistic and dangerous. The one thing about which both groups seemed to agree was that the issue of openness was central and bothersome. When I have been able to pursue these different reactions, it has always turned out that the issue of openness was intimately related to another one: How should decisions be made, by whom, and on what basis? In the case of new settings, openness as a bothersome and destructive issue seems always to be a consequence of dissatisfaction with some aspect of the decision-making process. The dissatisfaction may be about the nature of the decision or about those who were, or were not, involved, or the context in which it took place. In any event, in different people and for different reasons some aspect of the decision-making process produces thoughts and feelings which they would like to express but are unable to do so. They are afraid to do so because they are unsure about how it will be interpreted. In the early phases of a new setting the most formidable obstacle to such expression is the thought that one will be introducing conflict into an atmosphere dominated by the spirit of missionary solidarity. This can be the case for the leader as well as for each of those around him. Private feelings, like secrets, frequently have a "spread effect" and come to absorb increasingly more of one's experience, especially if the feelings are about deeply felt matters for which the social context provides frequent stimulation.

If in a new setting the history of the problem of openness is intimately related to the history of decision-making (the former frequently, if not always, a consequence of the latter), and if the fear of diluting group solidarity is a major obstacle to openness, we must direct our attention to the question of how the leader and his core group initially "decided" to live with each other. This, of course, is the constitutional question that has been raised if we are to understand how people get to the point where openness and group solidarity are perceived as incompatible. Since the leader is, so to speak, the convener of the "constitutional convention," and he is explicitly in the central role, the rules by which he and his group will live will be determined primarily by his ideas, feelings, and values. As I described in Chapter Four, the process by which the leader attracts and organizes his core group almost never permits focusing on the anticipation of problems and the basis on which they will be resolved, namely, how they will live with predictable problems and conflicts. On the contrary, the focus is on the marvelous opportunity the new setting presents whereby each individual will realize his ambitions within the context of shared values and team effort. The new setting will create its own traditions which, needless to say, are expected to prevent the organizational craziness each experienced in his previous setting. Everybody is starting fresh with the knowledge and resources that transform dreams into reality. When the beginning atmosphere is suffused with such goodwill and so alluring a future, how can one raise and deal with the fact that there will be conflict and serious differences of opinions and with the problem of how one will recognize and deal with their consequences? Caught up in such a cloudless atmosphere, how can one recognize that subscribing to the value of openness is a facile gesture full of feeling and empty of thought?

A major source of control missing in the leader in this situation is an organized conception of the nature of the process in which he and others are engaged, a conception based on knowledge of the dynamics of group interaction, of the inevitability of conflict, of the strength of fantasy and of the tendency to deny the obvious, of the disjunctions between overt and covert behavior, and of the fact that he is perceived as a model of how one should think and act.[1] In short, he needs to possess—literally to feel that he "owns"—a theory that tells him what he is assuming and what variables he is dealing with. By theory I do not mean a set of unconnected ideas, intuitions, and generalities, each of which may have merit but none of which does justice to the complexity of the process. By theory, I mean, for example, what is in the head of a psychoanalyst as he approaches his patients. He has a conception of what man is, how he develops and differentiates, the obstacles he encounters, criteria of abnormality, the interaction between biological and social factors, and so forth. It is quite a complicated theory, and the degree of its validity and internal consistency is not an issue here. It is, however, an example of efforts to take an explicit and coherent stand about the nature of man and how this stand influences how one works with individuals who seek help. It is not only a theory about people in general and patients in particular, but it is also about therapists and how their thinking and acting must reflect awareness of what they have in common with patients. The theory is both a guide and a form of control. It tells the

---

[1] These are not the only factors with which the conception must deal. For example, as I pointed out in earlier chapters, the conception basically must be longitudinal and social-historical in character.

therapist what to look for and sensitizes him to the pitfalls of action.[2]

Leaders of new settings have no theory about the nature of the process they are engaged in and the complications of their relationship to it. They do not come to the task with a theory which, so to speak, has a status independent of them and is formulated in a way so that it can act as a guide to and control of their thinking and actions. What is there to tell them, for example, that in the early stages the verbal commitment to openness is an easy gesture that can effectively prevent the anticipation of situations that will make openness difficult? That status differences work against openness? That competitiveness among those of similar status, like the core group, also works against openness? That being a leader accelerates the pace of the processes of self-discovery and self-deception? That absence of conflict may be symptomatic of trouble?

It seems obvious that the question is not whether one is for or against openness or for a little or a lot of it but rather why it is always a problem, namely, what factors make people feel that they cannot be open, and that this is interfering with the purposes of the setting. To have an answer to this question is a big first step toward being sensitized to the problem and dealing with it so as to dilute its destructive consequences. But an answer based primarily on considerations of feeling, intuition, or motivation is as effective with this problem as they are with other human problems. That is to say, they can carry you a certain distance to your goal, but they cannot carry you very far. Whatever advances have been made in dealing with human problems have been a consequence of new or old knowledge conceptualized in new ways which provide a foundation for new strategies in action.

---

[2] There is much in psychoanalytical theories that can be criticized, but one should not confuse the validity of the theory with the problems to which it is addressed. (For example, Freud's theorizing about the death instinct has been criticized by various groups, but that does not eliminate the significance of the problem with which he was dealing, namely, the origins and vicissitudes of aggressive behavior.) In my opinion, among the most productive aspects of psychoanalytic theorizing are those relating to the different ways in which the desire to help is affected by a variety of factors (for example, curiosity, fantasies of omniscience and omnipotence, money, status, and the reactions elicited by patients' expressions of love and hate). Psychoanalytic training centers like to believe that their criteria of selection and training procedures effectively dilute the adverse consequences of those and other factors. Freud was not so optimistic. He came to believe that being an analyst inevitably changed the analyst and usually in unfortunate ways, hence his suggestion that analysts should be analyzed every five years. Leaders of new settings do not have a theory that sensitizes them to the fact that being a leader is to engage in a process which will inevitably change and probably corrupt them.

It could be argued that I am asking leaders to be theoreticians, and that is silly because they are primarily people of action, not noted for their love of theory or theoreticians. Indeed, they ordinarily pride themselves on being practical people who have to deal with the world as it is, and not as theoreticians imagine it to be. The thrust of this book, of course, is that leaders of new settings are probably among the most unsuccessful people on earth by their own standards of accomplishment. I do not expect leaders of new settings to be theoreticians in the sense of developing new theories, just as I do not expect clinicians (psychological, medical, and so on) to be theory builders. They *are* practitioners, but that does not mean that they are incapable of understanding and being influenced by theory. In fact, in the past several decades in different spheres of public life, men of action have inceasingly been influenced by theoreticians from different fields, giving rise to the usual three opinions: it has been a boon; it has been an unmitigated disaster; or it is a difference which has not made a difference. We are far from this point in the case of the creation of settings because it has not been the focus of theory builders. When it does become a focus, the theoreticians will have to ponder the question that will be put to them by practical men: Since theoreticians are not noted for their immersion in the real world, how can they develop a theory of new settings without ever experiencing the process? The truth is that there are few Freuds who can experience a process, develop a theory, try it out, change the theory, and continue to do so until the end of their long life.

John Dewey is an instance of a theoretician who created a setting in order to test his ideas. At the end of the last century at the University of Chicago, Dewey, the educational critic and theorist, created a school which has been beautifully described by Mayhew and Edwards (1966). Their description is unusually comprehensive, and the reader who thinks that the world has caught up to or passed Dewey had better read Mayhew and Edwards' account (Sarason, 1971). Unfortunately for us, however, Dewey never seemed to spell out the conceptions which guided him as a leader of the new setting because he never saw the creation of a setting as a general problem. He viewed what he was creating within the context of education and not as an instance of a process occurring in many different spheres of life. Furthermore, Dewey seemed to view his school as a demonstration that would influence others to change existing schools. Dewey did not see that creating a setting and changing an existing one were not the same problems and that they required different (but overlapping) theories. Consequently, what people took from his school, and what

Dewey hoped they would take, was applied in a context quite different from that in which it arose. Dewey's school was a magnificent achievement in educational theory and practice because he had a theory of what a school should be, and it guided him throughout the venture. Implicit in that theory was the problem of how to create an appropriate setting, but it remained implicit.

There have been few practioners who could develop theories, and there have been few theoreticians who have engagd in the world of practice. But these few have had an influence far beyond their numbers.

External Critics

Another question frequently put to me can be phrased as follows: Granted that we have no adequate theory of the creation of settings, and granted that such a theory probably would help lengthen the time during which a setting would be true to its purposes, are you not overevaluating the role of theory (which in some measure is always incomplete and wrong) as well as the degree to which in the world of action man is capable of using theory appropriately? Is not theory a frail reed upon which to base one's hopes? The question is a legitimate one, but it is powered by and betrays the hope, so tenaciously held by those who create settings, that a setting can and should endure for a long time, if not forever. That is to say, there should and must be a way to create and maintain settings that will not lose their zeal or purpose. Why cannot new settings last as long as bridges, buildings, and highways? Should and can they last that long? These are questions with which theory has to deal because it obviously makes a difference how these questions are answered by those who create settings.

There are several characteristics of new settings which suggest a tentative answer to these questions. The first is that new settings are never viewed as merely duplicating what already exists but rather as an improvement, which is to say that in one or another way it will meet a need not now being met by existing settings. The basis for this view is either that existing settings have not been responsive to changes in the larger society or that those creating the new setting possess new knowledge of some kind not known to or utilizable by those in existing settings. Society or man's knowledge or both have changed. But these kinds of changes continue, and in their more reflective moments even those who create settings realize that these changes will continue. The odds are extremely high that these changes will at some point cause the new setting to be viewed as it had initially viewed its predecessors.

A second characteristic resides in the obvious fact that new settings arise from and exist within a context of existing settings over which it has little, and frequently no, control. The new setting is not only in danger from within but from without as well, and the interaction between these sources of danger sets limits to the degree to which the new setting will meet its goals or even to its duration. To assume that a new setting will fulfill all of its purposes and will last forever is to assume a degree of control over society and a view of society that has no justification in experience or social theory. The third characteristic is the most subtle and involves two factors: that a new setting presents those who create it with a challenge and novelty; and that when these inevitably decrease in strength, the setting begins to lose its excitement and creative push.

The interaction between internal processes and external forces insures that a setting will change in the direction of losing its impetus or realizing all of its major goals. This can be regarded as pessimism only if one views society as static, man as a noncurious organism, and social problems and their solutions as not bound by time. It can be regarded as fatalistic or cynical only if it leads to the conclusion that one should not create settings because they will in varying degrees fall short of their mark. I do not regard my position as pessimistic or cynical, but rather as a consequence of theoretical considerations, let alone the history of man's efforts to create new settings. It is a position which, if taken seriously by those who create settings, can heighten their awareness of what they are about, sensitize them to the adverse consequences of myth, facilitate their eventual separation from the setting, and permit them to rise and adapt to the possibility that the setting can no longer be justified. To be tied to a setting because of what it has been, to tolerate what it is because of what it was, is to stop productive growth. The task is not how to continue the setting into an indefinite future, but how to prolong the period in which individual and social needs are most creatively met.

The assertion that in the world of action the implementation of theory is fraught with dangers and, therefore, cannot be viewed as other than a source of partial control against error and decline is valid. But this assertion rests on the assumption that the controls against error (as well as the source of error) only exist *within* the setting. When those who must act are also those who must control for error and inconsistency, it usually turns out that both action and control are adversely affected. But why must a person (or theory) rely only on controls within the setting? Why do those who create new settings think (when they think about it all) only in terms of internal vehicles of control? What obscures recognition of the necessity to have an external source of control, namely, an external critic? Briefly, part of the answer is that those who create settings do not have a theoretical analysis which makes an external source of control a necessity, not a substitute for but a supplement to internal vehicles of control. Another part of the answer is that those who create settings and the zeal and excitement that surround their feelings of uniqueness and superiority make the role of an external critic seem superfluous and a distraction. The external critic is seen as a necessity when the setting is in trouble, the clearest testimony to the absence of a preventive way of thinking.

By external critic I refer to someone (or a group) who, at the earliest time possible, accepts the task of understanding and responding to the purposes and values of the setting, the consistency between words and actions, and the sources of actual and potential problems. He is *not* a member of the setting. He is an outsider, independent, knowledgeable about, and sympathetic to the purposes of the setting. He makes a long-term commitment and regularly spends time in the setting in whatever ways he deems necessary to gain knowledge and understanding. His relationship to the setting is explicitly based on agreement that his task is to contrast the reality as he sees it with the way those in the setting see it, that his goal is not to be loved or admired, and that his remuneration will not depend on the cheeriness of his perceptions. He paints reality as he sees it. He has no responsibility except to observe, study, and report. He is not someone who waits for problems to be brought to him; he seeks them out. His obligation is not to any individual, but to the purposes and values of the setting.

The external critic is an external conscience and a reminder that man's capacity to deceive himself is not one of his less obvious characteristics. Gardner (1965) has put this well.

I have collected a great many examples of organizations or institutions that have fallen on evil days because of their failure to renew themselves. And I want to place before you two curious facts that I draw from those examples. First, I haven't yet encountered an organization or institution that wanted to go to seed or wanted to fall behind in the parade. Second, in every case of organizational decline that I know anything about, there were ample warning signals long before trouble struck. And I don't mean warning signals that only a Monday-morning quarterback could discern. I mean that before trouble struck there were observers who had correctly diagnosed the difficulties to come.

Now if there are plenty of warning signals, and if no organization really wants to go to seed, *why does it ever happen?* The answer is obvious: eyes that see not, ears that hear not, minds that deny the evidence before them. When organizations are not meeting the challenge of change, it is as a rule not because they can't *solve* their problems but because they won't *see* their problems; not because they don't *know* their faults, but because *they rationalize them as virtues or necessities.*

Gardner's observations are of chronologically mature settings, but they are no less true of new settings. In fact, they are probably more true of new settings because their level of mission, excitement, and hope is so much higher. It is precisely these characteristics that inhibit the idea of an external critic from even arising as a possibility. The external critic is and should be a nuisance whose observations reflect the luxuries of independence. And who needs a nuisance, a constant reminder of imperfection? What leader of a new setting would willingly expose himself to an external challenge to his superiority, a challenge over which he would have to agree he would have no control? And therein lies a major source of the problem: the prepotent tendency of the leader (and his core group) to the *idea* of an external critic would be that it is a challenge to his conception of his role. He and others would not view it as a necessity or as a positive challenge, but as a negative and destructive one. This prepotent response is one of the clearest indications of how in the earliest phases of a new setting barriers already exist against external pressure for change and the recognition of internal sources of trouble.

There have been many times when those creating new settings have called in outsiders to respond to ideas, goals, and organizational plans. Whatever functions they serve bear little resemblance to those of an external critic whose major function is to focus on the relationship between words and action and on factors and relationships that lead to self-defeating conflict. It is only somewhat of a caricature to say that those who create settings tend to view themselves as saints possessed of a superior truth and armed against the evil traps into which so many others before them have fallen. The analogy, however, permits me to suggest that the external critic is in the role of the devil's advocate who knows all too well that sincerity of motivation is no guarantee of accomplishment. If my use of a venerable institution in the Catholic church seems odd or irrelevant to some, I should remind them that the rationale for the devil's advocate is one of the most distinctive features of the history of science. The insistence on replicability is testimony to the fact that what people say they did and how and why they did it are insufficient grounds for accepting it as truth. Publishing one's findings is acceptance of the principle that one needs an external critic. And, as is so often the case, the response to the publication confirms the wisdom of the principle.

There are many problems in the role and utilization of an external critic. Some colleagues and I (Sarason, Zitnay, and Grossman, 1972) have been in this role and have discussed some of the issues. Suffice it to say, we have no doubt that it is a productive role at the same time that it is a frustrating and thorny one, as indeed it must be. Our experience is too limited to merit further discussion of it here, and, besides, the role was not given to us but was the result of our initiative and special interests. What is deserving of emphasis is the response of leaders to the concept of the external critic. With unfailing regularity the initial response was favorable and a variant of: Of course, every setting could use somebody whose task it is to keep us honest. Reflection and discussion, however, led to the conclusion: It sounds good in theory, but it won't work in practice. The first objection was: Where do you find people able to fill such a role and willing to give so much time over a long period of time? You are not describing a consultant who comes in every now and then and talks and works with a few individuals or certain groups. The second objection was that the external critic could be a source of increased turmoil and conflict. As one leader said: "As you describe him, he *could* turn out to be a nuisance and not a help." The third objection was that the authority and centrality of the leader could be questioned by and obscured for others (namely, the core group) in the setting, and the same could happen with each core member and his group. The final objection, always made with the kind of pleasure experienced when one has checkmated a chess opponent, was: You describe your external critic as a kind of philosopher-king who would see all and know all. But isn't he capable of seeing and interpreting things just as wrongly as we do? Just because he has no responsibility for decisions and actions doesn't mean that he is free from error. The last objection, of course, as well as some of the others, concedes the point that regardless of their sources, the imperfections of men can be depended on both to create and ignore problems. In doing an experiment one employs controls of different kinds not because one is certain they will work but because one is convinced that they are supposed to control what requires control. What the external critic is supposed to control requires control.

The most interesting aspect of these objections was the sensitivity of the leaders to the possibility that their power, status, and centrality could be affected in their eyes *only* negatively by the external critic. It is not a concern without foundation, but it is also a concern revealing the sensitivity of leaders to the dangers of openness. In this respect it is significant that no leader with whom I have spoken had even thought of the idea of external controls. This despite the fact that each was poignantly aware of the limitations of whatever internal controls existed in his setting. In several cases, in fact, the new settings had died, and the leaders had earlier told me in some detail how their errors in thinking and action had been obvious to others but not to themselves.

The design of experiments is an endlessly fascinating human endeavor. It is also endlessly frustrating because it copes with man's seemingly infinite capacity to err and misinterpret what he sees and does and copes with the fact that the more one knows the more one has to know. The creation of settings is also endlessly fascinating and frustrating, but those who design them have not yet been provided with a rationale that forces them to confront the issue of what requires control. And when it is provided, it will be found wanting in some respects. The more one learns, the more one has to learn. This assumes, of course, that those who create settings, like those who design experiments, want not only to prove something but to learn something. That is to say, they want to experience the sense of growth.

CHAPTER 12

Skinner's Design of New Cultures

Literary utopias can be expected to receive a critical reaction because they are indictments of an existing society at the same time that they rest on a new conception of man and what social man can be. The designers of these utopias are, at best, viewed as impractical and, at worst, dangerous visionaries intent either on the enslavement of man or the internment of those values that have led to man's greatest achievements. There may be a few people who respond favorably; the bulk of people will laugh disparagingly and continue living in their accustomed ways, secure in the feeling that one need not clutter the present with thoughts of improbable futures.

B.F. Skinner has had a somewhat different fate. His book *Walden Two* (1962) had, and still has, a very wide audience. I well remember that when it was first published in 1948, there were more than a few students in universities around the country for whom the

book was a spur to thinking and action. Efforts were made to create
these new societies, although very few of these efforts ever got very
far. It is too simple, if not thoughtless, to say that the book's influence
was due to some combination of Skinner's eminence in psychology
and the gullibility of the young. Published after Hiroshima and the
end of World War II, at a time when it was already clear that the
modern world was ridden with conflicts and possibilities that could
destroy it, it could be argued that the fascination that book had for
many young people foreshadowed later developments in our universities. In fact, within the opening pages of *Walden Two* Skinner gives
us a picture of the minds of two returning veterans that is compellingly similar to what young people have said for themselves in recent
years. It is my impression that a much smaller percentage of older
people read the book, and in general they were more negative than
younger ones. For the most part, the critics (older people) damned
Skinner as a sinister influence who contemplated with glee a utopia
where people were controlled to enjoy a cattle-like social existence.
In their eagerness to demolish Skinner, critics have not confronted the
fact that *Walden Two* continues to enjoy wide readership among
young people. If they did, they might learn that what fascinates
younger people about the book is not only the heaven-on-earth
society he describes but also Skinner's assurance that the scientific basis
for creating new societies exists—a basis to which he feels he has made
the most significant contributions.

Skinner's most recent book, *Beyond Freedom and Dignity*
(1971)', is obviously being read, appearing on the best-seller lists
within weeks of its publication. Although the popularity of the book
is not hard to understand (Skinner's increased influence and reputation, well-planned and well-planted publicity, a provocative title,
front-page reviews), there is little in the new book that was not contained in *Walden Two*. For the most part the book is a presentation
of Skinnerian principles of behavior, his conception of man, their
implications for the design of cultures, or in my terms the creation of
settings. At the time this chapter is being written it is too early to
tell what the range of critical reaction will be. The reviews which have
already appeared confirm the prediction that the dominant reaction
will be negative and, in my opinion, will fail to come to grips with the
central issues Skinner poses. Like so many other people, Skinner sees
our society as being at a point where its accustomed vehicles for change
and innovation are no longer adequate and where its efforts to create
new settings will fail because they are based on a fallacious view of
man. We have available, according to Skinner, a scientific view of

man, which can serve as a foundation for designing new settings. It is precisely because Skinner claims that he has provided us with the basis for a technology for creating a new setting that he deserves serious analysis. Even if his claims should be found wanting, we should feel indebted to him for attempting to explain why attempts to create new settings so frequently fail and for trying to show us how it can be done better. It is a disservice both to Skinner and to the problems he poses to respond to his writings with emotions and generalities that satisfy our prejudices at the same time they divert us from recognizing the legitimacy of the problems with which he is grappling. It is one thing to say that one does not like Skinner, whatever that may mean; it is quite another thing to say that the problems to which he addresses himself are not legitimate. We should not make the error of the atheist who consigned all of Rennaissance art to the scrap heap of history because of its religious content.

Position

The following statements, brief and necessarily oversimplified, are some of the major aspects of Skinner's position.

(1) Behavior (that is, overt behavior) is not explainable by age-old mentalistic conceptions having the characteristics of internal gremlins. These conceptions have very effectively distracted us from recognizing the pervasive and ever present environmental aspects which shape and change behavior. As soon as one accepts this fact, one can begin to see how the environment acts as a shaper of behavior, there being different types and schedules of reinforcement. Skinner does not deny that things go on inside the heads of people, but he does deny that these internal phenomena are the shapers and controllers of behavior.

(2) There is now a voluminous research literature demonstrating that Skinner's principles of behavior are extremely effective in shaping, predicting, controlling, and changing behavior. He cites research with laboratory animals and various atypical individuals (for instance, the mentally retarded, psychotic), as well as the countless studies applying "behavior modification principles" for extinguishing maladaptive symptoms (for instance, anxieties, phobias, and disruptive behavior).

(3) Man is never free in the sense that his behavior is in its origins and maintenance independent of environmental sources of stimulation and reinforcement. The concept of freedom is a fiction that hides the fact that behavior is always shaped and controlled by the behavior-environment relationships Skinner has discovered.

(4) Behavioral science has attained that degree of understanding of the overt behavior-environment relationships that allows one now to begin to approach and solve the technical problem of creating or designing settings which not only would insure the survival of society but would also permit man to realize his manifold capacities. Society is no longer working for its own survival, and part of the problem is that the primacy given to individual values (and the conception of individual freedom) works against the value of group survival.

(5) Skinner recognizes that his position should evoke massive resistance because it runs counter to how people regard the nature and sources of their behavior. They like to believe that they are autonomous and uncontrolled. Man's behavior is always controlled by forces outside him. The future task is to utilize these controlling forces in ways less destructive (than is now the case) of the individual and the group.

Most people would agree with Skinner that there is something radically wrong with modern society and that past and present efforts at remediation of old and creation of new settings are no basis for optimism. Reflection should convince most people that Skinner is correct in saying that there is something wrong in our conception of man and that it will take a new conception to produce a better state of social affairs. He offers us what he considers to be a new conception that can provide us with a technology for designing better cultures.

In responding to Skinner I shall be concerned only with those aspects of his position that most directly concern the creation of settings. Although I shall find Skinner very wanting in several respects and regard his contribution as being far less than he believes—and that indeed he misses the most important problems—I regard what he has tried to do as a bold effort to grapple with the most important issues confronting society. Furthermore, as I shall indicate later, unlike some vocal critics who seem to regard Skinner as a sinister figure who contemplates with glee the possibility of manipulating individuals and settings, I regard him as in the humanistic tradition. I have never met Professor Skinner but a careful reading of *Walden Two* and *Beyond Freedom And Dignity* convinces me that he is for and not against man, for creative and not imprisoned man.

Individual Psychology

Among the most obvious features of the creation of a new setting is that it involves two or more people. In the kinds of settings we have been talking about the number of people increases and another feature emerges: many of the people are unknown to each other. In earlier chapters I emphasized that in the earliest stages the addition of each new person is a problem to himself as well as to the existing group. In fact, the addition of each new person is a danger point because it can change existing contingencies in disruptive ways. Today we are used to saying that one of the unfortunate features of modern society is the sheer size of its major settings, for example, government, schools, corporations, hospitals, state institutions. When we say that things have become too big, we mean that we cannot, or do not know how to, control the processes of growth in order to avoid inefficiency, conflict, alienation, and adaptation (among other things). And when we say big we usually mean hundreds or thousands of people as if there were a point below which we know how to handle the processes of growth. The study of new settings, however, reveals that almost every problem and social process we associate with overpopulated settings appears in the earliest stages of a new setting. From one standpoint this is not surprising because when each of a small number of individuals is a unique organism, and they are then brought into a sustained relationship with each other, there is no *a priori* basis for expecting that the result will be smooth. Indeed, the one thing one observes is that a new environment is created characterized, in Skinner's terms, by a new, and historically unique, array of reinforcements and schedules. What one experiences in observing is the sense of unpredictability and the feeling of impotence that one does not know what is causing or is related to what. Paradoxically, if you are in the role of impartial observer trying to make sense out of what you see, your task is more difficult phenomenologically than if you are a participant because then you are observing in order to act and you must come to some conclusion, which is to say you resolve uncertainty and unpredictability, frequently by the kind of mentalistic explanations Skinner derogates. In one sense Skinner is correct in maintaining that our usual mentalistic explanations distract us from discerning the environmental forces shaping and sustaining overt behavior. However, trying to ascertain these forces, let us say in the case of a leader and his core group, is at this stage of our knowledge and capabilities a staggering task. The task is not that of observing *an* individual but a group of individuals in an ever-changing, uncontrived environment. What is required is more than a conception of how one individual is shaped by his environment because such a conception simply cannot deal with the problem of individuals interacting in a social matrix in which everybody is part of everyone else's environment.

I shall illustrate the problem by asking the reader to imagine he is interested in the behavior of rats (or pigeons)', and he contrives a laboratory situation in which he thinks he can begin to study behavior, its shapers and consequences. If he does what almost all animal psychologists do, he will study individual rats, each of which will have an opportunity to be center stage, namely, with no supporting cast and the psychologist as an audience of one. He gets to know each of these rats extraordinarily well, and he is able to make certain generalizations about the behavior of rats. But then the idea occurs to him to repeat his observations with rat A, but this time he will also put rat B into the apparatus. He will observe new behavior, social behavior, and it is likely that he will not find it easy to use his earlier generalizations to explain the social behavior he has just observed. But he will try, and perhaps with a little conceptual straining he will explain what happened. (He could not, of course, have predicted what would happen). And then he decides that he should introduce rat C to rats A and B. At this point the experimenter is probably aware of several things: that he has to observe quite differently, that what he is observing is quite complex, that his ability to predict is not very good, and that he may need new concepts about social behavior. If he continues adding new but well understood individual rats into the situation, he will undoubtedly end up overwhelmed not only by the complexities of dynamic (ever-changing) social behaviors he observes and his inability to determine how things got related and changed but by the conceptual task with which he is faced if he is to make sense of it all. And this does not take place in the "real" world but in a situation in which the experimenter has as much control as he wants or can imagine over the animals and their physical environment.

Skinner's principles of behavior stem almost exclusively from studies of individual organisms. In fact, he is one in a long line of American psychologists who have spent much of their lives designing environments in which to study single organisms.[1] Over the years we have been presented with all kinds of learning principles and theories which were considered basic for understanding human social behavior. In fact, since almost every school teacher has been required in his training to take a course in learning, he was exposed to ideas based

---

[1] The Norway rat was for decades the most frequently used animal. Years ago in a delightful and incisive paper, "The Snark was a Boojum," the distinguished comparative psychologist, F. A. Beach (1950), pointed out the dangers of basing psychological theory on a single type of animal in an unnatural setting (alone to boot).

almost exclusively on the learning of individual rats. Nobody has ever demonstrated in anything resembling a compelling manner that these principles and theories were or are relevant to learning in the social matrix of a classroom.

I have witnessed a number of attempts to apply Skinnerian principles for changing an ongoing setting or creating a setting consistent with his principles. Three things can be said about these efforts. First, the leaders were unprepared for the complexities they encountered. Second, they used ideas and principles not contained in or readily derivable from Skinnerian principles (for instance, social structure, role, power). Third, in varying degrees they came to see that they needed but did not have a workable conception of social or institutional change.

I am not taking the position that Skinnerian principles could not be elaborated in a way to handle my objections. I believe they cannot, but that is not my major point which is that Skinner's principles are at present quite inadequate for dealing with the problem either of changing or designing new settings. Skinner's claim that he has developed a scientific conception of man possessing such unrivalled explanatory power that we can now begin the technological task of changing existing settings and designing new ones is, to say the least, unjustified. Skinner seems to believe that his principles of behavior represent a sharp break with the substantive traditions of American psychology, if not with all past thinking in Western civilization. Unfortunately for him he is but the latest example of a tradition in which isolated organisms are studied in contrived and unnatural settings. This is not inherently a bad tradition, except when it purports to serve as a basis for understanding and controlling behavior in complicated social settings.

Leadership and Control

The more polemical of Skinner's critics see him as advocating a massive kind of control over the lives of people that would rob them of all that has been good and great in human history. He is, his critics say, taking the stand that an elite group will have to assume the responsibility for determining how and for what purposes society shall survive. Visions of George Orwell's *1984* come to the mind of many as they read Skinner. According to some, Skinner's position will recreate in society what he has done so well in the laboratory, namely, to control and manipulate an individual and his environment according to Skinner's ideas and values, and his values leave much to be desired.

I shall leave to the next section a discussion of this type of criticism. However, what should not be postponed is an issue contained in these criticisms, and one that is central to the creation of settings regardless of one's position. I refer to the nature and the consequences of leadership in the context of creating a new setting or society. For someone like Skinner, who says that he has provided the scientific basis for designing new and better cultures, one would expect that he would rather directly raise and discuss leadership in the context of his behavioral principles. After all, his principles of behavior are applicable to all people, and leaders no less than anyone else are governed by the same forces. (Early on, Freud came to see that a general theory of human behavior was not only applicable to anyone who used it for the purposes of changing human behavior but was especially so, precisely because the lives of others were involved. Active as he always was in changing the behavior of others, it is not surprising that he was as concerned with the changer as with those who were changed.) But Skinner is remarkably silent on the issue, and it is not because he is unaware of it. The issue gets raised rather testily in *Walden Two*, but it can hardly be said to have been confronted. We are told that the different levels of leadership stay in office for a limited period of time, but the overwhelming impression one gets is that because everyone in the community is appropriately motivated and understands and adheres to its overarching values, there is a built-in regulating mechanism which acts as a control against the kinds of social craziness we know too well in our society. However, Skinner was describing a utopia, and one of their distinguishing characteristics is that they are virtuously different from society as we know it.

In light of the critical reception *Walden Two* received, one would expect that in his most recent book Skinner would have responded to the charges of elitism and the dangers of uncontrolled leadership. We get hardly a word. He reiterates the differences between his conception of man and that of his critics and hammers away at the point that man has always been controlled according to Skinnerian principles and that when we recognize, accept, and act on this fact, we are more likely to insure society's survival. It is strange that Skinner is so silent about where he stands in regard to what bothers his critics: Is there not abundant evidence that power, be it given or taken, frequently corrupts? That the role of leader brings out the best and the worst in people? That, historically, leaders, like scientists in the laboratory, need to be controlled against their capacity to subvert their own purposes? Why does not Skinner recognize that over the centuries one of the reasons people have adhered to the myth of freedom is their experience with leaders and their knowledge of the facts and consequences of power? Take, for example, the discussion in *Walden Two* about how children of ages three and four are taught self-control by building up their tolerance for annoying experience.

Take this case. A group of children arrive home after a long walk, tired and hungry. They're expecting supper: They find, instead, that it is time for a lesson in self-control; they must stand for five minutes in front of steaming bowls of soup.

"The assignment is accepted like a problem in arithmetic. Any groaning or complaining is a wrong answer. Instead, the children begin at once to work upon themselves to avoid any unhappiness during the delay. One of them may make a joke of it. We encourage a sense of humor as a good way of not taking an annoyance seriously. The joke won't be much, according to adult standards—perhaps the child will simply pretend to empty the bowl of soup into his upturned mouth. Another may start a song with many verses. The rest join in at once, for they've learned that it's a good way to make time pass."

Frazier glanced uneasily at Castle, who was not to be appeased.

"That also strikes you as a form of torture, Mr. Castle?" he asked.

"I'd rather be put on the rack," said Castle [p. 109].

Skinner's response is that the young children pass this off "as lightly as a five minute delay at curtain time. We regard it as a fairly elementary test. Much more difficult problems follow." To the aghast visitors to Walden Two Skinner has the guide point out that the innoculation of frustration tolerance is humane in the extreme compared to the ways in which many young children in our society are brutalized and maltreated, a sticky point for those appalled by the seemingly increasing frequency of child abuse in our society. But Skinner never asks if one factor in this is that those who abuse have the power to do so, and often this is legally sanctioned. That is to say, possessing and exercising power can lead to its abuse, and this possibility is no less in Walden Two than in our own society. Skinner is silent on the means of control over such a possibility, and for two reasons. First, Walden Two is a utopia. Second, Skinner's conception of designing new cultures is explicitly technological, and the problems of power and its controls are not contained in it.

At a later point in the book Skinner has one of the visitors to Walden Two express the skeptical view that in light of the failures of earlier attempts to create new and better settings, why should Walden Two not be expected to die at an early age? Skinner's angry retort is that there is no similarity between Walden Two and earlier efforts. Really, he says, we know very little about these earlier attempts, and we cannot say why they failed. "Some of them broke up because the members couldn't resist the temptation to divide the loot, and a few still survive. But the crucial thing is the psychological management, and of this we know very little. A few facts, yes, but an adequate picture, no" (p. 157). Just as he is unaware that he is applying to social behavior a set of principles derived from isolated, individual animals (mostly rats), Skinner seems unaware that he is comparing a utopia to real-world efforts to create new societies, and he concludes that he has nothing to learn from them. In refusing to try to explain these past failures, except by the blanket criticism that their conceptions of human behavior and management were obviously wrong, Skinner betrays his innocence about the relationships between principles and actions. It is as if he is saying that if your conceptions are right, your results will be right, and one does not have to worry about the implementer's (leader's) capacities to foul things up. Between conception and practice there are no dilemmas for Skinner, just technology. Rarely have the problems of leadership and power been so neatly solved! Skinner seems to have all the characteristics of people who start new settings: superior ideas, superior mission, and unimpeachable motivations. He has more in common with the earlier attempts than he knows.

I cannot answer the question of why Skinner does not deal with issues of leadership and power, but I venture to guess that he has never attempted to create a setting. He imagined Walden Two; creating a setting involves everything that precedes Chapter One in that book.

Skinnerian principles of behavior apply to leaders as well as to everyone else, and if those principles are taken seriously, they emphasize the significance of the leadership problem. As soon as an individual (or group) takes, or is given, the role of leader, his surrounding environment changes in terms of strength and types of stimulation and reinforcement and the leader is not always aware, indeed can never be completely aware, of these changes. Skinner makes the valid point that our fascination with what goes on inside the heads of people has made us pretty poor observers of environments and those aspects of them which relate to and maintain overt behavior.[2] Even

[2] This is a point that Roger Barker (1963) has made over the years and to which he has devoted a lifetime of research. Whereas Skinner has spent a lot of time looking at individual animals in a Skinner box, Barker has focused on a single community and has illuminated how complex and time consuming is the process of description, let alone of understanding. Skinner makes no mention of Barker, who has done more sophisticated conceptualizing and research in the structure of human environments than anyone else in American psychology.

if leaders had the keenest understanding of Skinnerian principles, the nature and requirements of action would prevent them from being able to know and assess the complexities impinging on them.

Skinner's failure to deal with the problems of leadership and controls is serious, if not fatal. If we take his conceptual position seriously, we should pay most attention to what he says and not to what *we* think *he* thinks and feels. If we do that, we must conclude that he has surprisingly little to say about the most thorny aspects of the design of new settings and that they are not very important. This conclusion is at such variance with past and present experience that we must hope that he will someday break the silence, hopefully on the basis of studies more relevant than his past ones to the questions for which he thinks he has provided answers. After all, what is at stake, and Skinner has put it there, is the design of new cultures. For those who wish to move towards a future society better than the one we now have, he puts them on a voyage guided by the sirens of the myths of freedom and dignity and faith in Skinner's behavioral science and technology. The traveler would be well advised to tie himself to the mast.

My objection to Skinner is not that his position is wrong but that it is incredibly incomplete. It solves the problem of the creation of settings by labeling it technological, a typically American solution to social problems. It pays homage to and genuflects before the experimental method and spirit as if that fully compensates for incomplete and inadequate observation and description of the problems under study. And by an exercise of assertion and faith the elegant simplicity of its principles is presented to us as isomorphic with the workings of the social world. Parsimony of principles is not an inherent virtue.

View Of Man in Society

One cannot understand Skinner unless one recognizes that he has posed and answered an age old question: What should be the relationship between the individual and the larger society? Put in another way: Should the value of individual freedom take precedence over that of group survival? Skinner's unambiguous answer is that although it may once have been justified to consider the rights of the individual as supreme over all else, this should no longer be tolerated

---

Although it is an *ad hominem,* I confess to the impression that Skinner's desire to be viewed as a thinker whose ideas could revolutionize man and society has caused him to overlook the works of others, present and past. It may even be that this desire accounts in part for his insensitivity to some of the points of his critics because if he dealt with the issues more directly, he might find he had conceptual kinship with many writers in the near and distant past.

because it threatens the very existence of society. And for Skinner, as for so many other thoughtful people, the number one question on the world agenda is how to save society from self-destruction. Furthermore, he points out, it is difficult to look at human history and be very impressed by the number of people who have enjoyed individual liberty and freedom. On the contrary, most people have lead miserable, unfulfilled, imprisoned lives. No, says Skinner, I have far less to defend than those who worship at the shrine of individualism. The individualist "has refused to be concerned for the survival of his culture and is not reinforced by the fact that the culture will long survive him. In the defense of his own freedom and dignity he has denied the contributions of the past and must therefore relinquish all claim upon the future" (Skinner 1971, p. 210). Fine, say his critics, but if Skinner's answer is *Walden Two,* then we have to decline to share his vision. Such a wholesale rejection misses some of Skinner's most cogent points, points that anyone interested in new settings should not overlook.

The most distinguishing features of Skinner's utopia are how willingly its citizens give priority to the needs of their society. Each of its citizens understands that however important his own needs and goals might be, and they are important in that society, they are secondary to those values and rules upon which the society rests and because of which it will survive. Phenomenologically no one experiences a conflict between individual and group values, and if such conflict should occur, it is resolved quickly in favor of the group values. Skinner's citizens are not selfless or automatons but rather individuals who have a crystal clear commitment to the survival of their community. And they are happy people. What Skinner describes is far from utopian because it is one of the most frequent characteristics of the earliest phases of the creation of a setting, namely, an unconflicted willingness to be part of a larger group, to give priority to its needs and survival, and to give of one's self in various ways that an observer would call selfless. And they are happy people. In fact, they are for the rest of their lives likely to look back at this period nostalgically, full of memories of belongingness, joy in work, and the excitement of shared accomplishments. These memories do not contain elements of coercion or stagnation or cattlelike contentment; on the contrary the memories are full of the sense of growth and challenge. It happened in their lives and not in a literary utopia. In earlier chapters I have tried to understand why this happens, why it is such a brief period in the life of the new setting, how it comes about that individual needs become dominant over group needs (and the level of unhappiness increases), and the setting loses its momentum and purpose. The point is that it is possible for the values of the group to be dominant over individual ones without loss of freedom and dignity. In fact, as I have tried to show in a new setting, the feeling that one has lost freedom and dignity appears after that early phase which is remembered, as so frequently it was actually experienced, with fondness.

If one cannot accept Skinner's assurances about the validity and completeness of his science of behavior or about our readiness to start the technological task of designing new cultures, one should not be blind to the fact that in raising the issue of the relation of the one to the many Skinner is asking the important question. And if one does not like his clear rejection of the primacy of the individual, one is not absolved from answering Skinner's argument that the primacy of the individual is not unrelated to the ills of modern society and threatens its very existence. Just within this century we have witnessed a level of human slaughter and abuse within and between societies that makes a mockery of the concept of progress. And if everyone who has rushed into print has not indicated how the world is going to hell, no one has verbalized that we are making a heaven on earth.

We must distinguish between two criticisms of Skinner's argument. The first is that the process of implementing Skinner's conceptions would create a society worse than the one we are now in. The second is that it is both wrong and impossible to give supremacy to group values and survival without sacrificing individual growth and creativity. To the second criticism I have again to remind Skinner's critics that in the earliest phases of a new setting one frequently finds the situation in which the primacy of group values can exist without sacrifice of the individual's growth. If this usually lasts for only a brief period of time (and very occasionally for a period of years), the explanation lies less in the inevitable clash between individual and group values than in the absence of an organized set of conceptions which does not permit the participants to bypass the problem. Skinner is wrong in assuming that the reason earlier new communities failed is that they did not possess his scientific principles of behavior. He would be on more secure ground if he said that with few exceptions they did not have any organized conception of what they were about, what they would experience, and what they could do to avoid early failure. My experience leaves no doubt that the failure of most new settings is contained in simplistic notions compounded of unbridled hope, the best of intentions, and the denial of present or future conflict. It is noteworthy that in *Walden Two* there are numerous vehicles which serve several functions, for instance, to remind its citizens about the group's rules and their rationale and to provide forums for raising questions about the rules. Awareness and discussion of the group's rules are not left to chance, and each aspect of the code reflects an anticipation of possible problems and conflicts. Walden Two is a highly verbal society, and much of the talk centers around the needs and goals of the community. The model for how to talk and act is its founder, Frazier, who never seems to let himself or others forget what the community is about, the necessity for confronting and not avoiding problems, that a rosy view of the future is no substitute for vigilance in the present, that courteous talk is too frequently a cover for straight talk, and that the primacy of group values is a necessary condition to permit individuals to live creative and diversified lives. Skinner, of course, attributes the wonders of Walden Two to the validity and force of his principles of behavior; he says nothing about the fact that Frazier's behavior and success as a leader are not readily explained by those principles. Since the inventors of utopias do not have to concern themselves with the processes of creation, we do not really know how Frazier did it, but Skinner obviously chose a leader with many of the characteristics that most leaders do not have and the wisdom behind that choice are not in Skinner's principles. One can only express regret again that in his most recent book Skinner does not discuss (or raise) the relationships among his principles of behavior the choice and behavior of leaders and (from his standpoint) the engineering of new settings. If he did so, I predict that he would readily discover that his set of principles is a very incomplete basis for action in the social world. But this kind of criticism should not distract us from recognizing the cogency of Skinner's point that the design of new cultures is not a problem in esthetics or an exercise in motivation but in conceptualization which guides action, maximizes consistency, and yet fosters change.

In earlier chapters I pointed out that what is so attractive to people about participating in the creation of a new setting is that it introduces welcome novelty and challenge into their lives. Most people experience some boredom in relation to work, and many experience a great deal of it. The feeling that one is locked into a particular job or line of work, that one will never have the opportunity to test one's self in diverse kinds of tasks, is one consequence of pyramidally, hierarchically organized settings, but not limited to them. Many professional people outside such settings also feel trapped by circumstances that they perceive as preventing them from exploring new roles and untested interests and capacities. There are those who would maintain that the frequency and depth of feelings of boredom and alienation are the best indicators that our society is based on a conception of man that is obviously faulty and self-defeating. A fair reading of *Walden Two* should leave the impression that Skinner believes that boredom is one of the most destructive feelings in our society and that one of the major accomplishments of his utopia is that it is organized in a way that permits an individual the time and support to lead a diversified existence in which boredom is the exception rather than the rule. If anything is clear, it is that Skinner believes that the happiness of an individual depends on an environment that permits him to remain curious about himself and his world and supports his efforts to move in new directions. Furthermore, he asserts in the strongest terms that in our present society we will never be able to see how protean man really is. Cursed as we are by rampant professionalism, making a fetish as we do of formal credentials that penalize those who do not possess them and imprison those who do, and unreflectively confusing education with wisdom, the cards are stacked against the experience of novelty, challenge, and diversification. (And long before Women's Lib became so fashionable Skinner provided its conceptual rationale, although he was certainly not the first to do so.)[3]

Skinner's analysis of the relationships among boredom, work, and the capacities of man seems identical to that which gave rise to the Yale Psycho-Educational Clinic (Chapter Three), Goldenberg's Residential Youth Center (Chapter Six), and the Central Connecticut Regional Center (Sarason, Zitnay, and Grossman, 1972). In each of these new settings a pyramidal structure was minimal or absent, absence of formal credentials was no bar to learning new roles, changing roles was considered a matter of course, specialization of function was considered a potential trap for the individual, and in relatively short order it all seemed natural. It did not seem natural to outsiders. An independent comparative study by Sarata (1972) of several settings, one of which was the Central Connecticut Regional Center, found the personnel of the CCRC to have the highest level of job satisfaction and the most traditional of the settings to have the lowest.

[3] Skinner's view of man is perfectly consistent with the rise and demands of the paraprofessional movement, i.e., that people should do what they can learn to do unfettered by titles and irrelevantly formal criteria of education. Also, his conception of the man-environment relationship suggests that he would look upon the conclusions of Jensen's (1969) report on intellectual differences between blacks and whites as but another in a long line of examples of premature conclusions based on wrong conceptions of the principles and origins of behavior.

In fact, the level of job satisfaction was very highly correlated with the setting's degree of role rigidity.

The several settings I have described in greatest detail in this book not only confirm Skinner's analysis of what is wrong with existing settings but demonstrate that it is possible to create new ones in which people's conception of themselves in relation to work is radically different from what is ordinarily experienced, a difference that in each case resulted in important innovations. Related as I was to each of these settings, my observations and conclusions are not above being suspect, although Sarata's independent study suggests that my opinions cannot be lightly dismissed. I must, therefore, add the observation, supportive of Skinner's basic point, that in each of these settings the commitment of its people to its survival was, at least, coequal as a value to that of the furtherance of individual interests. People willingly contributed (phenomenologically it was not a sacrifice) to the survival of the setting not only because they saw it as a vehicle for their own development but because it represented something desirable, a communality without which individual accomplishments would lose their flavor. We knew we needed each other and that as soon as we forgot that we were back on the road to individual freedom and loneliness.

Skinner's principles of behavior purport to explain why man is what he is and why he can become quite different. In the process of illustrating the elegant simplicity and power of his principles, he also gives us glimpses of his conception of the structure of modern society, a conception without which his illustrations would have no meaning. In his indictment of capitalistic society he shows us that he knows that it is organized on economic and political grounds so that man's relationship to this work constricts his horizons, extinguishes his capacities for growth, brings him into conflict with and separates him from his fellow man, and makes him view death as a "final solution" to a miserable existence. There is a striking similarity between the views of Skinner and those of Karl Marx in his philosophical manuscripts of 1844 (Fromm, 1961). And like Marx, Skinner believes that in the name of capitalistic freedom and dignity most people are condemned to a mental jail with a life sentence. Modern society is not for but against the individual. Skinner, like Marx, concludes that the fetish of individualism, however progressive it may once have been, is an obstacle to society's development and survival and must be denied its accustomed priority. The survival of society must take precedence over all else and over the long run will produce truly self-fullfilled man.

Marx's analysis included attributing purpose to history (the class struggle) and provided him with a program of action. In *Walden Two*, Skinner looks at Russia with both contempt and sorrow, contempt because in the name of man he was enslaved again, sorrow because the leaders of that revolution did not understand the principles of behavior. (Skinner becomes verbally livid at the use of force and punishment, something his critics have failed to mention or emphasize.) And to what actions does Skinner's analysis of *society* lead to? We are not told. Skinner avoids examining the consequences of his social analysis. It could hardly be otherwise if for no other reason than his principles of behavior have no logical relationship to his view of society. Marx maintained that it would make no sense to develop a theory of atoms which was independent of a theory of molecules. Skinner's principles of behavior are (humanly) asocial in statement and content; they are as applicable to rats or pigeons as they are to man or any other animal. Their presumed generality is considered one of their distinctive features. Their generality, however, is gained at the expense of an analysis of the structure of natural environments human or otherwise. They are principles in search of social contexts except that there is nothing in the principles to orient one to the structure of societies. His principles tell us nothing of the structure of human society, and what he tells us about human society is obviously not derived from his principles. This lack of relationship is particularly noteworthy and troublesome because Skinner is proposing social action and change. It makes no difference whether the proposals have to do with an entire society or one small part of it, with creating a large or a small setting. Proposals for action require a unified conception of principles and society, of man in society. Action based in behavioral principles unrelated to social principles is a guarantee of failure. Skinner wants to change the world, to design new cultures, and to reshape society. And yet he knows that this must take place in a highly structured, complex society. He also knows that this society will not willingly change because of the compelling attractiveness of his visions of a blissful future. I assume that he also knows (if only from his critics) that society will resist and derogate the changes he advocates. And I also assume that Skinner knows that between his principles of behavior and social action is a void yet to be filled by him. And we further know that in social action he is opposed to the use of force as a way of achieving desired consequence, even though our society reeks with force and violence. If Skinner knows so much, why is he telling us so little about action in his society? If he is opposed to tyranny and force, how does he tell us to avoid them?

How will his social engineering avoid confirming the actuarially sound maxim that the more things change the more they remain the same? These are legitimate questions to direct to Skinner, who said he has provided a scientific analysis of behavior that can serve as the basis for developing a new social technology at Walden Two for social change *now*. In this utopia he does not have to deal with our society as he knows it or worry about attaining power and the abuses of power; he does not have to worry about falling short of goals, or about hostile environments, or even about deviant people. He does not *have* to worry in his utopia. But if he is to engage in social engineering in our society, he *must* worry about these questions. What we require of Skinner, what his own devotion to the experimental spirit demands, is that he do what the founder of Walden One did for his particular purposes, and that is to act and learn. There is a difference between proclaiming and demonstrating the truth, and the difference is usually an increment in knowledge and understanding that alters the proclamation, and sometimes renders it worthless.

Skinner is a thoroughgoing humanist. He wants the best for man: for him to be happy, differentiated, and social rather than miserable, constricted, and alone. To design the new cultures he provides us with his principles of behavior and the social value of the priority of the group. When one reads *Walden Two* (for instance, when he discusses Jesus) and the later chapters of *Beyond Freedom and Dignity*, one gains the impression that Skinner has one more tool: love. It adds an important ingredient, but it is still not enough.

CHAPTER **13**

The New Setting
as a Work of Art

The creation of settings is a general problem. It is not a new one, and yet it remains relatively unformulated. Although settings are created at a fantastic rate, and man has always created them, is it justified to say that the problem remains unformulated? After all, man does not create settings in his sleep; he does use his head and heart. One of the points I have emphasized is that creating a setting is one of man's most absorbing experiences, compounded as it is of dreams, hopes, effort, and thought. In the lives of individuals few things rival their participation in the creation of a setting for poignancy, memories, and meanings. And in the lives of societies one of the distinguishing features of their histories is the new instrumentalities that emerged in relation to social problems. Steiner (1971, p. 11) has compellingly made the point that the catastrophic condition of the modern world is in large part a consequence of the excitement, enthusiasm, bright hopes, and the new instrumentalities that characterized the period between 1789 and 1815. "No string of quotations, no statistics, can recapture for us what must have been the inner-excitement, the passionate adventure of spirit and emotion, unleashed by the events of 1789 and sustained, at a fantastic tempo, until 1815. Far more than political revolution and war, on an unprecedented scale of geographical and social compass, is involved. The French revolution and the Napoleonic wars—*la grande epopee*—literally quickened the pace of felt time."

It is clear that the revolutionary and Napoleonic decades brought on an overwhelming immanence, a deep, emotionally stressed change in the quality of hope. Expectations of progress, of personal and social enfranchisement, which had formerly had a conventional, often allegoric character, as a millenary horizon, suddenly moved very close. The great metaphor of renewal, of the creation, as by a second coming of secular grace, of a just, rational city for man, took on the urgent drama of concrete possibility. The eternal "tomorrow" of utopian political vision became, as it were, Monday morning. We experience something of this dizzying sense of total possibility when reading the decrees of the Convention and of the Jacobin regime: injustice, superstition, poverty are to be eradicated *now*, in the next glorious hour. The world is to shed its worn skin a fortnight hence. In the grammar of Saint-Juste the future tense is never more than moments away. If we seek to trace this irruption —it was that violent—of dawn into proviate sensibility, we need look only to Wordsworth's Prelude and to the poetry of Shelley. The crowning statement, perhaps, is to be found in Marx's economic and political manuscripts of 1844. Not since early Christianity had men felt so near to renovation and to the end of night (pp. 13–14).

And what followed, Steiner maintains, was "the great boredom," the "sensation of history gone absurdly wrong." "How can an intellectual bear to feel within himself something of Bonaparte's genius, something of that demonic strength which led from obscurity to empire, and see before him nothing but the tawdry flatness of bureaucracy?" The collapse of revolutionary hopes was near complete, the "great ennui" had begun. The barbarism of the modern age, Steiner asserts, did not begin with World War I, but was already contained in the "insane vitality" of the Napoleonic era. We look upon most of the nineteenth century as a kind of golden age of progress and hope, but in truth it was nurturing the sense of frustration and hopelessness that would culminate in twentieth-century holocausts and massacres. Steiner's assessment of the past 150 years reflects implicit conceptions amazingly similar to those I have emphasized in viewing the history of the creation of a single setting. In the end, in a somewhat desperate effort to be hopeful, Steiner tells us that "mental inquiry must move forward, . . . such motion is natural and meritorious in itself." But where should we move? About what should we inquire that gives the possibility that the social creations of man will not fail as frequently or as catastrophically? And if the best that we can hope for is the excitement that accompanies understanding and the sense that one has learned, what shall we try to understand?

The creation of settings as a problem has been unformulated in several respects. First, there has been little attempt to seek the genotypical communalities underlying a bewildering array of phenotypically different settings, for instance, marriage, communes, helping institutions, a new business, a new university, Head Start, Job Corps. They are different, they look different, they have different purposes, they are populated by different kinds of people. These and other differences ordinarily prevent us from asking if the processes by which these settings are created are similar, if not identical. Egyptian, Byzantine, Renaissance, Impressionist, and Cubist art are unmistakably different, but no one would conclude that they reflect unmistakably different processes. Second, even in regard to a single type of setting, we do not have the concepts to direct us to the developmental tasks and problems which are encountered, including, as they should, prehistory and before-the-beginning phases. When we look at available descriptions, they appear to be clear, ordered, and reasonable, but they turn out not to be comparable in terms of what the writers consider to be relevant factors and information. As a result, it is impossible or dangerous to generalize, and one is tempted to conclude that each setting is unique and that whatever lessons one draws have no particular significance for future efforts. The third respect in which the problem is unformulated is reflected in the differences of opinion people have in understanding success and failure. More specifically, explanations of the frequency of failure are remarkably varied and seem to have but one thing in common: oversimplification. They are either simplistically psychological or broadly sociological, and neither does justice to what one observes about the creation of settings. Of course it is a psychological process, and of course the psychological is embedded in and reflects characteristics of the larger society. But this level of truth is only a starting point for the task of formulating conceptions about the process; it is not an explanation of the complexity of the process, let alone of success and failure.

The final respect in which I consider the problem unformulated requires some personal history. I was a teenager during the Great Depression, and I knew what it was to skip meals and to expect that

each new day would present our family with questions of sheer existence. Fortunately, teenagers can usually withstand a fantastic degree
of buffeting without losing completely the capacity to dream and hope.
(They may lose a lot of other things, like their sanity, but they still
dream of a better future.) Like so many of my peers, I concluded that
our society needed a radical overhaul, and I seized upon Marxism and
the Russian revolution as models for thinking and action. They provided all of the answers and frequently to questions I had never asked
or even knew existed. I joined the faction (Trotskyite) of the radical
movement that considered the Russian revolution to have been the
most progressive in human history but the potentials of which were not
being realized, namely, its goals were being perverted because of a
combination of psychological, social, and historical factors. By joining
this group (if my friends were in another faction I would have been
there) I was, so to speak, forced to become interested in why the Russian revolution was failing. Why was the golden opportunity turning
into a human nightmare (as described by Conquest, 1968)? This was
for me the beginning, albeit vague and unformulated, of my interest
in the creation of settings.

My first job as a professional psychologist was in a new setting
based on innovative concepts about the residential care of mentally
retarded children. Initially it was a magnificent social experience in
that diverse kinds of people were working together, no one lacked for
a sense of meaning and worth, and the needs of the children were all
important. We were aware that we had a golden opportunity, and we
were secure in the feeling that the revolutionary innovations could be
sustained. But that was initially. Unlike the Russian revolution it did
not turn into a human nightmare. It just became a setting riddled with
conflict, divided into departmental and professional empires, each with
imperialistic tendencies, and the needs of the children became increasingly perceived in fractionated ways. Needless to say, I had my own
explanations, and they were primarily in terms of an individual psychology, namely, if the leader was a different kind of person, if this
director was not so obtuse, if that director were not so narcissistic, and
so on. (And, of course, none of the explanations pertained to me!) So
this was another revolution that succumbed to counter-revolutionary
forces. The new began to resemble the old.

My entrance into academia after World War II coincided with
(indeed was only made possible by) governmentally sponsored programs for the training of mental health personnel who would be
necessary to man the new settings being created to service the needs of
returning veterans. My position required that I help create a new

setting within our department. More important, I was in a position to observe and to consult a wide variety of new helping settings. Again these were invigorating experiences. Money seemed to be no problem, many were resolved to break with the arid traditions of their academic disciplines (those were the days when psychoanalysis could enter *and* stay in the academic halls), hospitals were springing up like prairie grass, and our cities began to be dotted by new out-patient clinics. The mental health revolution was well under way, the third revolution in which I was a participant. In the fifteen years after World War II, I came to observe and know at least a score of new settings. With very few exceptions they became, and fairly quickly, what they had wanted to avoid being. This is not to say that they were not helpful to some clients but rather that as settings they lost the sense of shared mission, became caught up in all kinds of strife, turnover of staff began to zoom, the sense of hope diminished, and work became routine. It took a long time, but I began to be aware that although each had been a unique setting, populated by unique beings, they not only had similar fates but there was a way of viewing each of their histories that suggested that these settings had been created on the basis of some implicit assumptions and a conception of organizational development that were highly similar, indeed identical. The developmental aspects of the creation of a setting began to intrigue me, I reviewed the histories of the new settings I had known with new questions and concepts, and I began to look for new instances I could observe. I also began to search the literature for descriptions of how new settings had been created, with no marked success. At first I was amazed that the organizational literature was almost exclusively concerned with chronologically mature settings and their problems, but then I realized that people in this field tended to focus on problems for which they got paid, not unlike other people in other fields. Organizations ask outsiders to come in when they have serious problems, and this is usually when the setting is beyond its early phases. It also became apparent that we knew more about the industrial setting than about any other kind, again because they have more money or because when they are not making money, they are in danger of dying, and so they seek help. I began to talk to knowledgeable people in the relevant disciplines about the creation of settings, but the questions I asked seemed to intrigue no one. It was as if I was interested in the problems of infancy and most everybody else was intrigued with adulthood. One thing I assumed to be absolutely true (thanks to Freud): To use our knowledge of chronologically mature settings as a basis for understanding what their early characteristics and processes were was risky and inevitably distorting. You can learn things about childhood from working with adults, but there is more to childhood than that.

Later events in the larger society provided me with more instances of new settings than I could possibly observe and study. In the early sixties, the beginning of the war on poverty, new settings began to proliferate at a dizzying pace. It was also the time when I decided to start the Yale Psycho-Educational Clinic. That decision reflected many factors, but one of the most important was my feeling that I had to experience the creation of a setting from scratch, so to speak. Because this clinic would be very much involved in the new settings being created almost weekly gave me a marvelous opportunity to see how they unfolded—and how so many folded.

The point of this personal history is that I came to see that people who create new settings have no organized formulation of what they are about. Phenomenologically, they know what they are about, but it is not a phenomenology that reflects an independent, organized set of conceptions that guides and controls, that permits, indeed requires, one to take distance from the flow and clash of events. That a new setting has a prehistory, local and national; that locally many different individuals and groups have a role in its birth; that much of its past is in the living present and must be dealt with; that resources are always limited and usually overestimated because of a sense of mission and boundless enthusiasm; that conflict within the setting (and between settings) is a fact of social life exacerbated by conflicts between ideas; that verbal agreement about values is no substitute for forging a constitution that anticipates and helps deal with differences in values, ideas, and change; that the leader is inevitably a model for the thinking and actions of others and that in the usual unthinking course of things the leader visits on others his increasing sense of privacy, fear of openness, dependence on extrinsic factors as criteria of worth, and boredom; that the usual structure of settings as well as the definition of and credentials for work tend rather quickly to extinguish curiosity and the sense of challenge—these are only some of the ingredients that would have to be encompassed by a formulation of the creation of settings.

Although the problem has remained unformulated, there can be no doubt that in some vague way many people are approaching and groping with it. Take, for example, Boguslaw's interesting book *The New Utopians* (1965). His prefatory statement conveys well the sense of urgency so many people have.

This essay was begun as a relatively straightforward description of problems in the analysis and design of contemporary large-scale computer-based command-and-control systems. It was addressed to the professionals who work together as more-or-less interdisciplinary teams on terrestrial and extraterrestrial large-scale systems projects—to those who call themselves system engineers, computer programers, operations researchers, and the like. These are the persons who link the peoples of the world together in communication networks; insure the timely production, transportation, and distribution of bananas, beeswax, and bombs, and increasingly use high-speed digital computers in the process.

But it was not long before I became more and more impressed with the similarity between the intellectual underpinnings of the modern materials I was using and the formulations of social theorists in the Utopian tradition who analyzed existing social systems and designed new ones. I saw that modern system designers were unconsciously treading well-worn paths—that they were embracing the most fundamental errors of earlier efforts and were incorporating them into the fabric of even the most sophisticated of pushbutton systems.

The current preoccupation with computer-based systems and automation has, unfortunately, left the contemporary social scientist, together with the overwhelming majority of our population, occupying the role of bystander. His characteristic involvement in system-design efforts is ex post facto, and this greatly circumscribes the range of his possible influence on the design of these crucially significant frames for social behavior.

But the issues involved are much too critical to remain exclusively the preoccupation of our new utopians. What are the characteristics of technology and system design that shape the possibilities for social change in a given society? What characteristics of social change define the possible parameters for technological development and system design? In the face of all this, how *does* one proceed to design a successful system—or a utopia [pp. V–VI]?

Boguslaw maintains that the thinking of the modern breed of "social engineer," enamored as they are with the fantastic possibilities of computer programing and hardware complexes, is basically similar to the thinking behind the classical utopias. "They are designed to deal with some perceived limitation in the existing organization of men and materials, they attempt to improve an existing state of affairs, and they are frequently visionary in concept and disappointing in execution. They lack only the humanoid orientation characteristic of all classical utopian schemes" (p. 5). And, he points out, the humanoid type of question "seldom, if ever gets posed or analyzed prior to the construction of large-scale machined systems."

Although it does not do justice to the details and force of Boguslaw's reasoned analysis, his presentation can be reduced to several major points. First, there are alternative ways of viewing the design of large-scale systems, and none of them is without faults. Second, the nature of work and social living is and will be affected by these computer-based systems. Third, unless underlying human values are clarified and become central to the purposes of the new systems, the success of modern technology in conquering nature may very well turn into a more powerful means "for extending the control of man over man."

Boguslaw never really discusses the question he posed in his preface: "How *does* one proceed to design a successful system—or a utopia?" And when he posed that question there was no doubt that he meant how people would be brought together in new and sustained relationships to achieve certain stated goals. If he does not discuss the question (except indirectly), it is because of his preoccupation with the fact that system designers are making the same kinds of errors of those who designed the classical utopias. Both kinds of designers avoid coming to grips with existing social realities and how these realities affect and are affected by the introduction of these new systems.[1] In several places Boguslaw approvingly quotes Max Lerner's description of Machiavelli: "Where others looked at the figureheads, he kept his eyes glued behind the scenes. He wanted to know what made things tick; he wanted to take the clock of the world to pieces to find out how it worked." The designers of classical utopias and modern systems, says Boguslaw, are similar in that they "severed the threads between their brave new systems and the system control or power mechanisms of their times."

The fact is that those who create settings, including a far wider range of people than only system designers, have always overwhelmingly tended to proceed as if social realities were nonexistent or so simply structured as to be of little account. (At least the designers of the classical utopias were clear that they were not about to change or deal with existing social realities; they were imagining a new social reality and, with few exceptions, they had no intention to do more.) It is understandable that Boguslaw should be concerned with the frightful ignorance of the modern designers of the new utopias. But they are not the only ones who are or have been creating new settings. Long before they appeared on the scene with their computers and hardware, settings (large and small) were being created to make for

---

[1] What would have been fascinating and instructive is if Boguslaw had described the creation of one of the human settings the task of which had been to develop a non-people and people-substitute system. I would predict that all of the unfortunate social consequences of their "product" due to failure initially to ask the "humanoid" type of question are contained in the human setting from which the product emerged. That is to say, that the errors of omission and commission which characterize the creation of such a human setting are genotypically similar to those made in developing the non-human system.

better worlds, and the results have not been impressive, to say the least. And even today the number of new settings being created is far greater than those being designed by our unwitting social technologists. When I see how we go about creating human settings, I cannot look upon the social and conceptual ignorance of the computer-hardware people as a special instance of denseness. The long-range consequences of what they develop are undoubtedly enormous, and they will influence every type of new setting. The hospital of today is as different from that of fifty years ago as the hospital of today will be from that of the year 2022, different that is in terms of physical structure, use of computers, and so on. I have no reason to believe that when a new hospital is created fifty years from now that its social structure and relationships, its problems of rivalry and professional imperialism and preciousness, and its relative isolation from existing social realities will be little different than what they are today. Schools will also look different, but they will remain much the same in terms of their self-defeating human relationships. And when in those far off decades institutions are built for dependent and handicapped people, there will be another Burton Blatt (1970) exposing the scandalous conditions within them, just as he had to describe what Dorothea Dix did one hundred years before him (and in the same state!). If, as so many people hope, the designers of the new utopias start asking the humanoid type of question, their answers will probably be highly similar to those which have subverted the purposes of new human settings which were uncomplicated by computers and hardware. The ability of these system engineers to create new and fantastic systems has been possible only because of distinctively new ideas and theories. To create new and more socially productive human settings will also require distinctively new ideas and theories. We should not expect the system engineer to be the source of these new ideas and theories. At best, his formulation of the problem of the creation of a human setting will be no less oversimplified than that of others in the humanist tradition.

Boguslaw does an excellent job of exposing the Achilles heel of the system designer. Unfortunately, however, he does not see that humans creating real "people settings" are no less vulnerable. When he says that "It is precisely in the short run that our new utopias fail to fulfill expectations," he is also characterizing the fate of many new human settings. When the system designer was not on the scene, the creation of settings was an unformulated problem; with him it still is. His arrival on the scene has raised with a sense of urgency questions about the kinds of values by which we want to live. But clarifying and even reaching consensus about values is only a beginning point in creating a new setting. Indeed, it is a danger point because it is rarely accompanied by the knowledge that in acting on the basis of these values the degree of consensus will inevitably be diminished and the solidarity of the group threatened.

After agreement on values the hard work begins. Creating settings consistent with their purposes and sustaining them for more than brief periods of time are general problems in any society. These problems do not disappear as the socioeconomic structure of nations changes, slowly or through revolution. It would be foolish to deny that the creation of settings is unrelated to socioeconomic structure or to national ideology, but it would be equally foolish to assert that the former disappears as a problem as the latter changes. Whether in our own society or in Cuba, Russia, China, or the new African nations, the creation of settings consists of processes and tasks that cannot be bypassed without courting failure. A revolution makes possible the creation of many new settings, and it may give a distinctively new aspect to their goals and human cast. But it does not thereby insure the avoidance of those self-defeating features that are found in most new settings, as Lenin and Castro learned (see Chapter One).

There are those who maintain that the nature of man is too imperfect and that it dooms his efforts to lead the happy life, however that is defined. Others assert that the nature and even the requirements of civilization put constraints on man who, given his nature, reacts in self-defeating ways. The fact that so many people today feel that there is a fair chance that man is now at the point where he unwittingly can destroy all of human life is used as evidence that pessimistic explanations are rooted in reality. Although their numbers are diminishing, there are those who still view man as capable of creating a new society. The optimism may stem from religious beliefs, or political ideology, or as in the case of B. F. Skinner, from a "scientific" conception of man that provides us (finally!) with a technology appropriate to the design of new cultures. The optimistic no less than the pessimistic explanations use as evidence a special view of past and current history.

I do not feel compelled to accept one or the other of these extreme positions, and not because I am indifferent to the questions and issues which give rise to them. If I do not accept their answers, it is not because they are not talking to meaningful issues. The issues are too important and the evidence too ambiguous to take an extreme position. The scientist could argue that the questions are illegitimate because they are posed in operationally meaningless ways, that is, they are not capable of proof or disproof. At what future time and by what procedures can we say that one or the other position is proved? Although the scientist may be correct that these polarized positions are not capable of proof or disproof, he should not make the mistake of confusing poorly posed questions with the experiences from which they have emerged. The optimist recognizes that there is something about the settings that man creates that contains the seeds of their own destruction, but he hopes that man's capacity to gain new knowledge and understanding will alter the quality of his future efforts. The pessimist agrees with the first part of the optimistic position, but those who hold it are unimpressed with man's capacity to use new knowledge for the betterment of society. Although both positions take a different view of man, each position in part emerges from man's experiences in creating new settings. That these experiences have been poorly described, that they are even more poorly understood, and that there has been no clear formulation by which these myriads of experiences can be ordered are not evidence for either extreme position. They are evidence of our ignorance.

In Burckhardt's (1965) classic *The Civilization of the Renaissance in Italy*, he entitles his first chapter: The State As A Work Of Art. By this title he wished to make the point that in the early renaissance there appeared a new political spirit, a new kind of consciousness, which viewed the state "as the outcome of reflection and calculation, the state as a work of art." Just as the new art intimately reflected a new kind of consciousness about form, content, materials, and scope, but no less controlled than heretofore by the processes of reflection and calculation, there began to emerge in the European political mind a new awareness of the problem of "the deliberate adaptation of means to ends. And in certain centers this new awareness, this new self-consciousness, became manifest in how records were kept, changes described, and discussions recorded. That wondrous Florentine spirit, at once keenly critical and artistically creative, was incessantly transforming the social and political conditions of the state, and as incessantly describing and judging the change. Florence thus became the home of political doctrine and theories, of experiments and sudden changes. But also, like Venice, it became the home of statistical science and, alone and above all other states in the world, the home of historical representation in the modern sense of the phrase" (p. 48). It was a major conceptual feat for Burckhardt to recognize that the creative process, wherever it appears, ultimately requires a clear sense of purpose and a formulation that makes it hard for one to forget that between feelings, values, and ideas, on the one hand and successful outcomes, on the other hand, there should always be the controls of reflection and calculation.

Before the final run the artist thinks, sketches and resketches, organizes and reorganizes, puts intuition to the test of an external reality, always aware that he is engaged in a process in which he and the problem are constantly changing, in which he is always wrestling with the personal and the impersonal, with desire and necessity, and with the discrepancy between intent and outcome. And with all of this, the outcome may fall short of *his* mark, regardless of how others regard his effort. But if he feels he has learned and changed, he can try and try again. He knows that to please others at the expense of his sense of growth is the worst form of punishment.

Creating a human setting is akin to creating a work of art. It is also different. It involves more than one artist; it involves different problems of function, materials, and organization; its products are different; its place and relationships to society are different.[2]

Like a work of art the creation of a setting requires of a group that it formulate and confront the task of how to deal with and change reality in ways that foster a shared sense of knowing and changing and allows it to regard its development as a necessary antecedent to and concomitant of its efforts to serve or please others. Like the artist, its problems are never solved once and for all, they are ever present and varyingly recalcitrant, they discourage and distract, but it knows that this is the way it is and has to be and there is no good alternative to trying and learning. It treasures feeling and reveres reflection and calculation; it knows that there is always a tension between the two from which something new may emerge.

Although there can be a kinship between the creation of a setting and the artistic process, there ordinarily is none because of heightened self-consciousness that clearly differentiates between routine

---

[2] Comparing the creation of a setting to a work of art is not a metaphor. No one questions characterizing a dramatic production, a ballet, or an opera as a work of art and its participants as artists. Such a characterization recognizes that in these instances there has been and is a process in which people and things are blended into a complicated whole in which discrete elements take on meanings and functions they would not possess by themselves. The greater these works of art the less we are aware as audience that this has come about and is still accompanied by a heightened awareness in the artists that they are part of an organized and dynamic effort. They know that the survival of the desired whole requires subordinating part of themselves, which they do willingly, as well as transforming themselves in order to create a new reality. To the extent that these features are minimally at work or do not hang together, we are dealing with poor art, and in many failures the participating artists were the first to know.

and imitative thinking and innovative, imaginative thinking. To say that the creation of a setting can be like a work of art is to say that it can involve in an organized way the most productive attributes of the human mind.[3] If it can be like a work of art, it will only be after we have been helped to change our categories of thinking.

Where new knowledge and understanding will take us is not predictable. It is hard to accept the fact that the more you know the more you need to know and that it is an endless process that does not end in a utopia. There will always be problems. This is the consequence of all new knowledge just as it should be part of the perceived reality of all those who create settings today and dream of future societies.

[3] Most people regard art as the special product of the special mental activity of special individuals, a view reinforced and stimulated by what artists say about themselves. This is like the incomplete and misleading picture of scientists, which the public has been given by scientists. For a contrary and documented view the reader should consult Schaefer-Simmern's *The Unfolding Of Artistic Activity* (1948). Another stimulating book along this line of thinking is *Art As Experience* by John Dewey (1934) who also wrote an introduction to Schaefer-Simmern's book.

Bibliography

ALBEE, G. W. *Mental Health Manpower Trends*. New York: Basic Books, 1954.

ALBEE, G. W. "Models, Myths, and Manpower." *Mental Hygiene*, 1968a, *52*, 168–180.

ALBEE, G. W. "Conceptual Models and Manpower Requirements in Psychology." *American Psychologist*, 1968b, *23*, 317–320.

ANDERSON, J. R. L. *The Ulysses Factor*. New York: Harcourt Brace Jovanovich, 1970.

BARKER, R. G. *The Stream of Behavior*. New York: Appleton-Century-Crofts, 1963.

BARKER, R. G. *Ecological Psychology*. Stanford, Calif.: Stanford University Press, 1968.

BEACH, F. A. "The Snark Was a Boojum." *American Psychologist*, 1950, *5*, 115–124.

BENNIS, W. G., AND SLATER, P. E. *The Temporary Society*. New York: Harper and Row, 1968.

BERLIN, I. "The Question of Machiavelli." *New York Review of Books*, November 4, 1971.

BERRIGAN, D., AND COLES, R. "Dialogue Underground: Inside and Outside the Church." *New York Review of Books,* April 8, 1971.

BIKLEN, D. (Ed.) *Human Report: 1. Observations in Mental Health–Mental Retardation Facilities.* Syracuse, N.Y.: Division of Special Education and Rehabilitation, Syracuse University, 1970.

BLATT, B. *Exodus from Pandemonium.* Boston: Allyn and Bacon, 1970.

BLATT, B., AND KAPLAN, F. *Christmas in Purgatory.* Boston: Allyn and Bacon, 1970.

BOGUSLAW, R. *The New Utopians: A Study of System Design and Social Change.* Englewood Cliffs, N.J.: Prentice-Hall, 1965.

BROMBERGER, M., AND BROMBERGER, S. *Jean Monnet and the United States of Europe.* New York: Coward, McCann, and Geoghegan, 1969.

BUDER, S. *Pullman: An Experiment in Industrial Order and Community Planning.* New York: Oxford University Press, 1967.

BURCKHARDT, J. *The Civilization of the Renaissance in Italy.* New York: Praeger, 1965.

CHOMSKY, N. "The Case Against B. F. Skinner." *New York Review of Books,* December 30, 1971.

COLARELLI, N. O., AND SIEGEL, S. M. *Ward H: An Adventure in Innovation.* New York: Van Nostrand, 1966.

COLE, T., AND CHINOY, H. T. (Eds.) *Actors on Acting.* New York: Crown, 1970.

Community Mental Health Centers Act of 1963. Title II, Public Law 88-164. Reprinted from the *Federal Register,* May 6, 1964. Washington, D.C.: U.S. Department of Health, Education, and Welfare.

CONQUEST, R. *The Great Terror.* New York: Macmillan, 1968.

DEWEY, J. *Art As Experience.* New York: Putnam, 1934.

EDWARDS, L. P. *The Natural History of Revolution.* Chicago: University of Chicago Press, 1927.

EHRENREICH, B., AND EHRENREICH, J. *The American Health Empire: A Report from the Health Policy Advisory Center.* New York: Random House, 1970.

EICHLER, E. P., AND KAPLAN, M. *The Community Builders.* Berkeley and Los Angeles: University of California Press, 1967.

FREUD, S. *Analysis Terminable and Interminable.* Vol. 23. *Collected Works.* London: Hogarth, 1964.

FROMM, E. *Marx's Concept of Man.* New York: Ungar, 1961.

FULLER, R. B. *Operating Manual for Spaceship Earth.* Carbondale, Ill.: Southern Illinois University Press, 1969.

GARDNER, J. W. *Education for Renewal.* Occasional Papers 101. American Association of Collegiate Schools of Business, 1965.

GOFFMAN, E. *Asylums: Essays on the Social Situation of Mental Patients and Other Inmates.* Chicago: Aldine, 1961.

GOLDENBERG, I. I. *Build Me a Mountain: Youth, Poverty, and the Creation of a New Setting.* Cambridge: MIT Press, 1971.

GRAZIANO, A. "Clinical Innovation and the Mental Health Power Structure: A Social Case History. *American Psychologist,* 1969, *24*(1), 10–13.

HEILBRONER, R. L. *The Making of Economic Society.* (2nd ed.) Englewood Cliffs, N.J.: Prentice-Hall, 1968.

HEXTER, J. H. "The Rhetoric of History." *International Encyclopedia of Social Sciences.* Vol. 6. New York: Macmillan, 1968.

HOLLOWAY, M. *Heavens on Earth. Utopian Communities in America, 1680–1880.* New York: Dover, 1966.

HUGGETT, R. *The Truth about Pygmalion.* New York: Random House, 1969.

JENSEN, A. R. "How Much Can We Boost IQ and Scholastic Achievement?" *Harvard Educational Review,* 1969, *39,* 1–123.

JUNGK, R. *The Big Machine.* New York: Scribners, 1968.

KARLIN, R. *A Study of Newly Married Couples.* Unpublished paper, Yale University, 1971.

KLABER, M. "The Retarded and Institutions for the Retarded: A Preliminary Report. In S. B. Sarason and J. Doris, *Psychological Problems in Mental Deficiency.* New York: Harper & Row, 1969.

KOESTLER, A. *Darkness at Noon.* New York: Macmillan, 1941.

LACOUTURE, J. *The Demigods: Charismatic Leadership in the Third World.* New York: Knopf, 1970.

LEKACHMAN, R. "The Poverty of Influence." *Commentary,* March 1970, *49*(3), 39–44.

LENIN, N. "Better Fewer but Better." In *Lenin on Politics and Revolution.* Indianapolis: Pegasus, 1968.

LEVI, A. W. *Humanism and Politics.* Bloomington, Indiana: University of Indiana Press, 1969.

LEVINE, M., AND LEVINE, A. *A Social History of Helping Settings.* New York: Appleton-Century-Crofts, 1970.

LEWIN, K. *Dynamic Theory of Personality.* New York: McGraw-Hill, 1935.

LEWIN, M. *Lenin's Last Struggle.* New York: Pantheon Books, 1968.

LITTLE, S. W. AND CANTOR, A. *The Playmakers.* New York: Norton, 1970.

LYNN, K. S. *The Professions in America.* Boston: Houghton Mifflin, 1965.

MACHIAVELLI, N. *The Prince.* New York: St. Martin's Press, 1964.

MARCH, J. G. (Ed.) *Handbook of Organizations.* Chicago: Rand McNally, 1965.

MATARAZZO, J. D. "Some National Developments in the Utilization of Non-traditional Mental Health Manpower." *American Psychologist,* 1971, *26*(4), 363–365.

MAYHEW, K. C., AND EDWARDS, A. C. *The Dewey School.* New York: Atherton, 1966.

Mental Illness and Mental Retardation. Message from the President of the U.S. 88th Congress, first session, House of Representatives Document No. 58.

MERTON, R. K. "Behavior Patterns of Scientists." *The American Scholar,* 1969, Spring, 197–225.

MICHAELSON, M. G. "The Coming Medical War." *New York Review of Books,* July 1, 1971.

MOYNIHAN, D. P. *Maximum Feasible Misunderstanding.* New York: Free Press, 1969.

New York Times. December 17, 1970, p. 1.

NORDHOFF, C. *The Communistic Societies of the United States.* New York: Dover, 1966.

PREZZOLINI, G. *Machiavelli.* New York: Farrar, Straus, and Giroux, 1967.

ROBERTSON, C. N. *Oneida Community: An Autobiography 1851–1876.* Syracuse: Syracuse University Press, 1970.

ROSSITER, C. *1787: The Grand Convention.* New York: New American Library, 1966.

SARASON, S. B. *The Creation of Settings: The Beginning Context.* Paper prepared for presentation at the Kennedy Foundation Scientific Meeting in Chicago, 1968.

SARASON, S. B. *The Culture of the School and the Problem of Change.* Boston: Allyn and Bacon, 1971.

SARASON, S. B., AND DORIS, J. *Psychological Problems in Mental Deficiency.* (4th ed.) New York: Harper & Row, 1970.

SARASON, S. B., LEVINE, M., GOLDENBERG, I. I., CHERLIN, D. L., AND BEN-NETT, E. M. *Psychology in Community Settings: Clinical, Educational, Vocational, Social Aspects.* New York: Wiley, 1966.

SARASON, S. B., ZITNAY, G., AND GROSSMAN, F. *The Creation of a Community Setting.* Syracuse: Division of Special Education and Rehabilitation, Syracuse University, 1972. (Distributed by Syracuse University Press.)

SARATA, B. P. V. *The Job Satisfactions of Individuals Working with the Mentally Retarded.* Unpublished doctoral dissertation. New Haven, Conn.: Yale University, 1972.

SCHAEFER-SIMMERN, H. *The Unfolding of Artistic Activity.* Berkeley, Calif.: University of California Press, 1948.

SCHLESINGER, JR., A. (Ed.) *The Best and the Last of Edwin O'Connor.* Boston: Atlantic Monthly Press, 1969.

SILONE, I. *Emergency Exit.* New York: Harper & Row, 1968.

SILONE, I. *The Story of a Humble Christian.* New York: Harper and Row, 1968.

SKINNER, B. F. *Walden Two.* New York: Macmillan, 1962.

SKINNER, B. F. *Beyond Freedom and Dignity.* New York: Knopf, 1971.

SMITH, L. M. *Oral presentation,* pp. 201–205. In M. C. Reynolds (Ed.), *Proceedings of the Conference on Psychology and the Process of Schooling in the Next Decade.* Minneapolis, Minn.: Department of Audio-Visual Extension, University of Minnesota, 1971.

SMITH, L., AND KEITH, P. M. *Anatomy of Educational Innovation.* New York: Wiley, 1971.

STANTON, A. H., AND SCHWARTZ, M. S. *The Mental Hospital: A Study of Institutional Participation in Psychiatric Illness and Treatment.* New York: Basic Books, 1955.

STEINER, G. *In Bluebeard's Castle: Some Notes Towards the Redefinition of Culture.* New Haven Conn.: Yale University Press, 1971.

STREET, D., VINTER, R. D., AND PERROW, C. *Organization for Treatment:A Comparative Study of Institutions for Delinquents.* New York: Free Press, 1966.

STINCHCOMBE, A. L. "Social Structure and Organizations." In J. G. March, (Ed.), *Handbook of Organizations.* Chicago: Rand McNally, 1965.

WAISBREN, B. A. "Designing a Modern Hospital: A Physician's Point of View." *Delaware Medical Journal,* 1971, *43*(4), 102–104.

WAISBREN, B. A. *The Function of the Hospital in the Human Endeavor.* Paper presented at the Herman Miller Health Care Conference, Grand Rapids, Mich., 1971. Dr. Waisbren, St. Mary's Hospital, Milwaukee, Wis.

WATSON, J. D. *The Double Helix.* New York: Atheneum, 1968.

YASWEN, G. "Sunrise Hill: Post Mortem." *Win Magazine,* August, 1970.

Index